The Roman Empire

Bacchus, half-life-size bronze. This beardless, long-haired adolescent bends his head, slightly turned, to look out over the edge of his pedestal. His lips, eyes, and somewhat disquieting charm reveal his divine nature. (Paris, Petit Palais, Dutuit Collection.)

The Roman Empire

Paul Veyne

Arthur Goldhammer, Translator

The Belknap Press of
Harvard University Press
Cambridge, Massachusetts
London, England

Library of Congress Cataloging-in-Publication Data

Veyne, Paul, 1930–
   [Empire romain.   English]
   The Roman Empire / Paul Veyne ; Arthur Goldhammer, translator.
      p.   cm.
   "Originally published as 'L'Empire romain' in Histoire de la vie
   privée, vol. 1, De L'Empire romain à l'an mil, Editions du Seuil,
   © 1985"—T.p. verso.
   Includes bibliographical references and index.
   ISBN 0-674-77771-9 (paper)
   1. Rome—Social life and customs.   2. Rome—History—Empire,
   30 B.C.–476 A.D.   I. Title.
DG78.V49   1997
937'.06—DC21   97-15566

Contents

✕ Introduction

WITH them the mirror is soon broken: to know them we have only to look them in the eyes. They look back at us in the same way. It is not every age whose portrait art embodies such a direct exchange of gazes.

This man and this woman are not objects, for they look at us. But they do nothing to challenge or seduce or persuade us, nothing to show us a glimpse of inner life, which we would not presume to judge. They do not so much bare themselves to us as offer themselves tranquilly to the world's eyes. Our presence is taken for granted, and they take themselves for granted. They are what they are and stare at us as equals, sharing common values.

This Greco-Roman humanity was long regarded as classic. It seemed natural, neither dated nor constricted. Man and wife do not pose, nor do they mimic. Their clothing betrays no signs of social rank, no political symbolism. Clothes do not make the man. The background is empty. Against this neutral backdrop the individual is himself, and would be the same anywhere else. Truth, universality, humanity. The woman's elegance is in her hair; she wears no precious gems.

Today, however, we believe not in universality but in the arbitrariness of custom and the finiteness of history. To awaken ourselves from the humanist slumbers in which these Romans still sleep, a single argument, external though it is, will suffice: this man and this woman are wealthy enough to have had their portrait painted. Hence they are "individuals" only in appearance: this portrait, so like a snapshot, establishes their identity by depicting them, as if by chance, at a canonical age, when one is fully grown but has not yet begun to grow old. These are not flesh and blood people caught at some

Painting in the so-called Terentius Neo House, Pompeii: portrait of a couple, prior to 79 B.C. The "Fayoum portraits" of Roman Egypt were similar. (Naples, Archaeological Museum.)

6

arbitrary moment in their lives but individualized types belonging to a society that conceived of itself as both natural and ideal. The moment captured in the portrait coincides with a timeless truth, and the individual is an essence.

Husband and wife hold undeniable and personal attributes of their superior social status: not symbols of wealth or power such as a purse or a sword, but a book, writing tablets, and a stylus. This ideal of culture is taken for granted: the book and the stylus are obviously familiar tools and are not ostentatiously displayed. Oddly enough, given the reluctance of ancient artists to portray familiar gestures, the man is resting his chin expectantly on top of his book (actually a scroll), and the woman has brought the stylus meditatively to her lips. She is searching for a line, for poetry was an art practiced by women as well as men. Michelangelo would have relished these "unconscious" gestures (his Moses absentmindedly rubs his beard); for him, such gestures revealed the shadow of a doubt or dream. But here no one is dreaming; they meditate, sure of themselves. Their unconscious gestures prove that they are intimate with culture. They are not privileged people. If they hold books, it is because they are fond of reading. The subtlety and naturalness of a deceptive beauty create the grandeur of the Greco-Roman world. Are these people bourgeois, or are they nobles?

If friendship and grief have claims on us, let me dedicate the pages that follow to the memory of Michel Foucault, so towering a man that with him I felt the pleasure of living beside a mountain. One source of my energy is gone.

Detail from a sarcophagus, mid-2nd century. A woman seated in a high-backed armchair, a sign of privilege, nurses a baby. Holding a scroll, a mark of his class, the father leans nobly on a convenient pillar. (Paris, Louvre.)

✒ From Mother's Womb to Last Will and Testament

THE birth of a Roman was not merely a biological fact. Infants came into the world, or at any rate were received into society, only as the head of the family willed. Contraception, abortion, the exposure of freeborn infants, and infanticide of slaves' children were common and perfectly legal practices. They would not meet with disapproval or be declared illegal until a new morality had taken hold, a morality which for the sake of brevity I shall describe simply as Stoic. A citizen of Rome did not "have" a child; he "took" a child, "raised" him up (*tollere*). Immediately after the birth it was the father's prerogative to raise the child from the earth where the midwife had placed it, thus indicating that he recognized the infant as his own and declined to expose it. The mother had just given birth (in a seated position, in a special chair, away from male eyes). Had she died in labor, the child would have been cut out of her uterus. But birth alone did not signify that a scion had come into the world.

A child whose father did not raise it up was exposed outside the house or in some public place. Anyone who wished might claim it. An absent father might order his pregnant wife to expose her baby as soon as it was born. The Greeks and the Romans thought it peculiar that Egyptians, Germans, and Jews exposed none of their children but raised them all. In Greece it was more common to expose female infants than males. In 1 B.C. a Greek wrote his wife: "If (touch wood!) you have a child, let it live if it is a boy. If it is a girl, expose it." It is not at all clear, however, that the Romans shared this prejudice. They exposed or drowned malformed infants. This, said Seneca, was not wrath but reason: "What is good must be set apart from what is good for nothing." The Romans

Midwife's sign in terra-cotta. One midwife supports the woman about to deliver, who clutches the chair, while the other midwife prepares to deliver the child. (Ostia, Archaeological Museum.)

also exposed the children of their daughters who had "gone astray." More important, some Romans abandoned their legitimate children because they were poor, and others because they wished to bequeath a decent fortune to their surviving heirs. The poor abandoned the children they could not feed. Other "paupers" (in the ancient sense of the word, which we would translate as "middle class") exposed their children, "so as not to see them corrupted by a mediocre education that would leave them unfit for rank and quality," in the words of Plutarch. The middle class, the mere notables, preferred to concentrate their efforts and resources on a small number of offspring, for reasons of family ambition. In the eastern provinces, peasants agreed to divide their offspring. If a household with four children already had too many mouths to feed, the next three sons might be given to friends, who would welcome these future workers as "sons." Jurists never could decide whether children thus "taken in" (*threptoi*) were free or slaves of the family that raised them. Even the wealthiest Roman might have reasons not to keep an unwanted child, especially if the birth disrupted plans for division of his estate. A rule of law stated that "the birth of a son (or daughter) breaks a will" sealed previously, unless the father were willing to disinherit in advance any offspring that might be born after the will was sealed. Some fathers may have felt that it was better to do away with a child than to disinherit it.

What became of children who were exposed? Few survived, according to pseudo-Quintilian, who distinguishes, however, between the rich and the poor: when the rich exposed a child, they hoped never to see it again, while the poor, compelled by poverty alone, did all they could to ensure that the infant might someday be reclaimed. Sometimes exposure was faked: the child's mother would, without her husband's knowledge, entrust the newborn to neighbors or subordinates, who would raise it in secret. When the child grew up, it became the slave of its educators, who would eventually set it free. In extremely rare cases such a child might win recognition of its freeborn status. Vespasian's wife was one such.

A legitimate and deliberate act, the decision to expose a child was at times a statement of principle. A man who suspected his wife of infidelity would expose a child he believed to be the product of adultery. The little daughter of a princess was abandoned, "stark naked," at the gates of the imperial palace. Exposure could also be a political or religious statement: when the well-loved prince Germanicus died, the plebs indicated their displeasure with the gods' government by smashing their temples, and some parents apparently exposed their infants as a sign of protest. After the murder of Agrippina by her son Nero, an unknown person "exposed his child in the middle of the forum with a sign on which he had written: *I will not raise you, lest you cut your mother's throat.*" If exposure was a private decision, was there any reason why on occasion it should not be public? One day a false rumor circulated among the plebs: that the Senate, having learned from soothsayers that a king was to be born that year, would attempt to force the people to expose every newborn child. The Massacre of the Innocents inevitably comes to mind (this, I might add in passing, was probably an authentic occurrence and not a mere legend).

The "voice of blood" spoke very little in Rome. What mattered more than blood was the family name. Bastards took their mother's name, and legitimation or recognition of paternity did not exist. Forgotten by their fathers, bastards played almost no social or political role in the Roman aristocracy. This was not true of freed slaves, often quite wealthy and powerful individuals, some of whom pushed their children into the equestrian order and even the Senate. The ruling oligarchy replenished its ranks with its own legitimate children and with the sons of former slaves. Freed slaves adopted the

Fragment of vase with reliefs, 1st century. A servant hastens with a pail of water to a busy couple. A purifying bath after intercourse was ritualistic. (Lyons, Museum of Gallo-Roman Civilization.)

family name of the master who set them free. This custom accounts for the frequency of adoptions: the adopted child took the family name of its new father.

Birth and Contraception

Adoptions and the social advancement of freed slaves compensated for the low rate of natural reproduction, for the Romans made no fetish of natural kinship. Abortion and contraception were common practices, although historians have distorted the picture somewhat by overlooking the Roman use of the term "abortion" to describe not only surgical practices that we today would call abortion but also techniques that we would call contraceptive. Precisely when after conception a mother got rid of offspring she did not wish to bear mattered little to Romans. The most stringent moralists might argue that a woman had a duty to preserve the fruit of her womb, but even they never dreamed of according to the fetus a right to live. All classes of the population certainly made use of contraceptive techniques. Saint Augustine, who speaks of "embraces in which conception is avoided," gives no indication that these were rare; he condemns the practice, even between legitimate spouses. Augustine distinguishes between contraception, sterilization by means of drugs, and abortions, only to condemn them all. Alfred Sauvy (private communication) states his opinion that, "based on what we now know of the multiplicative powers of the human species, the population of the Roman Empire should have grown much more than it did and overflowed its borders."

What contraceptive procedures were used? Plautus, Cicero, and Ovid allude to the pagan custom of washing after sex, and a vase decorated with reliefs found in Lyons shows a man carrying a pitcher to a couple busily occupied in bed. Dressed up as a ritual of purification, the custom may have been contraceptive. The Christian polemicist Tertullian held that the sperm was already a child immediately after ejaculation (and hence that fellatio was in fact cannibalism). In the *Veil of the Virgins* he alludes, with obscene truculence that obscures his meaning, to false virgins who give birth to children who, oddly enough, exactly resemble their own fathers, only to kill them, apparently with a pessary. Saint Jerome, in his twenty-second epistle, speaks of young girls who "savor their sterility in advance and kill the human being even before its seed has been sown," an allusion to a spermicidal drug. As for the menstrual cycle, the physician Soranus taught the theory that women conceive either just before or just after their periods; fortunately, this doctrine remained esoteric. All these methods were the responsibility of the woman. No mention is made of *coitus interruptus*.

How many children did Romans have? The law accorded special privilege to mothers of three children, who were seen as having done their duty, and this number seems to have been canonical. The evidence of epitaphs is difficult to interpret with assurance, but the texts mention families of three children with particular frequency, almost proverbially. When a writer of epigrams wishes to castigate a woman who, out of greed, starves her offspring, he writes, "her three offspring." A Stoic preacher shouts: "Do you suppose you have done great things because by bringing two or three wretched brats into the world you have helped to perpetuate the human race?" These Malthusian attitudes served dynastic ends. As soon as a man has more than one child, Pliny writes to one of his correspondents, he must think of finding a wealthy son- or daughter-in-law for his younger offspring. No one liked to eat away at an inheritance. To be sure, the older morality eschewed calculation of this kind, and even in Pliny's time this was still the morality of certain old-fashioned heads of family, who "did not allow their fertile wives to lie fallow, even though in our time most people hold that an only son is already a heavy burden and that it is advantageous not to be

Ex-voto to the nurturing goddesses, 2nd or 3rd century. Mother and child offer a tray of fruit to the statue of the seated goddess, who is suckling an infant. The Nurses or Mothers or Matrones were protective deities of the Celts. (Marburg Museum.)

overburdened with posterity." Do things change as we move toward the end of the second century A.D. and Stoic and Christian morality begins to take hold? The orator Fronto, Marcus Aurelius' teacher, "lost five children" to childhood maladies. He must have had many more. Marcus Aurelius himself had nine sons and daughters. After three centuries Rome returned to that golden age in which the exemplary Cornelia, mother of the Gracchi, had given twelve children to the fatherland.

Education

Shortly after birth the newborn boy or girl was handed over to a wet nurse. Breast-feeding by a child's natural mother was a thing of the past. But the "nurse" did much more than just offer the child her breast. She was responsible for education up to the age of puberty, in conjunction with a "pedagogue," also called a "nurse" (*nutritor, tropheus*). Marcus Aurelius' pedagogue taught him to take care of himself and not to become excited by the races at the Circus. Children lived and took meals with their nurses, but dined in the evening with their parents and guests at what was something of a ceremonial dinner. Nurse and pedagogue remained important figures even after a child was grown. Marcus Aurelius speaks with suitable piety of his natural father, his adoptive father, and his (male) "nurse," and the emperor Claudius would hate his pedagogue throughout his life because of the free use the latter had made of the whip. When a girl married, her mother and nurse together offered last-minute advice for her wedding night. Pedagogue, nurse, and foster child formed a kind of surrogate family and enjoyed all sorts of indulgences in later life; they were free to ignore the law. Nero, murdering his mother, Agrippina, was aided by his pedagogue. Later, when he was abandoned by everyone and facing death at the hands of his rebellious subjects, only his nurse stood by to console him. It was she who, with the help of his concubine Acte, wrapped him in a winding-sheet after his suicide. Yet Nero had been harsh toward his foster brother, to whom he should have shown respect. A Stoic philosopher once delivered a sermon on love of the family. Filial love, he explained, is in accordance with Nature, and Nature is the same thing as Reason; hence it is reasonable for a child to love its mother, its nurse, and its *pedagogus*.

In noble households the surrogate family lived in healthy rural surroundings, far from temptation, under the watchful

Sarcophagus. Boy at play, driving a cart hitched to a small animal. Axle shafts had not yet been invented. (Paris, Louvre.)

Paintings from underground tomb, 2nd century A.D. Left: ball game. Below: child learning to walk with a wheeled walker. (Rome, Museum of the Baths.)

eye of a strict older relative. "To its [the surrogate family's] tried and proven virtues all the progeny of the household were entrusted. It governed the children's studies and disciplines as well as their games and distractions." Caesar and Augustus were raised this way. The future emperor Vespasian was "raised under the direction of his paternal grandmother on his Cosa estates," even though his mother was still alive. A paternal grandmother's duty was to be strict, whereas the role of the maternal grandmother was one of total indulgence. Uncles differed in the same way: symbols of severity on the one side and of indulgence on the other.

The truth about education may be far from what self-satisfied educators imagine. One Roman teacher tells a very different story, though, to be sure, he is particularly severe, as his profession required. (In Rome, philosophers and some rhetors occupied a place apart in society, rather like priests today.) The child raised in its parents' home received, in this teacher's estimation, an education in indulgence. He dressed as sumptuously as his elders and, like them, was carried about by porters. His parents delighted in his most impudent words. At dinner he heard off-color jokes and bawdy songs. He saw concubines and pet young men about the house. In Rome, as we shall see, common sense held that the world was perverted and decadent. It was also believed that morality consists not in the love or habit of virtue but in having the strength to

Child's sarcophagus. Figure of boy playing with hoop (*trochus*). (Rome, Vatican Museums.)

Child's sarcophagus, 2nd century. Girls throw a ball at the wall, while boys slide a nut down an inclined plane to demolish a tower of nuts. (Paris, Louvre.)

resist vice. The cornerstone of every individual character, therefore, was the strength to resist. In theory, the purpose of education was to temper a person's character while there was still time, so that later, when he or she was fully grown, the germs of luxury and decadence, omnipresent in these vicious times, could be successfully warded off. The Roman attitude toward the teaching of virtue was rather like our own insistence that children participate in sports because we know full well that they will spend the rest of their lives seated behind desks. In practice, the antidote to self-indulgence was activity, *industria,* which, it was thought, strengthened the moral sinew that self-indulgence withered. Tacitus tells of one senator who was born into "a plebeian family, but a very old and distinguished one. He impressed more by his good nature than by his energy, although his father had raised him strictly."

Only severity, which terrifies appetites susceptible to temptation, can give strength of character. Accordingly, says Seneca, "parents subject the still malleable characters of their children to what will do them good. Let them cry and struggle as they will, we swaddle them tightly lest their still immature bodies become deformed rather than grow up straight and tall. Later we instill liberal culture by means of terror if they refuse to learn." Severity was part of the father's role; the mother pleaded for leniency. A well-brought-up child always addressed its father as "sir" (*domine*). Parvenus were quick to imitate this aristocratic custom. The distance between parents and children was dizzying. The professor of rhetoric just quoted lost a son of ten whom he adored and who preferred him, he writes, to his nurses and to the grandmother who raised him. This son had been destined for a splendid career in judicial eloquence (the most visible, "high-society," and busiest part of literary life—rather like the theater today). The child's exceptional gifts justified the father's public mourning. As is well known, the so-called maternal or paternal instinct

does not exist. In some cases love between parent and child develops from natural affinity (which is neither more nor less likely to occur between parent and child than between any two individuals brought together by chance). More often, no doubt, parental sentiments are "induced" by the prevailing morality. In Rome the prevailing morality taught that fathers should love their children as bearers of the family name and perpetuators of its grandeur. Tenderness was misplaced. But it was legitimate to mourn the ruin of a family's hopes.

Our teacher had yet another reason to mourn his beloved son: a great personage, a consul, had just adopted the boy, thus ensuring that he would enjoy a splendid public career. The frequency of adoption is yet another proof that nature played little part in the Roman conception of the family. Apparently one gave a child for adoption as one might give a daughter in marriage, particularly a "good" marriage. There were two ways to have children: to conceive them in legitimate wedlock or to adopt them. Adoption could prevent a family line from dying out. It was also a means of acquiring the quality of paterfamilias, which the law required of candidates for public honors and provincial governments. Everything that could be had through marriage could also be had through adoption. Just as a testator, in choosing an heir, also made him the continuator of the family name, a man who adopted a youth was careful to choose a successor worthy to bear his name. The future emperor Galba was a widower, and his two sons died. Having long since discerned the merits of a young noble by the name of Piso, he had a will drawn up naming Piso his heir and finally adopted him. A man could adopt a son even if his own sons were still alive, as Herodius Atticus did. The histories mention the practice of adoption by will, but no trace of such a thing survives in legal documents. The most striking instance of an inheritance linked to adoption involves a certain Octavius, who became the son and heir of Caesar and eventually the Emperor Octavius Augustus. In some cases adoption, like marriage, was a means of controlling the flow of wealth. A father-in-law impressed by his son-in-law's deference might adopt him as a son after the young man inherited his father's fortune, in order to gain control of the inheritance. In return he would see to it that his adopted son enjoyed a brilliant career in the Senate. Adoption could have great influence on a man's career.

Adoption

Children who were moved about like pawns on the chessboard of wealth and power were hardly cherished and coddled. Such matters were left to the servants. It was the nurse who taught the child to talk. Noble households employed Greek nurses so that the child might learn the language of culture in the cradle. The pedagogue was responsible for teaching the child how to read.

School

Was literacy a privilege of the upper class? From Egyptian papyruses we can be sure of three things: there were illiterates who employed others to write for them; some people of the lower orders knew how to write; literary texts, classics, could be found in the smallest towns (here is the "culture" of which the ancient world was so proud). Books of the fashionable poets quickly found their way to the end of the world—meaning Lyons. Beyond this we have only hints. (Historians of literacy in early modern Europe are familiar with the problems involved.) In one fictional tale a former slave is proud of his ability to read capital letters. In other words, he did not know how to read the cursive script of books, private papers, and documents, but he could decipher shop and temple signs and posters publicizing elections, plays, houses to rent, and auction sales, to say nothing of epitaphs. Although only wealthy families could afford private teachers, Ulpianus tells

Funerary relief, 2nd century. Girls playing quoits. (Ostia, Archaeological Museum.)

Another detail of the sarcophagus shown at the start of this chapter. Grandly costumed, the son does his homework in rhetoric before his father (not his teacher). The boy's fingers are making a rhetorical gesture; these were codified and taught in school. The scroll in his left hand is not a genuine detail but a symbol of culture, hence of social rank. (Paris, Louvre.)

us that "in the cities and towns there were teachers who taught the rudiments of writing." School was a recognized institution. School vacations were determined by the religious calendar, and children attended school in the morning. We find large numbers of documents written by simple folk: artisans' accounts, naive letters, graffiti, magical tablets. To write for oneself was one thing, however; to write for people of higher station was something else entirely. One had to know the rudiments of high style and, to begin with, spelling (of which the graffiti writers were ignorant). So, when it came to drawing up a public document—a petition or even a simple contract— people who strictly speaking knew how to read and write felt that they were "illiterate" and turned to a public writer (*notarius*). Nevertheless, a fairly substantial number of young Romans attended school up to the age of twelve, girls as well as boys (as the physician Soranus confirms), together, in fact, in the same schools.

At age twelve the lives of boys and girls diverged, as did the lives of the rich and the poor. Only the boys continued their studies, and then only if they came from well-to-do families. Under the whip of a "grammarian," or teacher of literature, they studied classical authors and mythology (of which they believed not a word, but knowledge of mythology was the mark of a cultivated person). In rare instances fathers of young girls might hire a tutor to teach them classics. At age twelve a girl was considered nubile. Some were even married off at this tender age, and the marriages were consummated. By age fourteen a girl was considered an adult: "Men then call them 'madame' (*domina, kyria*), and seeing that there is nothing left for them but to share a man's bed, they dress themselves up and think of nothing else." The philosopher who penned these lines concluded: "It would be better to persuade them that nothing will make them more estimable than to appear modest and reserved." In good families girls of this age and older were confined in the wall-less prison known as "women's work," as visible proof that they were not misusing their time. If a woman learned to sing, dance, and play a musical instrument (singing, dancing, and music went together), people praised her and appreciated her talents, but hastened to add that she was nevertheless a decent woman. In the end, it was the husband who completed the education of a young woman of good family. A friend of Pliny had a wife whose epistolary talents earned her praise: either her husband was the real author of the letters attributed to her, we are told, or he had been clever enough to cultivate the talents of "this girl he married as a virgin" and hence deserved the credit for himself. Seneca's mother, on the other hand, was forbidden to study philosophy by her husband, who saw such study as the road to dissolution.

Meanwhile, young boys attended school. Why? In order to become good citizens? To learn a trade? To acquire the means to understand their world? No: to embellish their minds, to cultivate themselves through the study of *belles lettres*. It is a peculiar error to think that schools always perform the same function, that of shaping man or adapting him to society. Roman education was neither formative nor utilitarian. Rather, it conferred prestige, primarily through the study of such subjects as rhetoric. It is rare in history that the purpose of education is to prepare a child for life and equip him with an image of society. The history of education is generally a history of ideas about childhood; the social function of education does not explain why things change. In Rome the minds of little boys were decked out with rhetoric, much as in the last century the bodies of little boys were decked out with sailor suits or military uniforms. Childhood is an age that we disguise by embellishing, by using it to embody our ideals.

I have so far said nothing about education in the Greek

portions of the Empire, which differed from the foregoing description in several respects. Nilsson's views on this question are sound: Roman schooling was an imported product and, as such, separate from everyday life, from religious and political activity. Greek schooling, on the other hand, was a part of public life; it look place in the palestra and gymnasium. The gymnasium was like a second public square, a place where anyone could go and where activity was not limited to gymnastics. But gymnastics were an important part of schooling; in my opinion, the major difference between Greek education and Roman education was that sport took up half the time of the Greek student. Even literary subjects (Greek, Homer, rhetoric, a little philosophy, and a great deal of music, even under the Empire) were taught in a corner of the gymnasium or palestra. Schooling, which lasted until the child was about sixteen, was followed immediately by one or two years of ephebia, the program of which was identical.[1]

Apart from the public character of Greek education, its music and gymnastics, there was another difference between it and Roman education. No Roman of good birth could call himself cultivated unless a tutor had taught him Greek language and literature, whereas the most cultivated Greeks thumbed their noses at the thought of learning Latin and haughtily ignored Cicero and Virgil (with a few exceptions, such as the functionary Appian). Greek intellectuals who, like sixteenth-century Italians, went abroad and sold their talents naturally used Greek when practicing medicine or teaching philosophy, for Greek was the language of these sciences. In Rome they picked up a little broken Latin. Even in late antiquity Greeks would study Latin systematically only if they wished to make careers in the imperial bureaucracy.

Adolescence

At age twelve the young Roman of noble birth completed his elementary education. At age fourteen he shed his child's clothing and was allowed to do what every young man loves to do. At age sixteen or seventeen he might choose a public career or join the army—like Stendhal, who enlisted as a hussar at sixteen. There was no such thing as a legal age of majority. In Rome there were no minors, only prepubescents, who ceased to be so whenever their fathers or tutors judged they were ready to wear a man's garb and start trimming their mustaches. Take, for example, one senator's son. At sixteen he became an equestrian, and at seventeen assumed his first

Young prince, procession of the altar of the Peace of Augustus, 9 B.C. His great-uncle the emperor leads the procession. Beneath the gaze of the adults, the boy may as well not be there. This is unimportant, for the main thing is to belong to the imperial family, whose private life became public, as this image, as much a family as an official portrait, proves. The boy is characterized by his youth—not yet old enough to be officially himself. (Paris, Louvre.)

public office. He was put in charge of the Roman police, supervised executions, and governed the mint. From then on he rose steadily, becoming in turn general, judge, and senator. Where did he learn his craft? On the job. From his elders? More likely from his subordinates: he would have carried himself with enough aristocratic hauteur to seem to be making decisions that others in fact made for him. One noble was a colonel by age sixteen, as well as a state priest; he had already pleaded his first cases at the bar.

Civic and professional matters were learned on the job; culture was studied in school. (The lower orders *had* a culture but not the ambition to cultivate themselves.) School was the means by which one cultivated oneself, and this altered the nature of the culture acquired; certain writers came to be viewed as "classics." (Just as now, with the formation of a "canon" of tourism, there are sites that one "must" visit, monuments that one "must" see.) The schools taught subjects that brought prestige to anyone familiar with them but that actually interested only a few, even among those who admired from afar. And since any institution soon becomes an end in itself, the schools taught, and called "classic," what was easiest to teach. Ever since Athens' golden age rhetoricians had been developing a predigested doctrine, ready to teach. So, from age twelve to age eighteen or twenty, Romans learned to read their classics and then studied rhetoric. But what exactly was rhetoric?

It was most assuredly not utilitarian; it contributed nothing to "society." Eloquence at the podium and the bar played an important role in the Roman Republic, but its prestige derived from its brilliance as literature, not from its civic function. Cicero, who was not the son of an oligarch, enjoyed the rare honor of being admitted to the Senate, because his brilliance as an orator lent prestige to that institution. Under the Empire the public followed trials the way we follow literature; poets, for all their glory, were not wreathed with popularity to compare with the renown of talented orators.

Because of the popularity of eloquence, rhetorical art, or eloquence reduced to formulas, became the sole subject matter, apart from the classics, of Roman education. All Roman boys learned typical speeches suitable for use in politics and the courts, complete with model developments and catalogued effects (our "rhetorical figures"). Did they quickly learn to speak eloquently? No, because rhetoric as taught in the schools soon became an art unto itself, an art whose rules had to be learned. There was a gulf between true eloquence and rhetorical teaching, which the ancients never ceased to deplore even as they delighted in it. The subjects assigned to young Romans for their speeches had nothing to do with the real world. On the contrary, the more mystifying a subject was, the more it stimulated the imagination. Rhetoric became a society game. "Suppose that a law holds that a seduced woman may choose either to have her seducer condemned to death or to marry him, and, further, that in one night a man rapes two women, one of whom demands his death, while the other insists on marrying him." Such a theme gave free rein to virtuosity and to the Roman taste for melodrama and sex. It offered the pleasure of paradox and vicarious amusement. Amateurs long since done with school but highly trained in the rhetorical art continued to play such games at home, before an audience of connoisseurs. The genealogy of ancient education was as follows: from culture to the will to culture, from there to the school, and from the school to the scholastic exercise as an end in itself.

While the young Roman, under his teacher's watchful eye, "advised Sulla to abdicate the dictatorship" or weighed the choices open to the victim of rape, he also reached puberty. This marked the beginning of a period of indulgence. It was common knowledge that, as soon as a young man donned his adult garb, his first thought was to buy himself the favors of a servant or hasten to Suburra, Rome's quarter for mischief. Or perhaps a woman of good society might take it into her head to initiate the young man. (The ways of the Roman aristocracy were as free as those of the French aristocracy in the eighteenth century.) To physicians such as Celsus or Rufus of Ephesus, epilepsy was a disease that healed itself at puberty, that is, when girls have their first menses and boys their first sexual encounter. In other words, puberty and sexual initiation were synonymous for boys, while the virginity of young girls remained sacrosanct. For boys, the time between puberty and marriage was a time of parental indulgence. Such strict moralists as Cicero and Juvenal, as well as the Emperor Claudius in his capacity as censor, all admitted that allowances had to be made for the heat of youthful passions. For five or ten years young men chased prostitutes or lived with mistresses. Gangs of youths were known to break down the doors of a prostitute's house and rape her.

Youth

It was, moreover, a semiofficial practice for youths to form associations of their own. Organizations of young men were common in Greek sectors of the Empire and also existed (as *collegia juvenum*) in the Latin parts, although their precise role remains obscure, probably because they served many purposes and in any case tended to exceed the limits imposed on them (the blood of youth being hot). Young men participated in sports, duels, and hunting. They gathered in amphitheaters to grapple with wild animals, to the admiration of their compatriots. Unfortunately, they did not limit themselves to such laudable physical activities, derived from the physical education practiced by the Greeks. Taking advantage of their numbers and their official status, they created public disturbances. A privilege always accorded well-born youths in Rome was the freedom to wander the streets at night in gangs, beating passersby, manhandling women, and smashing shops. (The young Nero was no stranger to this custom; once he nearly suffered a thrashing at the hands of a senator attacked by his gang, who failed to recognize the Emperor among his attackers.) Groups of young men claimed this right as their due. "Come home from dinner as soon as possible," we read in one Latin tale, "for a gang of hotheaded youths from the best families is pillaging the city." These same youths cheered armies of gladiators and charioteers who clashed in pitched battle, for this, too, was considered sport by the Roman public. One jurist writes that "certain people, who usually call themselves The Young Men, have been seen to cheer the sides in certain public disturbances. If that is the extent of their crime, they should first be admonished by the governor, and, if they repeat the offense, they should be whipped and then released."

Tomb of the Haterii (detail), ca. A.D. 100. This child's face is a convention of Roman art, but a delightful one. (Rome, Lateran Museum; now at the Vatican.)

The privileges of youth were also the privileges of youths as a social group. Once a man married, the time for mistresses was over, and so was the time for handsome male lovers. That, at least, is what we are told by the poets who composed epithalamiums and who, in their nuptial songs, do not hesitate to describe the young bridegroom's past mischief, while assuring their audience that the bride is so pretty that none of these things will ever happen again.

Such was Rome's first moral code. But during the second century A.D. a new code gradually took hold, in theory supplanting the older morality. Backed by medical myths (and bear in mind that ancient medicine had about as much scientific validity as medicine in the time of Molière), the new morality attempted to confine sexuality to marriage, even for young men, and encouraged parents to keep their sons virgins until their wedding day. To be sure, love was not a sin but a pleasure; the only trouble was that pleasure, like alcohol, is dangerous. For the sake of health, it was advisable to limit the amount consumed, and more prudent still to abstain altogether. This was not puritanism but hygiene. Conjugal pleasures were another thing entirely. They were part and parcel of the civic, and natural, institution of marriage and hence a duty. The Germans, whom Tacitus describes as noble savages, "know love only late in life, so that the strength of youth in them is not drained," as it was among the Romans. The philosophers, rationalizers by vocation, supported the movement. One wrote: "Regarding the pleasures of love, you must keep yourself pure until marriage, so far as it is possible to do so." Marcus Aurelius, philosopher as well as emperor, congratulated himself "for having preserved the flower of his youth, for not having performed the virile act too soon, and for waiting perhaps even longer than necessary." He was also proud of having touched neither his slave Theodotus nor his servant Benedicta, even though he felt the desire to do so. Physicians prescribed gymnastics and philosophical studies to cool the sexual energies of young men. Masturbation was to be avoided, not because it sapped a man's strength but because it ripened him too quickly and hence produced fruit imperfect because immature.

Patricide

The new morality was bolstered by arguments drawn from the old morality, with its civic and patrimonial concerns. Over the centuries these gave rise to an idea new to the Roman Empire, the notion of majority. Coming of age ceased to be a physical fact recognized in customary law and became instead a legal fiction: the prepubescent child was replaced by the legal notion of the "minor" child. A young man who abused his license to indulge in pleasure lost forever the opportunity to temper his character. The emperor Tiberius, a severe ruler and a Stoic as well, sent his young nephew Drusus to command a regiment, "because he showed too great a proclivity for the pleasures of the capital." Early marriage was proof that one's youth was not misspent. Jurists had always been more concerned with patrimony than with morality. A youth of fourteen who had not yet come into his inheritance might borrow at usurious rates of interest to pay for his

Funerary statue: sorrow for the dead or of death. This statue, whose face is a portrait, is a masterpiece of Greco-Roman sculpture, the existence of which is too often neglected by a public that has eyes only for Greek originals, for the supposedly all-Roman art of portraiture, and for the elements of Roman originality. (Rome, Museum of the Conservators.)

pleasures, as he was legally entitled to do, and thus squander his patrimony in advance of receiving it. Usurers (which in Rome meant everybody) "seek the notes of young men who have only recently donned the manly toga while continuing to live under the cruel authority of their fathers." Laws, renewed on several occasions, decreed that anyone who lent money to the scion of a noble house forfeited the right to collect the loan even after the youth's father had died. No one was allowed to borrow money before the age of twenty-five. There were other ways of dealing with the problem: a grandfather or paternal uncle might compel an adolescent orphan to obey a pedagogue who had shown that he was capable of asserting his authority. As a matter of principle, however, any fatherless adolescent was his own master. Quintilian tells, with no particular astonishment, the story of a young noble who just had time to bequeath his fortune to his mistress before dying in the flower of youth, aged eighteen.

This brings us to a point that seems important and may in fact be so. A peculiarity of Roman law that astonished the Greeks was that every male child, past puberty or not, married or not, remained under the authority of his father and did not become a Roman in the full sense of the word, a paterfamilias, until the father's death. More than that, the youth's father was his natural judge and could privately sentence him to death. A testator had almost unlimited discretion: fathers could disinherit their sons. Hence it was possible for an eighteen-year-old orphan to make his mistress his heir, yet a grown man could take no legal action on his own while his father was alive. "Where a son is involved," one jurist writes, "public officials have nothing to say; though he were consul, he would have no right to borrow money." Such, at any rate, was the theory. What was the practice? Morally it was even worse.

There were of course legal limits to paternal power. Not every father disinherited his children, and to do so one had to be sure not to die intestate. A son deprived of his inheritance could contest the will in the courts. In any case, only three-quarters of his patrimony could be taken away. As for a father sentencing his son to death, a notion that played a large role in the Roman imagination, the last instances date from the time of Augustus and outraged public opinion. Still, a child had no fortune of his own: whatever he earned or inherited belonged to his father. The father could, however, grant him a certain capital, the so-called *peculum,* to use as he saw fit. Or

Greek funerary relief from Thyrea (Laconia), 2nd or 1st century B.C. This wealthy young horseman and hunter had been taught to wage war with the breastplate and helmet exhibited by his slave. In the upper right is the vase that adorned his grave. The man sets an example by feeding a serpent, who is none other than the deceased, now a good spirit to be fed by his survivors. (Athens, National Archaeological Museum.)

the father could decide quite simply to emancipate the boy. Sons therefore had grounds for hope and means to act.

But the latter were mere expedients, and hopes were attended by risks. Psychologically, an adult male whose father was alive found himself in an intolerable situation. He could do nothing without his father's consent: he could not sign a contract, free a slave, or draw up his will. He possessed only his *peculum,* like a slave, and even that could be revoked. Apart from these humiliations there was the risk—quite real—of being disinherited. Leaf through Pliny's letters: "So-and-so has made his brother residuary legatee, cutting out his own daughter"; "So-and-so has disinherited her own son"; "So-and-so, whom his father disinherited." Public opinion, which, as we shall see, exerted a powerful influence over upper-class attitudes, did not censure automatically; it weighed the facts of each case. "Your mother," writes Pliny again, "had a legitimate reason for disinheriting you." We know, in any case, the demographic facts of life before Pasteur: society was filled with widows and widowers; many women died in childbirth; many others remarried after their husbands died. And since fathers were almost entirely free to draw their wills as they saw fit, the sons of a first marriage feared their stepmother.

Sons had one last yoke to bear: without their father's consent they could make no career. A youth, if of noble birth, could always have himself named a senator—or, if a mere notable, a member of his city's Council. But how could he meet the considerable expenses attached to such honors in an age when bread and circuses were the means by which public men got ahead? No youth would attempt to become a senator or councillor without his father's consent, for the necessary funds could be taken from his patrimony only if his father approved. On many public buildings in Roman Africa—buildings built by councillors to honor themselves—we find inscriptions stating that the father has borne the expense on behalf of the son. The father exercised sovereign authority in deciding the fate of his children. The number of places in the Senate and municipal councils was limited, and few families could claim more than one for their sons. The attendant expenses were considerable, so only the son chosen by the father could enjoy the costly honor of a career. Other sons were duly praised for their sacrifice. I should add that the eldest son enjoyed no legal privilege, though tradition encouraged younger sons to respect the priority of the eldest.

Wills

The father's death meant that, barring mishap, his children could enjoy their inheritance. It also signaled the end of a kind of slavery. The sons became adults, and the daughters, if they had not married or had divorced, became heiresses, free to marry whomever they wished. (Although the law required that a woman consent to her own marriage, it also assumed that she always did consent, so in practice girls had to obey their fathers.) Of course I am assuming that the new heiress did not become subject to another authority, that of her paternal uncle. A strict uncle might forbid his niece to take lovers and assign her to work with distaff and spindle. The poet Horace took tender pity on the fate of such unfortunate women.

In these circumstances the obsession with parricide—a relatively common crime—is not surprising. The reasons for committing such a horrible act are quite comprehensible and require no Freudian feats of explication. "During the civil wars and their attendant proscriptions," writes Velleius of a time when denunciations were common, "the loyalty of wives was greatest, that of freedmen less great, that of slaves not insignificant, and that of sons nil, so hard it is to bear the postponement of hope!"

The only Romans who were men in the full sense of the word were therefore free citizens, either orphans or legally emancipated sons, who, married or not, were "fathers of families" and who possessed a patrimony. The paterfamilias occupied a place apart in the prevailing moral system, as the following discussion, reported by Aulus Gellius, suggests: "Must one always obey one's father? Some say, 'Yes, always.' But what if your father orders you to betray your country? Others respond subtly that one never obeys one's father because it is morality that one obeys, to whose dictates he gives voice." Aulus Gellius replies intelligently that there is a third order of things that are neither good nor immoral, such as the decision to marry or remain celibate, to enter one profession rather than another, to leave home or to stay, to seek public office or not. It is over this third order of things that paternal authority is exercised.

The symbol, and weapon, of the father's familial authority and social dignity was the will. The will was a kind of

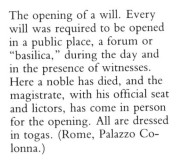

The opening of a will. Every will was required to be opened in a public place, a forum or "basilica," during the day and in the presence of witnesses. Here a noble has died, and the magistrate, with his official seat and lictors, has come in person for the opening. All are dressed in togas. (Rome, Palazzo Colonna.)

confession in which social man revealed himself fully and by which he would be judged. Had he chosen the worthiest heir? Had he made bequests to all his faithful clients? Did he speak of his wife in terms that would certify her as a good spouse? "What a long time we spend deliberating in our heart of hearts over whom we should name in our wills, and how much we should leave them! None of our decisions is more thoroughly examined." All kin, close or distant, were supposed to get something, along with all members of a man's household: deserving slaves were set free by their master's will, and loyal freedmen and clients were not forgotten.

The public reading of a will was an event of some significance. More was involved than just legacies and bequests; the will had the value of a manifesto. The custom of designating "substitute heirs," who received nothing unless the principal heir refused to accept his due, enabled the testator to name anyone he wished and to assign to each person he named a theoretical fraction of his estate, a measure of his esteem for that individual. A man could also insult, postmortem, anyone he had secretly despised, and praise anyone he had esteemed. The custom among nobles was to make a bequest to fashionable writers of the moment. Pliny, a famous orator in his day, went to every will-reading and remarked with satisfaction that he was always left the same amount as his friend Tacitus. (He did not lie, and epigraphists have found a will in which he is named.) Politics played a part. A senator who had always been taken seriously lost his reputation when his will was opened, because in it he flattered Nero (obviously to avoid having his will set aside and his estate confiscated by the Imperial Tax Collector). Others insulted the freedmen who served the sovereign as all-powerful ministers and even had rather unflattering things to say to the emperor himself, be he Nero or Antoninus Pius. A will was such a fine thing, of which people were so proud, that many a testator in his cups found it difficult to keep from reading his will so as to give his legatees a foretaste of their good fortune and win their respect.

In other societies the deathbed ritual and the dying man's last words were of great importance. In Rome what mattered was first of all the will, which expressed the social individual, and second, as we shall see, the epitaph, which manifested what can only be called the public individual.

Painting at Herculanum, 79 B.C. Unmarried life as it exists in painting. This couple, accustomed to it, are in no rush to take their pleasure. She is half nude, and he drinks wine from a raised vessel (with a hole in the bottom that one held closed with a finger; the vessel was usually emptied in a single swallow). (Naples, Archaeological Museum.)

✇ Marriage

ROMAN Italy, in the first century before or after Christ, was home to five or six million free citizens, male and female. They lived in hundreds of rural territories, at the center of which stood a cluster of monuments and private dwellings (the *domus*); these were called "cities." In addition, some one or two million slaves served as domestic servants and agricultural laborers. Little is known about how they lived, beyond the fact that marriage, at this time a private institution, was forbidden to them and would remain so until the third century. Slaves, it was believed, lived in sexual promiscuity, save for a handful of trusted servants who acted as stewards for their masters or, as slaves of the emperor himself, served the state as functionaries. These privileged slaves lived monogamously with a single concubine, sometimes given them by their masters.

Let us restrict our attention, then, to free men. Some of these were born free, the fruit of legitimate marriage between male and female citizens. Others were bastards, born to mothers who were citizens. Still others, born slaves, had been subsequently freed. All were nonetheless citizens, entitled to participate in the civic institution of marriage. To us this institution seems paradoxical: Roman marriage was a private act, which did not require the sanction of any public authority. Bride and groom did not have to appear before the equivalent of a priest or justice of the peace. No written document was necessary: there was no marriage contract, only a contract for the bride's dowry (assuming she had one), and the whole procedure was quite informal. Notwithstanding all that has been said on the subject, no symbolic act was required. In

Criteria for Marriage

short, marriage was a private event, like engagement today. How, then, could a judge decide, in case of litigation over an inheritance, whether or not a man and a woman were legally married? In the absence of a formal act or contract, he based his decision on certain signs, much as courts do today in establishing matters of fact. What signs? Well, for instance, such unambiguous actions as the constitution of a dowry, or acts that proved a man's intention to be a husband, such as referring habitually to the woman with whom he lived as his wife. Or witnesses might testify that they had attended a small ceremony whose nuptial character was manifest. Ultimately, however, only husband and wife could be certain that in their own minds they were married.

It was, nevertheless, important to determine whether or not a man and a woman were legitimately married. For even though marriage was a private institution, with no written instrument or even formal ceremony to certify its existence, it was a fact with legal consequences. The children of a marriage were legitimate; they took their father's name and continued his line; upon his death they inherited his estate, assuming he had not disinherited them. Divorce, from a legal standpoint, was as easy for the wife as for the husband and as informal as marriage. It was enough for either party to leave home with the intention of divorcing his or her spouse. Certain cases gave jurists pause. Was there a true separation or a simple quarrel? Strictly speaking, it was not even necessary to notify an ex-spouse of the divorce, and cases are recorded in which husbands were divorced by their wives without their knowledge. Whether or not a woman took the initiative in divorce, she left her husband's household with her dowry, if any. On the other hand, children apparently always remained with their fathers. Divorce and remarriage were quite common, and nearly every family had children born of different mothers.

A marriage ceremony involved witnesses, useful in case the marriage was contested. The custom of marriage gifts existed. The wedding night took the form of a legal rape from which the woman emerged "offended with her husband" (who, accustomed to using his slave women as he pleased, found it difficult to distinguish between raping a woman and taking the initiative in sexual relations). It was customary for the groom to forgo deflowering his wife on the first night, out of concern for her timidity; but he made up for his for-

bearance by sodomizing her. Martial and Seneca the Elder state this as a proverb, and the *Casina* confirms it. The same custom existed in China. Women abstained from sexual activity during pregnancy. Elian and pseudo-Quintilian found such modesty natural, because they believed it was shared by animals. Since conjugal pleasures were legitimate, wedding guests had the right and even the duty to praise them bawdily. In one epithalamium the poet went so far as to promise the bridegroom an afternoon of love. Such boldness was pardonable on the day after a marriage, but in other circumstances making love during the daylight hours would have been considered shamelessly libertine.

Why did people marry? For money (obtaining a dowry was one honorable way to get rich) and for children who, as legitimate heirs, were entitled to inherit an estate; those children, moreover, perpetuated the state by replenishing the ranks of its citizenry. Politicians called upon families to do their duty as citizens and preserve the city. Pliny the Younger, a senator no more pompous than most, added appropriately that there was another way to make new citizens: by freeing deserving slaves.

Wedding night, reproduction of a Greek original. The veiled bride sits on the edge of the bed, as Persuasion encourages her. At the foot of the bed sits the god Hymen, bold and relaxed, awaiting his moment. Venus, or one of the Graces, leans on a pillar, ready to perfume the bride in preparation for her lawful violation, from which, thanks to the woman's charm, matrimonial harmony would grow. (Rome, Vatican Museums.)

The Transformation of Marriage

Whether in legitimate marriage or concubinage, monogamy was the rule. But monogamy was not synonymous with "couple." I shall consider here not what everyday married life was actually like, but what prevailing moral codes required husbands to think about their wives in different periods. Was the wife a person in her own right, her husband's equal, his queen as it were, and as such entitled to appear together with him in a "royal portrait" (even if she served him as handmaiden under a more respectable name)? Or was she a perpetual child, whose only importance was as personification of the institution of marriage? The answer is simple. In the first century B.C. a man was supposed to think of himself as a citizen who had fulfilled all his civic duties. A century later he was supposed to consider himself a good husband; as such he was officially required to respect his wife. At some point people began to internalize, as a moral code, what had been a civic and dotal institution: monogamous marriage. Why this change? Michel Foucault thinks that the role of men, of males, changed when the Empire supplanted the Republic and the independent cities of Greece. The members of the ruling class, formerly citizen-soldiers, became local notables and loyal subjects of the emperor. The Greco-Roman ideal of self-discipline and autonomy was associated with the desire to exert power in public life. (No one is worthy to govern who cannot govern himself.) Under the Empire, sovereignty over oneself ceased to be a civic virtue and became an end unto itself. Autonomy secured inner peace and made a man independent of Fortune and of the power of the emperor. This was preeminently the Stoic ideal, and Stoicism was the most widespread of those sects of wisdom, or "philosophy," that enjoyed as much influence with the Romans as religions or ideologies do with us. Much Stoic preaching concerned the new conjugal morality. Note, however, that everything I am about to say applies to only a tenth or a twentieth of the free population, to the class of the wealthy, who also considered themselves cultivated. Given the nature of our sources, this is the best we can do. In rural Italy free peasants, whether smallholders or sharecroppers on the lands of the rich, were married. That is all we know about them. The choice between the civic and Stoic ideals was not an option for them.

The code of civic morality, then the morality of the couple. When, over the course of a century or two, the transition was made from one to the other, what changed was not the

Stabies, portrait of a couple, prior to 79 B.C. Mediocre but cruelly accurate. Between the man and the woman is a small Bacchus. (Naples, Archaeological Museum.)

way people behaved (let's not be overoptimistic), or even the rules they were supposed to follow, but something else, something more abstract and yet somehow more crucial: the very ground of morality, that which justified all the prescriptions, and hence the way in which moral agents were perceived—as soldiers with a civic duty to perform or as responsible moral individuals. Form determined content. The older moral code said: "To marry is one duty of the citizen." The newer said: "To be a good man, one must make love only in order to have children. Marriage is not a means to sexual pleasure." The older code did not question the reasons for the rules: the rule was that the only way to father a citizen was to take a wife, so citizens obeyed and married. Less militarist, the newer code sought to discover the grounds of social institutions. Marriage outlives the duty to produce children, it was argued, so there must be some other reason why it exists. Husband and wife, both reasonable beings, live together all their lives. Thus marriage, the Stoics deduced, must be a kind of friendship, a durable affection between two good people who make love only in order to perpetuate the human race. In short, the new morality sought to justify its prescriptions to reasonable people. But it was incapable of criticizing existing institutions. Rational grounds for marriage had to be found. This mixture of good intentions and conformity gave rise to the myth of the couple. In the old civic code, the wife was nothing but an accessory to the work of the citizen and paterfamilias. She produced children and added to the family patrimony. In the new code, the wife was a friend, a "life's companion." As a rational person it was her duty to recognize her natural inferiority and obey her husband. Her husband would respect her as a leader respects his devoted subordinates—friends but inferiors. In short, the couple came to the West when moralists began to wonder why a man and a woman should spend their lives together and ceased to regard marriage as a sort of natural phenomenon.

The new moral code said: "Here are the duties of the married man." By contrast, the old civic code had said: "Marriage is one of the duties of the citizen." Teachers of ethics accordingly had made a point of reminding their pupils of the existence of this duty. In 100 B.C. a censor could say to the assembly of citizens, "marriage, as we all know, is a source of trouble. Nevertheless, one must marry, out of civic duty."

Marriage as a Duty

Pompeii. Idealized figures conversing. A fabulous or theatrical model of elegance for the real world. Gynaeceum scene, perhaps a pastiche of Hellenistic painting. The figures are not placed at random; their respective positions establish the grandeur of the composition. (Naples, Archaeological Museum.)

Each citizen was called upon to ask himself whether or not he would fulfill this obligation. Marriage was not taken for granted but openly discussed as an issue. This created the illusion of a "marriage crisis," a spread of celibacy. (Such collective obsessions, as we know all too well, cannot be countered by mere statistical evidence.) The Romans suffered from this illusion before their historians took it up, and the emperor Augustus promulgated special laws to encourage citizens to marry.

Marriage was therefore perceived as a duty among other duties, an option to elect or reject. It was not a matter of "establishing a family" or setting the course of a life, but one of many dynastic decisions that a noble Roman had to make. Should he enter public life or seek to enhance his family's wealth in the private realm? Should he become a soldier or an orator? And so on. The nobleman's wife was not so much his life's companion as the object of a major decision. She was so much an object, in fact, that two noblemen could amicably pass her back and forth. Cato of Utica, that model of every virtue, lent his wife to a friend and later remarried her, picking up an enormous inheritance for his incovenience. A man by the name of Nero "affianced" his wife Livia to the future emperor Augustus ("affianced' was the word used).

Marriage was but one of a life's acts, and the wife was

but one of the elements of a household, which also included children, freedmen, clients, and slaves. "If your slave, your freedman, your woman, or your client dares to answer you back, you get angry," writes Seneca. Lords, heads of household, settled things among themselves, dealing with each other as sovereign to sovereign. If one of them had to make an important decision, he convoked a "council" of friends rather than discuss the matter with his wife.

Did husband and wife make a "couple"? Did the man of the house allow his wife to see visitors as we in the West do today, or did she quickly retire as in Islamic countries? When a man was invited out to dinner, was it proper to invite his wife as well? From the few indications in the sources, I have not been able to arrive at any firm answers to these questions. The one thing that is clear is that wives were allowed to visit women friends, albeit in the company of chaperones.

A woman was like a grown child; her husband was obliged to humor her because of her dowry and her noble father. Cicero and his correspondents gossip about the caprices of these lifelong adolescents, who, for example, might seize upon the absence of a husband sent to govern a remote province in order to divorce him and marry another. These women's antics nevertheless had real consequences for political relations among the nobility. Needless to say, it was impossible for a woman to make a fool of her lord and master. Cuckoldry (as we know it from Molière) was not a part of the Romans'

Painting of an underground tomb, 2nd century A.D. (Rome, Museum of the Baths.)

conceptual universe. Had it been, Cato, Caesar, and Pompey would all have been illustrious cuckolds. A man was the master of his wife, just as he was the master of his daughters and servants. If his wife was unfaithful, the man did not thereby become a laughingstock. Infidelity was a misfortune, neither greater nor less than the misfortune of a daughter who became pregnant or a slave who failed of his duty. If a wife betrayed her husband, the husband was criticized for want of vigilance and for having, by his own weakness, allowed adultery to flourish in the city—much as we might criticize parents for overindulging or spoiling their children, allowing them to drift into delinquency and thus making the cities unsafe. The only way for a husband or father to avoid such an accusation was to be the first to publicly denounce any misconduct by members of his family. The emperor Augustus detailed the affairs of his daughter Julia in an edict; Nero did the same for the adultery of his wife, Octavia. The point was to prove that the man had no "patience," that is, connivance, with vice.

People wondered whether the stoic silence of other husbands deserved praise or blame.

Because deceived husbands were aggrieved rather than risible and divorced women took their dowries with them, divorce was common among the upper class (Caesar, Cicero, Ovid, and Claudius married three times), and perhaps also among the urban plebs. Juvenal tells of a woman of the people who consults an itinerant soothsayer about whether she should leave her tavernkeeper husband to marry a secondhand clothing merchant (a prosperous profession in a time when the lower orders bought their clothing used). Nothing was more alien to the Romans than the biblical notion of taking possession of the flesh. Roman men did not hesitate to marry divorced women. The emperor Domitian remarried a woman he had divorced, who had subsequently married another man. For a woman to have known only one man in her life was considered a merit, but only the Christians would undertake to make such fidelity a duty and attempt to prohibit widows from remarrying.

The Harmonious Union

Since marriage was a civic duty and a private boon, all that the old moral code required of spouses was to have children and run the household. There were two degrees of virtue: one for discharging strict marital duties, and another, higher level of virtue for achieving a harmonious union. It is here that the couple makes its first appearance in the West, but the appearance is deceiving. The household is the household, and husband and wife each have their respective duties to perform. If they happen to get on well together, so much the better; but mutual understanding is not essential. People were glad to hear that husband and wife got on well, as did Ulysses and Penelope in ancient times, or even that they adored each other, as did the Philemon and Baucis of legend. But not every couple was so fortunate. Marriage was one thing, happy couples were another.

Love in marriage was a stroke of good fortune; it was not the basis of the institution. Marital difficulties were commonplace, and people resigned themselves to this. Moralists said that by learning to put up with a wife's moods and the flaws in her character, a man prepared himself to face the trials and tribulations of the world. In many epitaphs a husband will speak of his "very dear wife"; in others, no less numerous, he will say rather, "my wife, who never gave me any reason to

Probably 2nd century A.D. This is not a fanciful image but a funerary portrait set in a shell—a common device. Evidently there were women painters; this one, with her pots of paint, is working with a nude model. Note the sophisticated hairdo (a similar hairdo can be seen in the portrait of a girl in the Museum of Thessalonica). (Rome, Villa Albani.)

complain" (*querella*). Historians compiled lists of couples who remained together until they died. Nevertheless, when the time came to pay one's respects to a new husband, people emulated Ovid and said: "May your wife equal her husband in exhaustible good nature! May quarrels rarely trouble your life together!" Ovid was too shrewd and courtly a poet to have committed a gaffe and embarrassed his audience.

Because treating one's wife well was not compulsory, it was all the more praiseworthy, all the more meritorious to be "a good neighbor, amiable host, kind to his wife, and lenient to his slave," to borrow Horace's words. Ever since Homer, tenderness toward one's wife had been held up as an ideal beyond the strict obligations of marriage. Bas-reliefs depict husband and wife holding hands, and this, whatever may have been said on the subject, was a symbol not of marriage but of this desirable additional concord. Ovid, exiled, left his wife in Rome, where she administered his property and attempted to win his pardon. Two things united them, he said: the "marital pact," but also "the love that makes us partners." It was possible for conflict to arise between duty and these extraneous tender feelings. What to do, for instance, if one's wife turned out to be sterile? "The first man who repudiated his wife on grounds of sterility had an acceptable motive but did not

Bronze mirror bracket: Jupiter, Juno, and Cupid, 1st century B.C.? In Italy, for five centuries, scenes from Greek mythology were de rigueur in elegant boudoir decoration. (Paris, Louvre.)

escape censure [*reprehensio*], because even the desire to have children should not have outweighed lasting devotion to his wife," according to the moralist Valerius Maximus.

The New Illusion

Had the couple arrived in the West? No. A merit is one thing, a duty another. Note the shade of difference: harmony was praised where it existed, not held up as a norm implicit in the institution of marriage, in which case disagreement between husband and wife would have been seen as shocking rather than only too predictable. And this was in fact the case under the new moral code, related to Stoicism, which imposed the couple as an ideal that husbands and wives should emulate. Hypocrisy was the result. To suspect disharmony in a marriage was now regarded as slander or defeatism. One symptom by which we can recognize the champions of the new morality of marriage is their edifying style. When Seneca and Pliny speak of their married lives, they do so in a sentimental style that exudes virtue and deliberately aims to be exemplary. One consequence was that the place of the wife ceased to be what it had been. Under the old moral code she had been classed among the servants, who were placed in her charge by delegation of her husband's authority. Under the new code she was raised to the same status as her husband's friends, and friends played an important role in the social life of the Greeks and Romans. For Seneca the marriage bond was comparable in every way to the pact of friendship. What were the practical consequences of this? I doubt that there were many. What changed was more than likely the manner in which husbands spoke of their wives in general conversation or addressed them in the presence of others.

What can be said about this moral transformation is approximately the same that can be said of any "event" in the history of ideas. After a century of cultural sociology, many historians frankly admit that they are incapable of explaining cultural mutations and, even more, that they haven't the slightest idea what form a causal explanation might take. Let it be noted simply that the cause was not Stoicism. The new morality had its champions among the enemies of the Stoics as well as among Stoics and neutral onlookers.

Plutarch, a Platonist philosopher, was at pains to mark his distance from Stoicism, the still triumphant rival of neo-Platonism, its challenger for philosophical supremacy. He nevertheless sets forth his theory of conjugal love, which he regarded as a higher form of friendship. A senator, Pliny belonged to no sect; he had chosen eloquence rather than wisdom. In his letters he paints himself as a good man, and he pronounces his opinion on every subject with dogmatic certainty typical of the Roman senator. He decides, for example, that remarriage is laudable even if the age of the parties rules out procreation as its purpose, for the true end of marriage is the aid and affection that the spouses bring each other. He claims that his relations with his own wife are noble and sentimental and that he shows her the greatest respect and bears toward her the profoundest feelings of friendship, marked by all the virtues. The modern reader must make an effort to recall that the woman in question was a child bride who came to Pliny in a marriage of convenience made for money and for the sake of his career. Another neutral senator, Tacitus, admitted that, contrary to republican tradition, a woman might accompany her husband on a mission to govern a province, even though this was practically a military function and the female sex was barred from all things military. The wife's presence would lend moral support to her husband, strengthening rather than weakening his soldierly resolve.

In these circumstances it is hardly surprising that the

This couple, 1st century B.C., has such an "old Roman" look that at first we do not notice that the sculptor has clothed them in the Greek manner. The Greeks sculpted Romans without their togas, retaining only the shoes of their usual costume. (Rome, Museum of the Conservators.)

Stoics, too, adopted the new morality, for it had emerged triumphant and would henceforth be taken for granted. But because there were so many Stoics, and their voices were so powerful, they appear, misleadingly, to have been the propagators rather than the dupes of the new moral outlook. I use the word "dupes" advisedly, for nothing in Stoic doctrine obliged them to preach submission to the reigning morality. Indeed, the contrary was true. Stoicism, in its original version, taught that mortals should strive to become the equals of the gods, self-sufficient and indifferent to Fortune's blows. They could achieve this end by applying critical reason to discover the natural route to self-sufficiency and then courageously sticking to this path. Individuals were obliged to accept their social roles only insofar as these were compatible with the end of achieving self-sufficiency and with the natural sympathy that each man feels for his fellow human beings. Such a philosophy could easily have led to a critique of the institutions of politics and the family, and originally Stoicism did lead to such a critique. But it became the victim of its success with a clique of rich and powerful men of letters and was reduced to little more than a sophisticated version of prevailing morality: a man's duties to himself and others were identified with institutions, which this bastard doctrine ingeniously sought to internalize as moral precepts. Marriage, for example, was conceived as a friendship—an unequal friendship—between a man and a woman. We are far from the time when Stoics speculated about desire for beauty and love for boys (which they considered typical of love in general).

Typical tomb of Byzantium and Mysia, 1st century B.C., showing a couple (but not their children) and a symbol of marital harmony. At the left is a servant; in the middle a slave standing with his legs crossed (ready to obey his master's orders). The omnipresent scroll indicates the husband's high social class. (Paris, Louvre.)

Chaste Spouses

Apart from the deliberate conformity of the later Stoic philosophy, there was a more genuine affinity between Stoicism and the new conjugal morality. The new morality did more than just prescribe certain marital duties. It exhorted husband and wife to emulate a certain ideal of the couple, relying on feelings of friendship, constantly tested, to dictate their duties. Stoicism was a doctrine of moral autonomy, which held that the reasonable individual ought to guide himself, from within. But it was essential that he pay constant attention to every detail along life's path. This had two consequences: first, all the rigor of the matrimonial institution was incorporated into conformist Stoicism; and, second, the institution was made more rigorous than ever, by requiring husband and wife to control their every gesture and to dem-

Cameo. Octavia, sister of Augustus. Beautiful princesses, treated as stars, added luster to the new monarchy. (Paris, Bibliothèque Nationale, Cabinet des Médailles.)

onstrate, before giving in to any desire, that it conformed to the dictates of reason.

Perpetuation of the institution. One must marry, according to Antipater of Tarsus, in order to provide one's country with new citizens and because the divine plan of the universe requires propagation of the human race. The foundation of marriage, according to Musonius, is procreation and mutual support. Adultery is theft, according to Epictetus: to take one's neighbor's wife is as thoughtless as to snatch his serving of pork from his plate. "Similarly, for women, the portions have been distributed among men." Marriage, according to Seneca, is an exchange of obligations, possibly unequal or, rather, different, that of the woman being to obey. Marcus Aurelius, the Stoic emperor, congratulated himself on having found in his empress "so obedient a wife." Since husband and wife were both moral agents and contracts were mutual, adultery on the part of the husband was considered as grave an offense

Detail of sarcophagus, 3rd or 4th century. Muse with bare arms in melancholy daydream, leaning against frame of cultivated man's epitaph. (Paris, Louvre.)

as adultery on the part of the wife (in contrast to the old morality, which judged sins not according to a moral ideal but according to civic reality, recognizing male privilege as a fact).

It is clear that the requirements of marriage had become more stringent than ever. Because marriage was friendship, husband and wife could make love only in order to have children, and even then with care not to indulge in too many caresses. A man must not treat his wife as he would a mistress, Seneca admonishes, and Saint Jerome cites him approvingly. His nephew Lucan was of the same opinion. He wrote an epic, a sort of realistic historical novel, in which he describes in his own fashion the story of the civil war between Caesar and Pompey. He shows Cato, model of the Stoic, taking leave of his wife (the same wife he lent for a time to a friend) as he prepares to go off to war. Even on the eve of such a lengthy separation, they do not make love, as Lucan is at pains to point out, explaining as he does the doctrinal significance of the fact. Even that semigreat man Pompey, although no Stoic, does not sleep with his wife on the farewell night. Why the abstinence? Because a good man does not live for petty pleasures and is careful about every action. To give in to desire is immoral. There is only one reasonable ground for a couple to sleep together: procreation. It was a question not of asceticism but of rationalism. Reason asked: Why do this? By nature a planner, reason found it difficult to accept "Why not?" as an answer. Stoic *planism* bears a misleading resemblance to Christian asceticism. In any case, Christianity was not a monolithic religion. In its first few centuries it evolved far more than Stoicism did; and it was quite a varied religion to begin with. The Christian Clement of Alexandria was influenced by Stoicism to the point of copying out the conjugal precepts of the Stoic Musonius, without mentioning their true author. Saint Jerome would have found this doctrine far too sensual. As for Saint Augustine, one of the most prodigious inventors of ideas the world has ever known, it was easier for him to create his own doctrine of marriage than to copy someone else's.

Clearly we must not argue in terms of stereotypes and imagine a conflict between pagan and Christian morality. The real cleavage lay elsewhere: between a morality of matrimonial duties and an internalized morality of the couple. The latter, which originated somewhere in the heart of pagan culture, was commonplace by A.D. 100, shared by both pagans and Christians under Stoic influence. Stoics believed that this mo-

Venus. Roman replica of a Greek original from the 5th century B.C., cloaked in "wet drapery." (Rome, Museum of the Conservators.)

Portrait of an unknown
woman, early Christian era.
(Paris, Petit Palais, Dutuit
Collection.)

Portrait of an unknown man,
found in Annecy, 2nd century.
(Paris, Petit Palais, Dutuit
Collection.)

rality was morality par excellence, hence necessarily their own invention. To affirm, on abundant evidence, that late pagan morality was identical with almost all Christian morality is not to confound paganism and Christianity but to blur the outlines of both. There is no point arguing about those massive but flimsy inventions; rather, we must take them apart in order to study the more subtle mechanisms at work within them, mechanisms that do not correspond to traditional blueprints.

Besides, a moral code is more than just a collection of precepts. Even if some pagans and some Christians shared identical rules of marital behavior, questions would remain. At a certain point in history both pagans and Christians said: Do not make love except to have children. But the consequences of such a declaration differ, depending on whether it is made by a philosophy that offers advice to free individuals, who may take it or leave it as they find its arguments convincing or not, or by an all-powerful Church, which sees its mission as one of securing salvation in the hereafter through the regulation of consciences here below and seeks to lay down the law to all men without exception, whether convinced or not.

Rome, statuette of Venus or a Season. The hairdo would have been fashionable in the early Christian era. Did she once hold a mirror? This would account for the resigned gesture of the index figure beneath the chin. At the waist is the buckle of a girdle that lifted the woman's dress so that it would hang with more folds. (Paris, Petit Palais, Dutuit Collection.)

Fragment of sarcophagus, 2nd or 3rd century. Scenes like this occur infrequently on tombs. Either the man buried here was a wealthy landowner, or the plowing depicted had something to do with a myth, such as that of Triptolemus. Summer carries a full basket of fruit. The yoke is attached, not very efficiently, to the ox's withers. (Museum of Benevento.)

✒ Slavery

AT any moment, Seneca says, death may catch you una-
wares: you may fall victim to shipwreck or bandits, "and,
leaving aside higher powers, the least of your slaves holds
over you the power of life and death." A worried Pliny wrote
to alert one of his correspondents that his friend Robustus had
left on a journey accompanied by some of his slaves and had
disappeared. No one had seen him since. "Had he been the
victim of an attack by his servants?" In Mainz an epitaph
immortalizes the tragic end of a thirty-year-old slaveowner
murdered by his slave, who then committed suicide by jump-
ing into the Main. The Romans lived in unspoken fear of their
slaves. Though by nature an inferior being, the slave was a
member of his master's family, one whom the master "loved"
and punished paternally and from whom he expected obedience and "love" in return. The slave's relationship to his master was ambivalent, hence dangerous. Love could suddenly
turn to hatred. The annals of modern criminology record any
number of bloody crimes committed by maids who had previously given every appearance of being devoted servants.
Ancient slavery is a subject for Jean Genet.

Opinions to the contrary notwithstanding, the slave was
not a thing; he was considered a human being. Even "wicked
masters," who treated their slaves inhumanely, set them the
moral duty of being good slaves, of serving with loyalty and
devotion. One does not impose moral obligations on animals
or machines. Yet this human being was also a possession, the
property of its owner. There were two kinds of property in
the ancient world: men and things. My father, wrote Galen,
always taught me not to look upon material losses as tragic.
If an ox or a horse or a slave of mine dies, therefore, I do not

Tomb of the freedman Cornelius Atimetus, who manufactured and sold knives, 1st century A.D. In this scene knives are being sold. According to his epitaph, Atimetus owned several slaves. Shown on the right wearing a tunic, he displays his merchandise to a client wearing a toga. (Rome, Vatican Museums.)

carry on. Plato, Aristotle, and Cato shared these sentiments. Similarly, in our own day an officer may say, I lost a machine gun and twenty men.

Because a slave was owned property, he was an inferior being. And since this inferiority of one man made another man, his owner, a man of power, the master, confident of his majesty, consecrated that power by holding that the slave's inferiority was a fact of nature. A slave, it was said, is subhuman by fate and not by accident. Today's closest psychological analogy to ancient slavery is racism. Furthermore, the master's power over his human implement was not governed by rules; it was absolute. The personal relation between master and slave was therefore unlike the relation between employer and employee; the slave was a devoted servant who obeyed in his very soul. Though unequal, the master-slave relationship involved two human beings. The master "loved" his slave, for what master does not love his dog, what employer does not love his good workers, what colonist does not love his loyal natives? The officer who lost twenty men loved them and was loved by them. Ancient slavery was a peculiar legal relationship, which gave rise to common sentiments of dependence and personal authority; it was an emotional relationship between individuals, with little about it that was anonymous.

Slavery was not, or at any rate not simply, a relation of production. Though sharing a common inferiority, slaves played the most varied roles in the economy, society, and even politics and culture. A handful were richer and more powerful than most free men. Their ethnic origin was of no significance. The subjugation of vanquished peoples and slave trade at the borders of the empire supplied only a small fraction of the servile work force. Slaves reproduced themselves; their ranks were swelled by abandoned infants and free men sold into slavery. Children born to a slave mother belonged to her master, regardless of who the father was, just as the offspring of livestock belonged to their owner. It was the master's choice whether to raise his slave children or expose them—or even drown them as one might drown unwanted kittens. A Greek tale tells of the distress of a slave-mistress, who trembles at the thought that her master-lover might kill the child she is expecting by him. A collection of "jokes," the *Philogelos*, contains this good one: "The Absent-minded Fellow had a child by one of his slaves, and his father advised him to kill the child. But the Absent-minded Fellow responded, 'You tell me

Top: Relief, 1st or 2nd century. A family workshop (note the child at the left) in which metal vessels were manufactured. A vessel's price depended on its weight, which accounts for the scales. (Naples, Archaeological Museum.) Bottom left: Tomb of Cornelius Atimetus. Knives are being forged. Bottom right: Detail of a sarcophagus, 2nd or 3rd century. A cobbler and a ropemaker who lived together were buried together because they were friends. (Rome, Museum of the Baths.)

to begin by killing my children; next thing you'll be telling me to kill yours.'" As we have seen, the abandonment of children was common, and not only among the poor. Slave traders picked up babies exposed in temples or at public dumps. Last but not least, poverty drove the indigent to sell their newborn to slave traffickers (who took children scarcely out of the womb and still covered with blood, before their mothers had had a chance to see and develop affection for them). Many adults sold themselves in order not to die of hunger. Some ambitious men did the same in the hope of becoming the stewards of noblemen or imperial treasurers. This, in my view, was the story of the all-powerful and extremely wealthy Pallas, scion of a noble Arcadian family, who sold himself into slavery so that he might be taken on as steward by a woman of the imperial family and who wound up as minister of finance and *éminence grise* to the emperor Claudius.

The True Nature of Slavery

In the Roman Empire the emperor's slaves and freedmen played a role analogous to that played in French history by such illustrious royal ministers and advisers as Colbert or Fouquet. Most of those whom we would call functionaries or bureaucrats were also imperial slaves and freedmen: they handled the administrative chores of the prince, their master. At the opposite end of the spectrum were slaves who worked as agricultural laborers. To be sure, the age of "plantation slavery" and Spartacus' revolt belonged to the distant past, and it is not true that Roman society was based on slavery. The system of large estates cultivated by slave gangs was limited to certain regions such as southern Italy and Sicily. (The slave system was no more essential a feature of Roman antiquity than slavery in the southern United States prior to 1865 is an essential characteristic of the modern West.) Elsewhere, estates were worked by sharecroppers and hired laborers as well as slaves; in some provinces, such as Egypt, rural slavery was virtually unknown. Large landowners used slaves to cultivate portions of their estates not rented to sharecroppers. These slaves lived in dormitories under the authority of a slave overseer or steward, whose official concubine prepared meals for all the slaves. Philostratus tells the story of a modest vintner who resigned himself to tending his vineyard by himself because his few slaves cost too much to keep.

Most artisans seem to have been slaves. Slaves and freed-

men made up the entire staff of the pottery shops at Arezzo, where a host of small, independent businesses employed from one to sixty-five workers. In agriculture we find mainly small independent peasants and sharecroppers, who worked for large landowners. Additional labor was needed at times, however, and we find both hired day laborers, free but miserable, and "chained slaves," a phrase I interpret to mean slaves who had misbehaved and were punished by being sold on condition that the buyer keep them as prisoners in a kind of private prison. Slave labor supplemented the vast peasantry already on the land. For slavery to have become the primary relation of production, the Romans would have had to subjugate this free peasantry. At a rough estimate, slaves accounted for a quarter of the rural work force in Italy. Given that the peasants were the beasts of burden of the Roman Empire, the lot of the slave was harsh indeed.

A slave who did not work the land was most likely to be a domestic servant. An upper-class Roman employed dozens of servants in his household, and a middle-class Roman (who would have been wealthy enough to live without doing anything) had one, two, or three. According to Galen, "there was at Pergamum a grammarian who had two slaves. Every day the grammarian went to the baths with one of them [who dressed and undressed him] and left the second locked up at home to watch the house and prepare the meal." Domestics lived in a variety of situations, ranging from that of the slattern to that of the powerful overseer mentioned by Galen, who had charge of all of his master's affairs and who was seen by the greatest doctors when he fell ill. Relations between servants and their masters varied just as widely, and the slave who was the accomplice of his master and led him about by the nose was not just a figure of comedy (although the master could, in a fit of rage, send him off to a life of hard labor should their ambivalent relationship turn sour). Master and mistress could set trusted slaves to spy on their "friends" and clients or on preceptors, philosophers, and other freeborn servants. These slaves reported the scandals and absurdities of the household directly to the master. Certain types of work were normally performed by slaves, who obtained secure positions in the service of some great personage: grammarians, architects, singers, and actors might be slaves of the master who employed their talents. Intimacy with one of the great was less sordid than working for a daily pittance, and eventually the masters of these slaves would set them free.

Chariot race at the Circus. This relief telescopes two different phases of the race. The magistrate who presides over and pays for the games (identifiable from his scepter) prepares to throw down a handkerchief signaling the start, and one chariot pulls ahead of the others, indicating the finish. (Rome, Vatican Museums.)

Roman physicians were normally succeeded by slaves whom they trained and then manumitted (there being no medical schools at the time). The relation of employer to hired labor was not seen as a neutral one governed by rules; it was looked down on because it was not a personal bond. Personal ties were highly unequal, and it was this inequality that was common to all slaves, however different their conditions might be in other respects. This common condition—involvement in an unequal personal relation with a master—is what makes "slavery" a meaningful word. Whether powerful or wretched, all slaves were spoken to in the tone and terms used in speaking to children and inferior beings. Slavery was an extraeconomic relationship, and it was more than just a legal category. What is inconceivable and distasteful (to us) is that it was a social distinction not based on the "rational" criterion of wealth, which is why we compare it to racism. In the United States fifty years ago a black could be a famous singer or wealthy businessman and yet whites would speak to him in familiar terms and address him by his first name, as though speaking to a servant. As Jean-Claude Passeron has observed, there can be hierarchies, evident from visible signs of esteem, that have nothing to do with wealth or power. Slavery, racism, and nobility offer numerous examples.

Cover plate, 1st century. Prior to construction of the Coliseum, fights between gladiators and wild animals were held in the Circus. The seven boulders indicate that the chariots have completed seven laps. (Rome, Museum of the Baths.)

Slave collar in bronze, found around the neck of a skeleton in southern Rome: "If captured, return me to Apronianus, minister in the imperial palace, at the Golden Napkin on the Aventine, for I am a fugitive slave." (Paris, Petit Palais, Dutuit Collection.)

Bronze plaque, 3rd–4th century. "I am Asellus, slave of Prejectus attached to the ministry of markets, and I have escaped the walls of Rome. Capture me, for I am a fugitive slave, and return me to Barbers' Street, near the Temple of Flora." A slave who managed to escape had virtually no way to earn a living other than to sell himself to a slave dealer in the hope of being resold to a better master than the one from whom he had fled. (Paris, Petit Palais, Dutuit Collection.)

The slave was inferior by nature, whatever he was or did. This natural inferiority went hand in hand with legal inferiority. If the master decided to set the slave up in business in order to claim the profits for himself, he gave the slave a sum of money called a *peculum* and full financial autonomy, along with the right to sign contracts on his own initiative and even to plead in court, so long as his master's affairs were involved and the peculum was not revoked. Despite such useful sham freedoms, the slave remained a person who could be sold at any time. If the master, who had the right to punish a slave at will, decided that he deserved the ultimate punishment, he would hire the municipal executioner to do the job, paying only the cost of the pitch and sulfur needed to burn the unfortunate victim. In the public courts slaves could be subjected to torture to force them to confess crimes of their masters; free men were exempt from the threat of torture.

The barrier between humans and subhumans was supposedly impregnable. It was indecent to point out that such and such a slave had been born free and sold himself into slavery, indecent even to speculate about the possibility that a

The Unquestioned Nature of Slavery

Scene from a Greek comedy (or a Latin comedy with Greek costumes). Four masked actors: an angry master, ready to beat his slave, is restrained by an old friend. At right, the slave seeks the protection of a third party. Meanwhile, a woman plays a double "flute" (actually, a double clarinet). (Naples, Archaeological Museum.)

free man might sell himself that way. It was legitimate to buy futures—for example, a harvest "whenever it is ripe"—but it was not legitimate to offer a price for a man, "whenever he is forced to sell himself into slavery." This taboo was similar to one that existed in the Ancien Régime in France, where a respectful silence was maintained about the numerous offspring of poor nobles who lived obscurely as commoners. Since no ambiguity between freedom and servitude could be tolerated, Roman law had a rule of presumption "in favor of liberty," which held that when in doubt, a judge should decide in favor of liberty. If, for example, there was doubt as to the interpretation of a will that seemed to emancipate a late testator's slaves, the judge should choose the more positive interpretation, in favor of emancipation. Another rule was that once a slave had been freed, the decision could not be revoked, for "freedom is the common property" of all orders of free men, as the Senate reaffirmed in A.D. 56. To cast doubt upon the manumission of a single slave would be to threaten the liberty of all free men.

The principle of deciding in favor of the more humane alternative was humanitarian in appearance only. Suppose we had a rule that if a jury is divided equally between acquittal and execution, the verdict should be innocent; it does not follow from this that the execution of persons proven guilty will give anyone pause. The principle is established in the interest of the innocent, not in the interest of the guilty. The paradox in the Roman case is clear: judges should opt for freedom, but only in case of doubt. No one was concerned about those slaves whose servile status was unambiguous. To hate judicial errors is not to challenge the sanctity of justice but to uphold it.

Slavery was an undeniable reality. Humanitarians did not attempt to free slaves, merely to behave as good masters. So assured were the Romans of their own superiority, that they looked upon slaves as overgrown children. A slave was usually called "little one" or "boy" (*pais, puer*), even if he was an old man. Slaves addressed each other in the same way. Like children, slaves fell under the jurisdiction of that domestic court over which their master sat in sovereign judgment. If their crimes brought them before the public courts, they could be subjected to corporal punishment, from which free men were exempt. Lacking social importance, slaves had neither wives nor children. Their lovemaking and childbearing were like the breeding of livestock: the master rejoiced when his herds increased. Their proper names differed from those of free men (just as we call our dogs Fido and Rover). Slave names were of Greek origin, at least in appearance. (Greeks did not use these names, which were merely Roman pastiches of Greek names, made up for the purpose.) Slaves being children, slave rebellions were like parricide. When Virgil consigned to the lowest circle of his Hell all "those who have taken part in impious wars and renounced the faith due their masters," he had in mind Spartacus and his followers.

Romans looked with contempt on slaves' private lives, which they regarded as puerile. Yet slaves did have a life of their own. They participated in religion, for example, and not just the religion of the household, which was after all their own. Away from home a slave might well serve as the priest of some sect or even of the Christian Church—which never for one moment considered abolishing slavery. It is plausible that slaves should have been particularly attracted to things religious, whether pagan or Christian, for few other areas of life were open to them. They also took a passionate interest in public spectacles—theater, Circus, and arena—for on holidays they were given leave to stop work, as were the courts, the schools—and the beasts that toiled in the fields and on the roads.

Romans smiled or smirked about such matters. The feelings of slaves were not those of adults. A Roman would have found it as humorous to imagine a slave passionately in love as a Frenchman would to imagine a peasant of Molière's racked by Racinian passions and jealousies. And what if masters had been obliged to concern themselves with the sentimental caprices of their servants? "They fall in love now, do they, the slaves from around here?" asks the shocked hero of one of Plautus' fey comedies. A slave was supposed to live for his work, and that was all. Horace amused his readers with stories of the private life of his slave Davus, who went with cheap whores in the back streets and stared wide-eyed at paintings immortalizing the great matches of the gladiators. Judges were less amused: religious fanaticism, excessive lust, and immoderate passion for spectacles and paintings ("posters" may be closer to the mark) were all defects that slave traders were required to make known to prospective buyers. "Defects" in the sense of defective merchandise? No: slaves were men, and their defects were moral wrongs and psychological flaws.

It was commonly agreed that the psychology of servants was different from that of their masters. A slave's psychology came down to this: was he fit or unfit for his work, and did he have feelings of loyalty toward his master? Historians and moralists approvingly recount instances of slaves who carried devotion to the point of performing humble acts of heroism, who died to save their masters or who followed them to their deaths. But there were far too many "bad slaves." The adjective says it all. A bad slave was not a slave with certain flaws, as we might say, an "overweight plumber" or a "lazy lawyer." He was rather a slave unfit for his purpose, a "bad tool," a slave who was not a slave.

Like the psychology of a child, the psychology of a slave was the result of the influences he had absorbed and the examples he had been set; his soul had no autonomy. It was often said that imitating bad slaves could make any slave a

Small bronze of a grotesque character of fantasy, 1st century (?). A short, fat man should not take such long strides, especially when dressed in an improvised garment held together with one hand and ever so slightly too short. (Paris, Petit Palais, Dutuit Collection.)

gambler, a drunkard, or an idler, and that the example of a wicked master could make a slave lustful or lazy. The law permitted recourse against any person who corrupted one's slave. It was an offense to knowingly offer asylum to a fugitive slave or to encourage a slave to flee. Victims were all too often primarily responsible for their slaves' misdeeds. A master who wants to be respected by his servants should not joke with them, says Plato, and he must be the first to rise each morning. Many masters were weak and were censured for their weakness by public opinion. A Roman grammarian offers a curious detail: "In light comic sketches comic poets are allowed to show slaves wiser than their masters, something that would not be permissible in more formal comedies." In a short sketch it was possible to envision a maliciously inverted world; realistic comedy had to show the noble truth.

How did slaves endure such misery and humiliation? Did they feel smoldering rage or cunningly harbor thoughts of rebellion that occasionally erupted in slave uprisings or slave wars? Or did they resign themselves to their fate? Between utter passivity and active rebellion lies a middle term, which no doubt comes closer to describing everyday life: accommodation. Like a Pullman traveler in an uncomfortable berth, slaves adjusted their frame of mind so as to minimize their suffering: unable to burn the master, they loved him. In the slaves' argot the master was *ipsimus* or *ipsissimus* (roughly, "most himself"). "I was a slave for forty years," a freedman tells Petronius, "yet no one could tell whether I was a slave or a free man. I did all I could to gratify my master, who was an honorable and worthy man. And in the house I was dealing with people who would have liked nothing better than to trip me up. But in the end I came out on top, praise be to my master! Now, that is real merit, because to be born free isn't very hard at all." Thus, some saw slavery as a kind of career in which to outperform other slaves.

With nothing else to guide them, slaves shared the values of their master, admired him, and served him jealously. Like voyeurs they watched him live his life with a mixture of admiration and scorn. They took up his cause, defended his person, and jealously guarded his honor. In case of riot or even civil war they were the master's right hand, his soldiers. Let the master assert over a slave or his slave's concubine his *jus primae noctis*; the slave bore the blow with the aid of a

Evidence of Slavery

proverb: "There is no shame in doing what the master orders." When a master came to visit his farm, his steward's wife naturally slept with him. Obedience was the slave's cardinal virtue, and slaves reproached other slaves for their refusal to bend to discipline. "Your stupid masters don't know how to make you obey," said one former slave to a "bad" slave.

It is not hard to imagine how such love, if frustrated or offended, could turn to bloody rage against a master deemed unworthy of affection. The slave uprisings led by Spartacus and his emulators had a different cause, however. The down-trodden did not think of fighting for a less unjust society from which slavery would have been banished. To escape their wretched condition, they embarked upon an adventure comparable to that of the Mamelukes or the buccaneers, attempting to carve a kingdom of their own out of Roman lands. A generation before Spartacus, at the time of the great rebellion of slaves in Sicily, the rebels established a capital, Enna, made one of their number king, and even began striking coinage. It is hard to believe that in this kingdom of former slaves slavery would have been prohibited. Why should it have been?

No man has ever been able to look beyond the changing backdrop of the historical dramas in which he is caught up and peer deep into the wings of history's theater, for there are no wings. No slave, no master, was ever able to imagine a world in which the institution of slavery did not exist. What slaves wanted—or what most of them wanted (for it was better to serve than to be free and die of hunger)—was to escape from servitude individually, to be set free. Masters themselves regarded the manumission of slaves as a handsome deed. "My friends," declaims Trimalchio in his cups, "the slaves, too, are men and have sucked the same milk as us, even if fate has struck them down. They shall nevertheless taste the water of freedom before too long (but let us not tempt fate by speaking of this, for I wish to remain alive!). In short, I set them all free in my will." In speaking and acting this way a master honored himself. Far from undermining the legitimacy of slavery, he was in fact drawing the logical consequences of the paternal authority he enjoyed over his slaves. A master who loved his slaves would set them free, since freedom was what they wanted most. By setting them free, he did not show that he believed slavery to be an injustice rather than an accident of fate; he proved only that he wished to be a good master.

To free slaves was a merit but not a duty: everything hinges on that distinction. A king acts within his rights when he condemns a criminal to death, and commands respect when he grants him pardon. But the pardon is a free act, and the king is not in the wrong if he refuses to grant it. The pleasure masters took in freeing their slaves confirmed the authority that allowed them not to free their slaves. The master commanded with love, and love knows no law. The subordinate could not claim clemency as his due. The father had a double image: he punished and he pardoned. Because granting the pardon was not a duty, it could not be solicited by the slave himself, but only by a third party, born free, like the master. The intermediary honored himself by persuading the father to substitute clemency for severity. At the same time he honored the authority of masters in general over slaves in general.

A free man solicits a master to pardon one of his slaves: this is a typical episode of Roman life, which writers and even the *Digest* delighted in portraying because they sensed vaguely that its paradoxical flavor somehow contained the key to the authority of the slave system. Ovid counseled the clever lover to cast the woman he desired in the role of kindly aunt, while the lover himself played the severe father: "When you might easily on your own do something that you must do in any case, always use your mistress as an intermediary. Have you promised freedom to one of your servants? See to it that he begs your mistress to intervene with you on his behalf. Do you exempt a slave from his punishment? Let it be your mistress who persuades you to do what you were going to do anyway." Roman law did not regard as a fugitive a slave who fled in order to ask a friend of his master to beg indulgence of the latter. A master could be severe in individual cases without damaging the reputation for kindness of the master class as a whole. For clemency could be requested and decided only between peers. A slave who asked for clemency would have been regarded as impudent for having taken it upon himself to prejudge which of the two paternal masks the master would choose to wear.

If the master's indulgence was not the homage that slaveholding paid to humanitarianism but merely the merit of an individual, cruelties and even atrocities committed by some masters were demerits that attached to individuals only, not to the master class. Cruelty to slaves was not unusual. This is clear from the advice that Ovid gives in his manual of seduction: a woman who scratches her hairdresser or stabs her with

The Two Aspects of the Master

Hydraulic organ, 4th-century tombstone. Water pressure caused the pipes to vibrate. The sonority of the organ contrasted with the usual high pitch of ancient music. (Rome, Museum of Saint Paul's Outside the Walls.)

a needle does not make herself attractive. One day the emperor Hadrian, refined though he was, stabbed one of his slave secretaries in the eye with his pen. He later called this slave in and asked him what gift he would like as compensation for the loss of his eye. The victim stood silent. The emperor repeated his question, adding that the slave could have whatever he wished. The answer was: "I want nothing but my eye." Shortly before Christianity's final triumph, the council of Elvira condemned Christian mistresses who, "out of jealous rage beat their servingwomen so severely that they die, provided that said death occurs within four days."

A cruel or wrathful master brought moral condemnation upon himself and could do himself material harm. Once their rage had passed, many repented of cruel acts. Consider this incident from the second century A.D. The physician Galen had left Rome bound for his home in Pergamum (near the Turkish coast), accompanied by a man from Crete. This fellow was not without virtues: simple, friendly, and honest, he was not too demanding when it came to the daily expenses of travel. But he was susceptible to fits of rage, during which he went so far as to beat his slaves personally, kicking them and beating them about the head with whip or cudgel. Upon reaching the Isthmus of Corinth, the travelers dispatched their baggage to Athens by sea from the port of Cenchreae. They hired a coach to carry themselves and their slaves to Athens by the coastal route via Mégara. They had passed Eleusis when Galen's companion noticed that his slaves had loaded on the ship some baggage that should have been kept for the road. He fell into a rage and, finding nothing at hand with which to beat his men, took his sheathed traveling dagger from his belt and proceeded to beat his slaves about the head. But the knife cut through the scabbard, and two slaves received head wounds, one quite serious. Thereupon the master, overwhelmed by what he had done, went from one extreme to the other: handing a whip to Galen and removing his clothes, he begged Galen to beat him, "as punishment for what he had done under the influence of this accursed anger." Galen laughed in his face, gave him a philosophical sermon on anger (he was a philosopher-physician), and drew from the incident the following moral for his readers: A master should never punish his slaves with his own hands, and he should always postpone the decision to punish until the following day.

This anecdote sheds light on one piece of conventional wisdom: the idea that slavery, under the influence of Stoicism, became progressively more humane during the three centuries of High Empire. This alleged humanization of slavery was in reality a moralization, resulting not from some "natural" tendency of civilized humanity but from a particular historical development, which we have already described in discussing the origins of the couple. This moralization of master as well as slave was in no sense humanitarian, nor did it cast doubt on the legitimacy of slavery, nor was it a ruse or ideological camouflage intended to preserve the institution from some sort of agitation by slaves. Once we refuse to allow our thinking to be confined by these rigid yet inept generalizations, it is easy to see that the moralization of slavery made it no less harsh than before. Nor was the moralization of slavery the consequence of imperial legislation. This legislation, alleged to have improved the slave's lot, comes down to a single edict, whose real significance was quite different. Under Antoninus, anyone who killed his own slave was subject to death or deportation unless he could prove to the satisfaction of a judge that he had good reason for what he did. What must be understood, however, is that for a master to kill his own slave was different from sentencing the slave to death before the domestic tribunal over which the master presided. Antoninus' edict merely revived the ancient distinction between legal murder and murder pure and simple. If an enraged master sentenced a slave to death with a minimum of formalities, no one could reproach him. But if, in his rage, he killed the slave with his dagger, he would have to trouble himself to explain to the judge that his rage had been legitimate (so legitimate that, had he been given the time to set himself up as domestic judge, he would surely have sentenced to death the slave he had just stabbed). As long as the formalities were respected, anyone could punish his slaves as he pleased without difficulty: Antoninus confirmed this. Similarly, Hadrian condemned a father who had killed his son during a hunt, claiming that the murder had been committed in the name of paternal authority.

Other measures aimed to moralize, if not improve, the condition of the slave. Imperial legislation became more and more prudish as time went by, and what we shall now consider is a minor chapter in the history of sexual morality. The new laws that afforded the slave moral protection could be enforced only by the master, through exercise of his paternal power. Slaves were commonly sold under restrictive conditions (for

Morality

example, a seller might stipulate that a bad slave be kept in chains). When females were sold, it was sometimes specified that they could not be used as prostitutes by their new owners. If an owner went ahead and made a prostitute of a woman sold under such a condition, the emperor declared that the slave must be set free and that the buyer should lose his property. A less well-known aspect of the moral order was the new custom of allowing slaves to marry (mentioned by Tertullian around A.D. 200). It had previously been unthinkable that these childlike creatures should have families. Later, however, when marriage came to be looked upon less as a sign of a power than as a token of morality, it was opened to slaves. More married slaves are mentioned in the *Digest* than one might think. Michel Foucault found the earliest reference to a married slave in Musonius. Remember, marriage was nothing more than a private decision marked by a private ceremony, so slave marriage was more a matter of evolving custom than of revolution in the law.

Moral evolution. Free men in republican Rome had been hard on themselves as well as on their slaves, because their sense of duty was based on civic status, without the illusory but comforting involvement of moral conscience. There were as many codes of ethics as there were statuses, and the morals of a slave were different from those of a citizen. "Tolerance of adultery," said one orator, "is infamous on the part of a free man. On the part of a freedman with regard to his master, it is the effect of a proper sense of gratitude. On the part of a slave, it is duty pure and simple." But now morality seemed to derive from the conscience of mankind in general. The slave remained a slave, but ethics became universalist.

Slave owners have, at different times, conceived of slavery in different ways, without making the institution any less tyrannical. In the southern United States masters had their blacks baptized because they believed that all God's creatures have souls. They were no less authoritarian as a result. In the Roman Empire the prevailing morality gradually shifted from a concept of "political man" to a concept of "inner man." Stoicism and Christianity would shape in their different ways this new conception of man, which also affected ideas about slaves. No longer was the slave always a human being whose inner life was limited simply to understanding his duty to submit to his masters. He became a human being with a moral conscience, who obeyed his master not so much out of loyalty to his private duties as out of a sense of moral duty in general.

To the slave were imputed duties to his wife, for he was now allowed to marry, and duties to his children, for he was now allowed to raise children, who became his morally even if they remained indisputably the property of his master. Legal and literary documents provide evidence of a growing tendency not to separate families of slaves, not to sell the husband without his wife and child. And Latin and Greek epitaphs show evidence of a growing tendency to bury slaves according to the proper formalities rather than simply disposing of their corpses or leaving it to other slaves to bury their own.

The institution of slavery thus changed from within, because everything around it was changing. We would be taking too sanguine a view if we ascribed these changes to humanitarian scruples, and it would be pedantic to try to explain them as safety valves. They are signs of an autonomous change in the prevailing moral climate. What is most striking of all is the inability of Roman society to question or even alleviate the harshness of the institution for a single moment. It was all well and good to remind the paterfamilias of his duties as a judge to respect the formalities and to allow slaves to marry, but the formalities altered none of slavery's cruel punishments, malnutrition, physical and moral misery, or tyranny.

This was all that the moralists, including the Stoics, were able to accomplish. What some scholars say about Seneca's attitude toward slavery is no more than projection of our own brand of moralism. For Seneca, slavery was not a product of "society" but an individual misfortune, a misfortune that might befall any one of us, for we are all men, subject to the same tricks of fate as these unfortunates. In wartime even the noblest of men could be reduced to slavery. It is Fortune that determines each man's fate. What, then, is the good man's duty? To do whatever he has to do wherever fate has placed him, be he king, citizen, or slave. If he is a master, he must be a good master. The Romans had more respect for good masters and good husbands than for bad ones. Philosophy took this merit of some individuals and imposed it as a duty on all who would be wise. Thus, Seneca taught his disciple to comport himself as a good master toward those "humble friends," his servants. Had he deigned to give lessons to the slaves themselves, he would have taught them to comport themselves as good slaves—as Saint Paul and Epictetus actually did.

The Household and Its Freed Slaves

A ROMAN household consisted of a number of domestic slaves or former slaves, a paterfamilias, his legitimate wife, and two or three sons and daughters, along with a few dozen free men known as "clients," who waited each morning in the antechamber of their protector or "patron" to pay him brief homage. A household was not a "natural" family. The affections it induced are as dated as our own nostalgic family emotions—though certainly more picturesque.

Nor was the Roman household a clan, an extended patriarchal family—the *gens* or some weakened or disintegrated form of that vast, archaic entity (despite the legend to the contrary, which Yan Thomas has attempted to debunk). It is not true that the father gradually ceased to reign over the family as a monarch. In fact he never did reign. Archaic Roman society did not consist of a number of clans, each ruled by an ancestral monarch. Archaic Rome was an Etruscan city, one of the largest. It does not hark back to some prehistoric stage of human development. Let us therefore set aside these political myths of origin and consider the facts: the father was a husband, a propertyowner, a slavemaster, and a patron to freedmen and clients. Over his sons and daughters he exercised judicial authority delegated to him, in a manner of speaking, by the city. This amalgam of heterogeneous powers did not derive from any primitive unity.

Once orphaned and emancipated, every son became the head of a family in his own right and felt no attachment to his brothers and uncles but that dictated by private feelings or family strategy. Whether or not a group of brothers would live together in the family mansion was simply a question of convenience and money. The family was a conjugal unit; every

An elegant dressing room. Was it permissible to paint a lady smaller than the slave who does her hair? Yes, provided the lady was very young. This woman (a child becomes a woman at the magic age of fifteen) is being dressed for her wedding. (Naples, Archaeological Museum.)

family head preferred to have a home of his own, and every son wished for the same thing. The sons of Cicero and of his friend Celius rented an apartment so they would no longer have to live at home with their fathers. If they damaged their neighbors' property, the law held that they themselves should be held responsible and that their fathers should bear none of the blame. These children led their own lives. The father was master primarily of the patrimony and the patrimonial rights. His children were bound to him by money and hopes of inheritance. But he did not insist that they remain at his side, and newlywed couples, if they had the means, preferred to live in homes of their own.

The Mistress of the House

The paterfamilias was, in principle, head of the household. It was he who, every morning, gave the slaves their orders and assigned their duties, he who went over the accounts with the steward. And the mistress of the house? This was a point of friction: some husbands, but not all, put their wives in charge (*cura*) of the household and, if they deemed her worthy, gave her the keys to the strongbox. Cicero's sister-in-law made a scene one day when she was treated as a stranger in his house, because a servant had been put in charge of preparing lunch. Division of power over the household gave rise to frequent quarrels, if we are to believe the Church Fathers, enemies of marriage that they were. To marry was to submit to a woman's authority, they said, or at least to oblige oneself to suffer her recriminations. Physicians, for their part, recommended that wives be given charge of the house, because it was healthy for women to have some activity: "to supervise the slave baker, oversee the steward's purchases of supplies, and tour the house to make sure that everything is in order." These duties were not insignificant, for normally a wealthy woman had nothing to do but occupy herself with distaff and spindle, killing time in a traditional and honorable way.

Remember that these people had slaves constantly at their beck and call and were never alone. They were not allowed to dress themselves or put on their own shoes (although they could brush their teeth rather than have them brushed by a slave). On funerary steles in the museums of Piraeus and Larissa we see maids kneeling to remove their mistresses' shoes. The gospel phrase "I am not worthy to undo his sandals" means precisely that "I am not even worthy to serve him as a slave."

Woman's toilet kit, found at Cumae. (Naples, Archaeological Museum.)

The vast Roman houses we can visit at Pompeii, Vaison, and a hundred other places did not allow their owners to enjoy the pleasures of wide, open space; they were more densely occupied than today's low-rent apartment houses. Were husband and wife alone in the bedroom at least? Not always. A lover taken by surprise in one lady's bedroom claimed that he was there not for the lady of the house but for the servant girl who slept in the same room. The lady slept alone, but she had a slave, or several slaves, close to her bed. More commonly, slaves slept at the door to the master's bedchamber, over which they stood guard. "When Andromache mounted Hector," one satirist tells us, "their slaves stood with their ears glued to the door, masturbating." Slaves apparently slept all over the house. When the master or mistress wished to spend an evening alone, they had the slaves move their cots to some remote corner of the house.

The omnipresence of slaves was tantamount to constant surveillance. True, slaves did not count, and their presence could easily be overlooked. The poet Horace says: "I am accustomed to walking alone." Five lines later we learn that one of his three slaves is with him. Lovers never knew where to meet in secret—his place or hers? Their servants would know everything, and they gossiped. The only solution was to borrow the house of an indulgent friend (who risked being charged as an accomplice in adultery) or to rent the chamber of a sacristan, whose sacred office compelled him to maintain a loyal silence. Decency and concern for station required that ladies of rank never go out without maids, companions (*comites*), and a mounted servant known as a *custos*, often mentioned by erotic poets. This mobile prison, which followed a woman everywhere, was the Roman equivalent of the gynecaeum, or monogamous harem, in which a Greek woman concerned for her reputation insisted that her husband lock her up during the night. Even boys never went out without a *custos*, for there was as much concern for their virtue as for that of the fair sex. In any case, old-fashioned women proved their modesty by going out as little as possible and never showing themselves in public without a partial veil.

To be the mother of a family was an honorable prison, a rather constricted dignity to which a proud noblewoman could devote herself. But the daughters of the nobility inherited the pride of their fathers, who lent them as it were to their husbands. (An unhappy Roman wife who left her husband did not "go home to mother"; she went home to father.) Aristocratic pride was bolstered by wealth; wives often had fortunes

Statue of deceased woman, 1st–3rd century. The posture mimics that of draped statues in the Hellenizing manner; the artist's intentions are evident in the drapery of the left shoulder. This may be an early example of the ornamental, graphical style that supplanted the plastic naturalism of antiquity. We see here the decadence of the classical style. (Aquileia, Archaeological Museum.)

Silver from the 4th-century
crypt of Mildenhall, found not
far from a small villa. (London,
British Museum.)

of their own, which did not become the property of their husbands. Women were the equals of men insofar as the laws of inheritance were concerned, and they had the same right to make a will. Brides also had their dowries. Some women, nobler and wealthier than their husbands, refused to submit to their authority. Some played important political roles because, along with their patrimony, they inherited their lineage's hereditary clienteles. Others, not content merely to devote themselves to their husbands, showed the quality of their blood by following them into exile or even suicide. (Seneca, jealous of his wife's influence over his entourage, attempted to extort from her and from his disciple Lucilius promises of suicide.) Women were more than capable of defending their marital interests when their husbands were exiled or forced into hiding. They were also capable of an act that earned them far less praise and that is symptomatic of the impasse in which women found themselves: using a misfortune such as the loss of a son as a pretext, they deliberately renounced the world and cloistered themselves in perpetual mourning.

What if our wealthy heiress was a widow, or, rather, a *vidua*, a woman without a man, widow or divorcée? Or a virgin, yet the "mother of a family" because her father was dead? Relatives would hasten to fortify her virtue by providing her with a custos. An imperial edict compared the loves of a vidua to adultery and rape, but it was never enforced. Imagine a woman or girl, mistress of her own house and her own patrimony: the wealthy widow was a period figure. She was not flirtatious but "imperious," because she no longer had any master over her. She was surrounded by suitors, who lusted after her inheritance. She might remarry or take a lover. Such liaisons, sometimes made respectable by promises of marriage, were often known and almost openly admitted. The affairs of young girls, by contrast, had to remain secret. They were always suspected of having lovers, and people liked to think that the guilty party was the girl's slave steward. For how could a woman possibly manage her life without a lord and master? The Church Fathers were horribly malicious about the morals of widows and orphans, though they uttered no slander. Had the state of affairs they described not been true, where would Ovid have found the bevy of wealthy and independent women to whom he taught the art of sin with his

Widows, Virgins, and Concubines

Funerary stele, 1st century. A woman half-faces the spectator; a freedwoman looks at her. (Arles, Lapidary Museum.)

Lover's Handbook (Ars amatoria)? These women enjoyed the best fate Rome had to offer the female sex. Their lovers had to take pains to please them in bed, to the dismay of Seneca and Martial.

What about the opposite situation—the widower father? He might sleep with his servants or remarry, or he might take a concubine. The word concubine had two different meanings: pejorative at first, "concubine" eventually acquired an honorable interpretation. Originally the word was applied to the woman or women with whom a man, married or not, habitually slept. Emperors, even when married, kept a harem of slave concubines in the palace, and Claudius was known to sleep with more than one at a time. But public opinion eventually came to tolerate relations with a concubine, so long as they were durable and exclusive, like marriage; and only the social inferiority of the woman prevented the man from converting the liaison into a legitimate marriage. The jurists followed suit. For them, concubinage was a de facto situation, but an honorable one, which did not degrade a woman to the level of those whom decent men were obliged to hold in contempt. It was necessary, however, that concubinage should resemble marriage in every respect. In the second—and only honorable—meaning of the word, a concubine had to be a free woman (slaves were not allowed to marry), and the union had to be monogamous. It was unthinkable for a married man to have a concubine or for any man to have two concubines at once. In short, concubinage was a substitute where marriage was impossible. The typical case was that of a man who had sexual relations with a freed female slave but who was reluctant to marry a woman of such inferior station. The emperor Vespasian, a widower, took as his concubine his secretary, a freed imperial slave, and "treated her almost like his wife." Some fifteen cases are known in which a man had an epitaph written for himself, his late wife, and the concubine who replaced her. Other epitaphs honor the memory of a man's two successive wives.

Unlike lawful marriage, concubinage had no legal consequences. The jurists, notwithstanding their indulgence toward concubinage as an institution, were uncompromising on this point. Children born of an honorable concubinage were free, since they were the children of a free mother; but since the woman was not married, they were bastards and bore their mother's name. They could inherit from their mother, but not from their natural father. Hence concubinage had nothing but its honorable status: it conferred upon the woman a dignity that would not have been possible had her relations with the man not been stable and monogamous. Finally, what about the case in which a patron overcame his initial hesitation and decided to marry his freed slave and concubine? The woman would have been proud to have been deemed worthy of donning the traditional robes of the true "mother"; however, aware of her definitive inferiority, she would always refer to her husband, in their epitaph, as "patron and husband," as if the first quality were indelible and even conjugal affection could never erase the taint of slavery. These, then, were the families of the left hand, composed of a man, his concubine, and his natural children. There were also more irregular combinations, with which jurists did not concern themselves: a man, his servingwomen, and his "pets." Before saying more on this subject, we must penetrate the secret recesses of the slave system and remind ourselves that the Roman Empire, like colonial Brazil, was an empire of miscegenation.

Bronze keys. Some keys turned in the lock, causing a bolt to advance or recede; others withdrew a pivoting bolt. (Paris, Louvre.)

After Vespasian lost his cultivated concubine, he whiled away his hours in the company of one of his many servants. Anyone who owned slaves might have done the same: opportunity creates temptation. There was a word for husbands who gave in to that temptation: *ancillariolus,* maid-chaser. Their wives despaired of them. One cruel master drove his slaves so far that they murdered him, castrating him as well; they must have had their reasons. When the bloody news reached the house, "his concubines hurried in, screaming and sobbing." Slavery had its lyrical side. Horace delicately, even poetically, described the emotions of a master following the movements of a young female slave with his eyes. She is not far from the age when she might know a man, and the master savors the moment in advance. In short, the master might have good reason to believe that some of the infants born to his servants, who became his property, were his own children. Neither he nor anyone else was supposed to say so, however. It was essential that free status be above suspicion, unambiguously distinct from the condition of slavery; it was unthinkable that a master should scheme to recognize a slave as his own son. This was one of the tacit laws of the slave system. Yet everyone knew what the real story was: as one jurist put it, "It sometimes happens that a slave is the child of his master by a slave mother." Of course the master could always free

Unrecognized Bastards

"The *fanciulla* (maiden) of Anzio"; found in one of Nero's villas at Anzio. This celebrated flat-chested "young woman" is, in my opinion, a young male. He carries various cult objects on a tray. This statue-portrait was probaby consecrated in a temple by the model (or by his parents, if he was a *pais amphithales*). This is either an original from the 4th or 3rd century B.C. or a Roman copy, as the somewhat sketchy indication of the folds in the drapery suggests. The lower portion was carved in different marble from that used for the head and bust, so it may be a Greek original whose lower part was restored in Roman times. Original or copy, this masterpiece is a landmark in the history of imperial art and taste. (Rome, Museum of the Baths.)

his child without saying why he chose to favor that particular slave, but he could not recognize or adopt the child, even after manumission: the law forbade it.

A curious custom permitted him to do more, however, while keeping up appearances. The Romans liked to have about the house a little boy or girl slave or foundling, whom they brought up (*alumnus, threptus*) because they were fond of the child (*deliciae, delicatus*) and found it cute. They kept the child with them at dinner, played with it, put up with its whims; sometimes they gave it a "liberal" education, in principle reserved for free men. This custom was useful because of its ambiguity: the pet child might be a plaything, but it might also be a sexual object. It might have been adopted in all innocence, or it might be the master's own child, enjoying his secret favor. I should also mention the corps of adolescent valets that, had they been well born, we might be tempted to call pages; but they, too, were slaves.

Keeping a boy for sexual purposes was a minor sin for gentlemen of quality, and their inferiors smiled respectfully. Brutus, Caesar's murderer, loved a boy so beautiful that reproductions of a sculpture of him could be seen everywhere. The lover of the terrible emperor Domitian and Antinous, Hadrian's celebrated lover, were praised by court poets (whose successors would praise Madame de Pompadour similarly). Jealous wives refused to allow their husbands to kiss a beloved boy in their presence. Did husbands go further still when out of sight? By convention no one in good society asked such questions. The pet usually served his master as a squire or cupbearer, pouring his drink as Ganymede, Jupiter's boy lover, had done for the god. The corps of "pages" (*paedagogium*) consisted of handsome boys who had no other responsibility but to serve at table, to grace the hall with their presence and add pomp to the ceremonial trappings. The first sign of a mustache resulted in a major change in the life of a page. The pretext of ambiguous sexuality having been eliminated, it would have been scandalous to treat the now adult male as a passive sex object. The pet lamented the loss of his position, but the master caused his long, girlish locks to be cut—to the great relief of the mistress of the house. Some stubborn masters kept their pets even after they had stopped growing (*exoletus*), but such behavior was considered reprehensible.

Masters sometimes had more innocent motives to delight in their pets. A boy might be a sort of plaything with which the master amused himself affectionately at table, as he might

Antinous, after 131. This Greek work from the Roman era bears the "signature" (or name, if it is a replica) of Antoninianos of Aphrodisias (Turkey), a celebrated artistic city. Hadrian's deceased lover is compared to the god Sylvanus, whose pruning knife he holds. This apotheosis may have been a poetic notion of the artist, implying no cult, or the work may have been commissioned by an individual or confraternity that championed the monarchy and worshiped Antinous as a "new Sylvanus." The first explanation is more in keeping with the pictorial nature of the work. (Rome, Museum of the Baths.)

do with a pet animal. In those days the most valued toys were living creatures—birds, dogs, and, for little girls, rabbits (cats were not yet domesticated in Rome). A master might even feel genuine affection for a slave child. Plutarch writes: "Sometimes people who are unalterably opposed to marriage and children are eaten away by regret and freely mourn the death of a servant's child or a concubine's infant." This was not always because a man believed the child to be his own. There were men with a vocation for fatherhood, who took under their wing children born to members of their households; the kisses lavished on these children were quite innocent. Though opposed at first, kissing on the lips as a sign of affection between men became fashionable; the adolescent Marcus Aurelius exchanged some very sentimental kisses with his mentor Fronto. The poet Statius has left some moving lines about the death of a child whom he loved so well that he freed him at birth: "No sooner was he born that he turned toward me, and his wailing enveloped me and penetrated to my heart. I taught him to use words, I comforted his hurts and sorrows when he was still crawling on the ground, and I bent down to take him in my arms and cover him with kisses. As long as he was alive, I desired no son." These are the poet's best verses. Was he the child's father? That is not certain: paternal sentiment could be lavished more easily on a child without social importance than on one's legitimate son, who, as the scion and secret enemy of the man who now possessed what would one day be his, had to be raised strictly. It is true that in other poems by Statius or by Martial, the pet boy or girl is certainly the father's unrecognized child. Such children were treated like free men: dressed like princes, covered with jewels, they never went out without an escort. All they lacked was the garb worn by free-born adolescents (*praetexta*). The poet is at pains to make this clear. These children are freed slaves and must remain so.

Epitaph of a young girl, 1st or 2nd century. This important historical document is one of the two earliest pieces of evidence for the domestication in Europe of the cat. (Bordeaux, Aquitaine Museum.)

The question remains: Whose freedman was the slave? Forgive this insistence on precision, but it will lead us into another circle of hell: unusual relations among freed slaves. Suppose a master had a child by a servant, whom he then freed. Too late. The infant, conceived in the womb of a slave mother, was born a slave of its own father. Suppose, further, that the father freed his newborn child; then the child would have its own natural father for its patron. But sometimes the

The Tribulations of the Freed Slave

Sign for shop of the fuller Verecundus, Abundance Street, Pompeii, shortly before 79. In the center four men in short pants wring out cloth around an oven. Three men kneeling at benches draw cloth. At right, the master shows off a clean piece of fabric. The inscription, which pertains to an election, should not have been affixed to this sign.

mother, a wealthy freedwoman, could afford to purchase the child from its master. Then her child became her slave or freedman or -woman. Nor was it unusual for a son, out of filial piety, to purchase his mother, who had remained a slave; she then became the slave or freedwoman of her son. Epitaphs and legal documents prove that such situations were not at all hypothetical but in fact quite common. From here anything was possible. A son who became the freedman of his mother might have his own father for a slave, or a man might be the freedman of his own brother. Family feeling may have counted for more than the provisions of law in such matters. Yet feelings, however powerful, had to contend with the authority that legally belonged to anyone who purchased his or her blood relative as a slave. Such purchases often involved heavy financial sacrifice. The laws of inheritance also played a part. The family life of former slaves must have been a veritable hell, filled with conflict, ambivalence, and resentment. A father might never forgive his son for his crushing generosity; a son might never forgive his father for behaving like a ingrate.

Freed slaves usually did not live in the home of their former master, although they continued to come there to pay him homage. Set up in business as artisans, shopkeepers, or merchants, they accounted for less than 5 percent of the total population; yet they formed a group that was highly visible socially and very important economically. Although not all shopkeepers were freed slaves, all freed slaves were shopkeepers and traders. Hence a certain image attached to the group, earning it the enmity of many. Freedmen were seen as avaricious exploiters, especially since many former slaves were wealthier, sometimes far wealthier, than the majority of the free population, which deemed itself dishonored by the prosperity of individuals not born to freedom. People found it hard to accept opulence in a freedman that they would have found legitimate and admirable in a noble. The status of freedmen was ambiguous, at once superior and inferior to that of most of their fellow citizens. Privately they suffered from this ambiguity and accordingly developed a culture of their own.

It seems that freedmen lived more often in concubinage than in marriage. This at least is the conclusion that emerges from comparison of the views of Plassard and Rawson. Clearly the reason for this was not the concubine's social inferiority. Many slaves during their years of servitude lived as couples, especially the luckier ones—stewards of large estates and imperial slaves, or state functionaries. A servingwoman who lived for a long period with a single man might be called a concubine. If the servingwoman and her companion were both freed, their union, which now became a union between a free man and a free woman, would have been considered honorable. The problem was that the couple, while

Funerary relief commemorating a well-known merchant. Rome, 1st century(?). Two customers are seated; five clerks are standing, including one woman, shown in profile (a slave). The architecture is remarkable, but it seems likely that the columns were of stucco rather than marble. Note the arrangement of round and flat roofing tiles ("Roman tiles"). The floor is not tiled. (Florence, Uffizi.)

Tomb of freedman and freedwoman with their son and his
pet pigeon. Note the faces and
the clumsy attempt to enliven
the composition by the tilt of
the man's neck. The man holds
a number of tablets rather than
a book; though not educated in
the liberal arts, he knows how
to read and write. The woman's hairstyle is typical of the
fourth decade of the first century or the second decade of
the second century. (Rome,
Museum of the Baths.)

still slaves, might have had children; legally speaking, those children would have been either bastards or slaves of their mother. Even if the two freed slaves married legitimately, the father was not permitted to acknowledge his natural son. Even if the freed couple redeemed their slave son from his master, they could not make him their son, only their freedman. In Ancona is the tomb of the freedman Titius Primus, who became so notable a figure in that city that he asked the stonecutter to represent him dressed in a toga, which had become a ceremonial costume. At his right hand he had the sculptor carve his "concubine" (this is the word used in the epitaph), a freewoman (no doubt a freed slave) by the name of Lucania Benigna, who holds in her arms a baby girl named Chloé. Since the child has only one name, she is a slave: she was born when her mother was still a mere servingwoman. The best her natural father could do was to take her for his pet (*delicium*), and in the epitaph she is given no other title. Nature and affection were powerless in the face of the law. On the right is another freedwoman (there is nothing surprising about this grouping: household tombs were commonplace). It is hard to think of any reason why this couple should have wished to "remarry" in a legitimate ceremony. Theirs was a second type of concubinage, which stemmed from indifference to marriage.

Further Tribulations of the Freed Slave

Everywhere we encounter signs of what tormented freed slaves: uncertainty as to their true place in society. The scale of social conditions did not coincide with the status hierarchy, and freed slaves fell in the gap between the two. They suffered from a lack of legitimacy. Their wealth enabled them to live luxuriously. In Rome many a costly tomb with sculpted portrait belonged not to a noble but to a freedman. With their dress, clients, slaves, and freedmen of their own, they imitated good society—but, as demi-citizens, without hope of entering it. With cruel lucidity their totally imitative existence is portrayed in Petronius' *Satyricon*. Their base origins were betrayed by their lack of cultivation; the children of slaves did not attend school. They were not parvenus, as some have said, but refugees who bore an indelible stain that kept them out of good society: the barriers between status groups were unbreachable. People of good society found the freedmen's imitation of good manners absurd; they saw only pretentiousness and vulgarity. Worse still, freedmen did not even constitute a social class

Tomb of the freedman Titius Primus. (Museum of Ancona.)

worthy of the name. They could not console themselves with class pride. There could be no "dynasties" of freedmen, for the status died out after a single generation. The son of a freedman was a full-fledged citizen. It would be a mistake to regard as a social class what was only a transitional group. What is more, the Roman upper class replenished its ranks largely by admitting the sons of wealthy freedmen and freed imperial slaves: many a senator was the grandson of a freed slave. All in all, the chance of rising socially was somewhat better for slaves than for men born free but poor, who had virtually no chance at all.

The possibility of upward mobility was available to freedmen because of wealth. This wealth they owed to their vocation for trade, and that vocation must in turn be understood as a result of the conditions under which they had been set free. As much as, or even more than, the relations of production, it is such minor details, the consequences of which are often unexpected, that explain social structure. Roman nobles preferred their freedmen to their impoverished fellow citizens because, as we shall see, freedmen remained loyal to their former masters, who knew them personally.

What factors moved masters to free slaves? At least three are worth mentioning. The impending death of a slave was one. Masters often felt compelled to give slaves the consolation of dying in freedom and being buried as freedmen. When a master died, he might free some or all of his slaves in his will, leaving them freedom as a legacy just as he distributed other bequests to all his loyal retainers. Since the will was a kind of manifesto, the master who freed his slaves upon his death proved that he was a good master by giving them what they most desired: freedom. Finally, manumission often involved a financial arrangement of some sort. A master might use his slave as an agent in a business venture in which he offered the slave a share of the profits; the two would agree beforehand on the price of the slave's freedom. Or the master might offer the slave his freedom as a reward, in return for which the latter would continue to act as the master's agent with the rank of freedman. Manumitted slaves were rarely turned out to face life without some resources. When a master freed worthy old servants at his death, he left them a small plot or a pension (*alimenta*), as, later, wealthy people used to do with their servants. A slave businessman's future was assured. Last but not least, I imagine that many freed slaves remained in the master's household and went right on doing what they always had done, but with greater dignity than before. Others were set up in business or a trade, the profits of which they would share with the master as the price of freedom. The number of conceivable arrangements is limitless. Usually slaves were freed only if they were capable of earning money. One type of slave was never freed, however: the slave who handled his master's finances, even if the master was the emperor himself and the slave the imperial treasurer. Freedom, to which imperial slaves looked forward as a promotion at a certain stage in their careers, was not accorded the treasurer. This would have precluded the possibility of torturing him, and it was thought useful to retain the threat of torture and private justice in case the slave should be tempted to dip into his master's funds.

Some freed slaves remained in the household of their former master, in his service; others were set up on their own elsewhere and became completely independent. In either case the freed slave maintained a symbolic tie with the household of his master, who now became his "patron." He was obliged to pay homage (*obsequium*) to his master, who set great store by this custom. This homage was due the master in gratitude for his good deed in freeing the slave. If a freed slave neglected this duty (which was difficult to enforce), he was stigmatized

Mosaic from Pompeii, of "three itinerant musicians wearing theatrical masks, with an urchin looking on." (Naples, Archaeological Museum.)

Mosaic from Carthage, 4th century. These buildings at the water's edge might seem to be figments of the artist's imagination. But when it comes to architectural landscapes, Roman reality was stranger than fiction. In the islet of Brioni (Istria), a bay was surrounded by an unbroken semicircle of buildings: a magnificent villa with hemicyclic portico, three temples, baths, docks, a covered promenade along the water, and so on. The entire bay was turned into a decorative scene. (Tunis, Bardo Museum.)

by all of society as an "ingrate." Ingratitude, said to be one of the major problems of the day, provoked the Romans to outrage. Freed slaves who left a family were supposed to surround it with an aureole of obsequiousness, thereby proving to the world how great the family was. The role of "clients" was identical.

Romans were torn between two concepts of society: one was civic, the other based on relations of loyalty between man and man. On the one hand, because freedom was supposed to be unquestionable, a master was not supposed to hinder that of a freed slave by hedging it about with obligations. On the other hand, the freedman owed a debt of gratitude to his master and was supposed to remain forever his loyal servant. If he did not, his patron had good grounds for punishing him by striking him from the list of legatees and banishing him from the household tomb—or, indeed, by beating him with a stick. In principle, no Roman was allowed to raise a hand against a free man. Yet it was "not to be tolerated that an individual who was only yesterday a slave should come to complain of his master, who has turned him out, beaten him a little, or inflicted some punishment on him." The club, after all, was a symbol! Still, the family and monetary interests of even a newly liberated slave were sacred. A patron could not require the freedman to do more work than had been agreed upon beforehand, and he could not subject manumission to restrictions so severe that the former slave would have been free in name only. In particular, he could not make the freedman promise to forgo marriage and children in order to secure the patron's own rights as master to the former slave's estate. He could not even (as a general rule, at any rate) forbid the slave to go into competition with him in his own line of work.

Materially free within the limits of the manumission agreement, the former slave remained symbolically under the authority of his patron, and the Romans, much given to vaguely paternalistic pronouncements, often repeated that a freedman had the duties of a son—duties of piety—toward his former master, whose family name had become his own. At one time freed slaves were required to appear twice a day at the home of their former master, to bid him good morning and good evening, but this duty fell into neglect. Piety required that freedmen pay their respects, however, and the *Cistellaria* shows how grim the scene was. The freedman was exasperated by the burden of a symbolic yoke that had outlived its real power to compel. The master knew that his power was gone and that his ex-slave, if he did not still fear him, hated him, so he played up his own importance all the more. These unduly prolonged relations were particularly burdensome when the slave had obtained his freedom by agreeing to perform certain specified work for his master after being set free (*operae libertorum*). It seems that freedmen, unlike clients, were not required to pay the patron a protocol visit (*salutatio*) every morning. But they were often invited to dinner, where they found the master on his couch surrounded by those same clients. Dinnertime brawls between the two groups of loyal but unequal retainers were common. Poor clients

Clientage

Silver found at Pompeii. (Naples, Archaeological Museum.)

resented having to compete with prosperous ex-slaves for the master's attention. The poets Juvenal and Martial, reduced to paying court to the great in order to live, hated wealthy ex-slaves as well as Greek clients, for these were their competitors.

With a "court composed of clients and toilsome, not ungrateful freedmen," as Fronto puts it, a household made a brilliant place for itself on the public stage—a necessary and sufficient condition to be deemed worthy of membership in the ruling class. "I had many clients," wrote one very wealthy former slave as proof of his success. What was a client? A free man who paid court to the paterfamilias and openly declared himself the client of his patron; he could be rich or poor, miserable or powerful—sometimes more powerful than the patron to whom he paid respects. There were at least four kinds of clients: those who wished to make a career in public life and counted on their patron for protection; men of affairs whose interests could be served by the patron's political influence, particularly when he stood to profit from their success; poor devils such as poets and philosophers, often Greek, many of whom had nothing to live on but what their patron gave them and who, not being commoners, would have found it dishonorable to work rather than live under the protection of a powerful man; and, finally, those clients who were powerful enough to move in the same circles as the patron himself and who might legitimately aspire to be remembered in the patron's will in gratitude for their homage. This last-named group would have included leading statesmen and imperial freedmen, all-powerful administrators. A wealthy old man without heirs would have had many clients of this kind.

Such was the mixed crowd that lined up in regulation order every morning in front of the patron's door at the hour when the cock crows and the Romans awoke. The clients numbered in the tens, sometimes even hundreds. Neighborhood notables were also besieged, but by smaller crowds. Far from Rome, in the cities of the Empire, the few powerful rural notables also had their clienteles. That a wealthy or influential man should have been surrounded by protégés and self-seeking friends is hardly surprising. But the Romans erected this unremarkable custom into an institution and a ritual. Unimportant people, Vitruvius wrote, are those who make visits but receive none. A man who was the client of another man proclaimed the fact loudly, boasting of his own importance and stressing the patron's influence. People re-

Small bronze pot, 8 inches in diameter, found at Doudeville. Probably used to carry to the bath or gymnasium the oil that the ancients used instead of soap. The scene depicts a goatherd leaning on his crook, with his goats. (Paris, Petit Palais, Dutuit Collection.)

ferred to themselves as "the client of So-and-so" or "a familiar of Such-and-such a household." Those who were not themselves commoners would pay for the erection of a statue of their patron in a public square or even in the patron's own home. The inscription on the base would list the patron's public duties and spell out the name of the client. When shrewd patrons protested that the word "friend" was more appropriate than "client," "friend" became a flattering synonym for client.

The morning salutation was a ritual; to fail to appear was to disavow one's bond of clientage. Clients lined up in ceremonial costume (*toga*), and each visitor received a symbolic gift (*sportula*), which enabled the poorest to eat that day; in fact this custom supplanted the earlier practice of simply distributing food. Clients were admitted into the antechamber according to an inflexible hierarchical order that duplicated the civic organization by ranks. At dinners, too, guests of different rank were served different dishes and wines of different quality, according to their respective dignities. Symbolism reinforced the sense of hierarchy. The paterfamilias did not simply receive individual greetings from certain of his friends; he admitted into his home a slice of Roman society, respecting public rank and inequalities. Over this group he exerted moral authority, and his knowledge of proper behavior always exceeded that of his clients: "A wealthy patron," writes Horace, "governs you as a good mother might do and requires of you more wisdom and virtue than he possesses himself."

Moral Authority

The economic power that the household exerted over its peasants, bound by sharecropping contracts, was coupled with a kind of moral authority. When the Christian Church was being persecuted, frightened Christian landowners who decided to sacrifice to the idols compelled their farmers and clients (*amici*) to emulate their apostasy. Other masters, with a stroke of a magic wand, converted all the residents of their estates by deciding one fine day that the rustic religion of their peasants should henceforth be supplanted by worship of the one true God; the pagan sanctuary was demolished and a church erected in its place. The aura of prestige that surrounded the household defined the limits of its authority. Three centuries earlier Catiline had involved his sharecroppers in his revolt against the Senate. And Cicero, on the eve of his exile, had the consolation of hearing his friends offer to place at his disposal "their bodies, their children, their friends, their clients, their freedmen, their slaves, and their property."

The household exerted both material and moral power over those who lived in and around it. In the public mind what qualified a family for membership in the governing class of its city, and indeed of the Empire as a whole, was its power over this small group of people. Even in Rome, Tacitus tells us, "the sound segment of the populace saw everything through the eyes of the great houses." Wealth and power (the two were one and the same) over a small circle qualified a man for political leadership. Obviously I do not mean to imply that the collective consciousness was somehow directly aware of the power that each household exerted over its circle of clients. Underlying this state of affairs was an implicit idea: that governing men is not a specialized activity but the exercise of a natural right, that the larger animals are entitled to rule over the smaller. Because social importance and political legitimation went together, the performance of public duties was not a specialized profession as it is, say, in the civil service today. Nobles and notables physically made up the membership of the Roman Senate and city councils. This was true even when the number of seats was so limited that not all could be accommodated.

On the subject of social and political power, a more general if less important point should also be made: any man who bore a great name was obliged to take part, to play an honorific role, in all activities of interest to his clients. This was one of the more harmless aspects of that multifaceted phenomenon, clientage. The Roman Empire, an indirect form of government, was a federation of autonomous cities. Every member of the nobility, whether senator or equestrian, sought to be named or to earn the title of patron of one of those cities or, if possible, of several. The title was in fact nothing more than an honorific. Some gift or service to the city by the patron was its cause or consequence. Patrons might donate money to the municipal treasury, build or repair an edifice of some kind, or defend the city in court in a dispute over boundaries. In exchange, the patron was allowed to display in his antechamber an official letter of honor sent him by the city. Deaths in his family became local events: duly informed of the death, the city would respond with a decree of consolation. If the patron visited the city, he was received officially and made a formal entry, in the manner of a king. The collecting of cities as clients was one of the careers open to those avid for symbolic tokens. Even the many associations (*collegia*) where common people met for the pleasure of one another's company had noble patrons. Because the main purpose of these "colleges" was putting on banquets, the patron had no real power other than deciding, perhaps, the menu of the feast paid for by his donation. Ambition for symbols was one of the leading passions in the Greco-Roman world. No celebrated person could go out without a train of admirers. Actors and charioteers had fans, as did even some physicians, who had become "stars" in their profession.

There were minor variations from region to region. Italy was the kingdom of clientage. In Greek areas, as everywhere else, the influence, economic power, and powerful contacts of the wealthy—natural allies of the Roman occupiers—were of great importance. Powerful men periodically tyrannized the cities whose patrons they were. But in these places the ceremonies and salutations associated with clientage were unknown. Freedmen did not play leading roles (in Athens they accounted for about half the demi-citizens whose epitaphs mention no deme), nor did they form entourages around former masters. The ruinous passion to accumulate symbols of patronage—recently dubbed "evergetism"—was particularly prevalent in Greece, however. The Italians picked up this vice from the Greeks.

Oil lamp, 6 inches long, in the shape of a foot, with a chain for hanging. (Paris, Petit Palais, Dutuit Collection.)

Statue portrait, early Christian era. A faceless noble (the head is a modern restoration) exhibits the busts of his ancestors; the busts capture likenesses but neglect small details. The dynastic purpose of Roman portraiture is here displayed with impressive naiveté. Roman portrait art was a byproduct of Hellenistic portrait art, and the Romans never matched the Greeks when it came to recreating reality. (Rome, Museum of the Conservators.)

⚛ Where Public Life
Was Private

WHAT did a Roman possess? What did he lose if sent into exile? His patrimony, his wife and children, his clients, and also his "honors." Cicero and Seneca tell us so. Honors were public offices that a man might hold, generally for a year's tenure, after which his having held the office served as a token of nobility. Roman nobles had a keen sense of the authority and majesty of their Empire, but nothing like our notion of public service. They made no clear distinction between public functions and private rank, or between public finances and personal wealth. The grandeur of Rome was the collective property of the governing class and the ruling group of senators. Similarly, the thousands of autonomous cities that formed the fabric of the Empire were controlled by local notables.

In these cities, as in Rome, legitimate power was in the hands of the governing elite, which stood out by its opulence. The elite had the exclusive right to judge whether or not a particular family was worthy of membership. Legal criteria such as election or wealth of some specified amount were fictions, necessary conditions perhaps, but not at all sufficient. If wealth had been the real criterion, thousands of landowners might have contended for every seat in the Senate. The real method of selection was cooptation. The Senate was a club, and club members decided whether or not a man had the social profile necessary for membership, whether or not he could add to the prestige of the group. Senators did not select new members directly, however; this chore was left to innumerable clientage networks. Public offices were treated as

Cooptation

Sacrifice, A.D. 2. The four priests wear ritual veils, as does the oboist. Telescoping time, two of the priests burn incense, while the other two appear to be pouring a libation. At the left is a lictor, because this sacrifice was part of a public cult. (Rome, Museum of the Conservators.)

Above right: Libation on a table of offerings, prior to immolation of an ox, 1st or 2nd century. At left, a man representing the crowd tweaks his ear, a gesture whose conventional meaning was: "Look meditative." (Milan, Archaeological Museum.)

though they were private dignities, access to which depended on private contacts.

Too many historians, forgetting that Rome was not a modern state, have mistaken these ancient principles for a perversion of modern ones. Some have protested that Rome was rife with corruption, bribery, and clientage; others have passed over these matters in silence, on the grounds that such "abuses" hold little more than anecdotal interest. To our modern way of thinking, a man ceases to be a true public servant if he lines his pockets with the spoils of office or if he places personal ambition above the common good. But the modern state is not the only effective form of rule: organized crime, for example, functions quite well under different rules. The Mafia that protects and exploits Italian immigrants in some American cities and immigrant workers in France performs a "public" function. It administers justice in an immigrant population and, relying on ethnic solidarity, protects it from a hostile society. It must serve its community well or risk losing credibility; by serving the interests of its clients, it rules paternally, and it is particularly assiduous in this because otherwise it could never extort money from the immigrants it is supposed to protect. Whoever protects controls, and whoever controls pillages. Like an old Roman, even the most insignificant Mafia *capo* will make edifying speeches about his devotion to the common cause and try to establish personal and confidential relations with each of his protégés. A Roman noble (or even a mere notable) has more in common with this "godfather" than with a modern technocrat. Getting rich through public service has never stood in the way of taking public service for one's ideal. If it had, it would be surprising.

The honest functionary is a peculiarity of modern Western nations. In Rome every superior stole from his subordinates. The same was true in the Turkish and Chinese empires, where baksheesh was the general rule. Yet all these empires proved capable of governing effectively for many centuries. Similarly, the Roman army was quite a capable fighting machine in spite of some rather curious customs. "Soldiers traditionally bribed their officers for exemption from service, and nearly a quarter of the personnel of every regiment could be found idling about the countryside or even lounging around the barracks, provided their officer had received his kickback . . . Soldiers got the money they needed from theft and banditry or by doing the chores of slaves. If a soldier happened to be a little richer than the rest, his officer beat him and heaped duties upon him until he paid up and received dispensation." It is hard to believe that these are the words of Tacitus. Every public function was a racket; those in charge "put the squeeze" on their subordi-

Arch of Lepcis (Libya), A.D. 203. According to Epictetus, people are always cursing either the gods or the emperor, on whom they blame all their woes. But the emperor was also the champion of Romanness: on a chariot, Severus and his two heirs apparent enter a city as conquerors. At the right, a child is carried away with enthusiasm. Figures are shown frontally in this naive work. The youth who holds the horses' bridles and who wears a portrait of the prince around his neck is probably a slave page (*paedagogium*).

nates, and all together exploited the populace. This was true during the period of Rome's greatness as well as during the period of its decline.

Even the least important public positions (*militia*), such as apparitor or clerk of the courts, were sold by their incumbents to aspiring candidates, because every position carried with it a guaranteed income in the form of bribes. A new officeholder was supposed to pay a substantial gratuity (*sportula*) to his superior. In the Late Empire even the highest dignitaries, appointed by the emperor, paid such a gratuity to the imperial treasury. From the very beginning of the Empire, every dignity bestowed by the emperor, from consul to mere captain, imposed upon the person honored the moral duty to make a bequest to his benefactor, the emperor. Failure to fulfill this duty meant running the risk of having one's will set aside for ingratitude and one's estate confiscated by the imperial treasury. And, since every nomination was made on the recommendation of "patrons" with court connections, these recommendations (*suffragia*) were sold or, in any case, paid for.

The heart of Rome. The open space shown in the middle of this photo originally was tiled (the agora at Athens was not). This was the center of Rome, the forum, from 600 B.C. to A.D. 700—or what was left of the forum after the construction of various monuments. In the foreground are three columns from the temple of the Greek demigods Castor and Pollux, founded in 494 B.C. In the background, on the left, is the arch of Severus (after 203) and, on the right, with a modern roof, the Senate, between which stood the republican electoral enclosure, destroyed during the Empire. To the top left of the photo, imagine the Capitoline Hill, the acropolis of Rome, on which stood the temple of Jupiter (founded in 509 B.C.), god of Rome. Agora and acropolis constituted the city.

If the patron did not keep his word, the victim did not hesitate to complain to the courts. Courtiers (*proxenetae*) specialized in buying and selling recommendations and clientage (*amicitiae*), though their profession was denounced as disreputable.

Public officials paid themselves. The troops that patrolled the countryside and were responsible for rural administration forced the towns and villages under their jurisdiction to vote them gratuities (*stephanos*). Every official had his palm greased before taking the slightest action. But, because it was important not to skin the animals one fleeced, an official schedule of bribes was eventually established and posted in every office. Supplicants were careful to bring gifts whenever they visited a functionary or high dignitary. The gift was a tangible symbol of the superiority of rulers over ruled.

In addition to bribery, high mandarins practiced extortion. After the Roman conquest of Great Britain, the military administration forced the conquered tribes to take the grain they paid as tax to remote public storehouses and then took bribes for granting permission to use storehouses located closer to home. Demanding payment of illegal taxes was big business among provincial governors, who bought the silence of imperial inspectors and split the profits with their department heads. The central government allowed these abuses to continue, content to receive its due. To pillage the provinces of which one was governor, Cicero said, was the "senatorial way to get rich." A good example was Verres, who ran his province, Sicily, with an iron fist and conducted a bloody reign of terror.

The notion that the government of a province was like a private economic enterprise persisted, albeit on a less spectacular scale, as long as the Empire. It was no secret. Erotic poets waited impatiently for the husbands of their beloved paramours to leave town for a year to make their fortunes in the provinces. The poets professed to live for love alone and to care nothing for career or wealth (the two being interchangeable). Officials enriched themselves in part at public expense. One governor was paid colossal sums for costs incurred in the course of his mission; he never rendered an accounting. Under the Republic, these costs accounted for the bulk of the state budget. Apart from extortion, moreover, the governor engaged in business. In the first century B.C. Italian traders took over the economy of the Greek Orient with the help of gov-

The Empire of Baksheesh

A high-ranking officer wearing a "muscled breastplate" (which reproduced the pectoral muscles in its relief) and a smaller centurion with a "swagger stick." (Museum of Syracuse.)

Rome, Trajan Column, ca. A.D. 110, detail: civilization conquers Romania. Trajan (lower left) oversees the construction of a fortified bridgehead. We see ramparts, haystacks for the horses, and crenellated walls of sun-dried brick (instead of the indigenous wooden construction). The column tells the story of an annexation, and its 200 yards of comic strip depict much building of this type, in contrast to the battles and massacres of the barbarians shown on the Column of Marcus Aurelius. Without composition or style, this art was intended to be a pastiche of the painted signs used to explain military conquests to the populace.

ernors sent to the region, who profited from their complicity. Roman governors backed Roman merchants because of corruption, not "economic imperialism."

Until the past century it was not considered improper to enrich oneself through government service. In Stendhal's *Charterhouse of Parma,* when Count Mosca resigns his ministry he is able to give the grand duke incontrovertible proof of his honesty: when he took office he had only 130,000 francs; on leaving it he has only 500,000. Cicero, after a year as governor of a province, was making the equivalent of a million dollars a year and prided himself on his scrupulousness: the sum was considered quite small. Ancient bureaucracy was nothing like our bureaucracy. For millennia sovereigns relied on racketeers to extort taxes and control their subjects.

The cardinal virtue of the official was tact, not honesty—rather like the merchant who must not let his clients think that he is in business for his own sake rather than theirs. Even as governors served themselves in serving the emperor, oppressed people wanted to believe that their paternal masters oppressed them for their own good. "Be obedient and the governor will love thee," Saint Paul wrote. A good governor knew how to fill his coffers without undermining such beliefs. Just because officials get rich by governing does not prove that government itself is not disinterested. Now and then an example was made of some unfortunate governor, subjected to public trial and then executed or, if lucky, disgraced. One particularly clumsy governor displayed his cynicism in a letter to his mistress that unfortunately fell into the wrong hands: "Joy! Joy! I am coming to you free of debt after selling out half the people in my charge." (This is one of three or four extant examples of ancient love letters.) The emperor and his high officials proved their disinterest by disowning their subordinates. The emperor openly criticized the tax collector, who was merely the governor of the imperial estates. Occasionally he granted the request of peasants who came to him complaining of exactions made by his agents. And periodically he would issue an edict outlawing corruption: "An end must be put to the rapacity of all officials. I repeat: an end." Top officials established a regular schedule of bribes, an act tantamount to legalizing bribery.

Dignity

Functionaries, soldiers, and governors did not think of themselves as members of a corps whose reputation had to be preserved but as an elite group with no specialized role—simply superior in every way. Within this elite, gradations of rank were created by the level of office that an individual held, whether in the state apparatus or, in the case of local notables, in the municipalities. Officials told themselves that by serving their emperor or their city for a year, they enhanced their own "dignity" as well as the dignity of their house; henceforth they could appear in the ancestral portrait gallery in official garb. "Dignity" was a great word. It connoted not a virtue, like respectability, but an aristocratic ideal of glory. To the great of the world, dignity was as much a matter of importance as honor to El Cid. Dignity was acquired and increased; it could also be lost. Cicero, exiled, fell into despair; his dignity was gone, he was reduced to nothing. Because public dignity was private property, it was acknowledged that holding public office was a matter of pride and that a man might defend his possession of office as legitimately as a king might defend his crown. If he acted on such grounds, he was absolved of guilt. No one could hold it against Caesar that he crossed the Rubicon, marched on his fatherland, and plunged it into civil war. The Senate had taken away some of his dignity, when Caesar had made it clear that dignity mattered to him more than anything else, including his life.

Certain outward signs indicated membership in the ruling

Fragment of scene of sacrifice, 1st or 2nd century. It shows man with an axe, who will immolate the ox, and two lictors (rather than five or more), whose knouts have no blades for decapitation of the condemned. These were indications of rank that everyone could read: these two lictors serve a municipal magistrate, not a representative of the remote and awesome state apparatus. (Museum of Portogruaro.)

class. Manners, however, were not the most important sign in Roman society, which set little store by salons and the like. Not aesthetes to the same degree as the Greeks, Romans were suspicious of elegance and attached no social significance to it. Gravity of gesture and language was a better indicator of the man of authority. Every notable was supposed to have a good education (*pepaideumenos*), capped by literary culture and knowledge of mythology. In choosing senators and even department heads preference was given to men known for their culture, on the pretext that they would be able to draft official papers in fine prose. Schools of rhetoric became the training ground of future administrators because culture enhanced the image of the governing class in its own eyes. The first naturalized Greeks to become members of the Senate were aristocrats renowned for their culture. What effect this had on the lower orders is doubtful, but it certainly proved disastrous for the conduct of government affairs. By the first century, imperial edicts were couched in language so euphuistic and archaic as to be almost incomprehensible and all but unenforceable, for cultivated writers eschewed technical terms, even in decrees pertaining to matters of finance.

Broadly speaking, the governing class sought to recruit not capable rulers but individuals who would reflect the private qualities that it held in esteem: opulence, education, natural authority. It preferred to judge these qualities with its own eyes because they could not be pinned down in regulations. That is why cooptation tacitly continued to govern entry into the ruling class and promotions in rank. The choice of the elect was not made by the class as a whole. Each of its members had his own stable of protégés whom he would recommend to his colleagues, who in turn recommended their protégés. Even the emperor depended on these recommendations for nominations to the highest positions. This system guaranteed that every important personage could enjoy the pleasure of reigning over an army of aspirants—his clientele, if you will, but be careful of this vague and misleading term. There are two kinds of clientele: in one the client needs a patron; in the other the patron courts clients for the sake of his glory. In the former, the patron exercises real power. In the latter, patrons compete for clients; the clients are the real masters, for the patron needs them.

Alas, not every clientele system was of this sort! "In Istria," Tacitus wrote, "the house of Crassus always had clients, lands, and a name forever renowned." In rural areas there prevailed a form of patronage comparable to the South American caciquism. Large landowners tyrannized and protected the peasants who occupied the land surrounding their estates. Whole villages delivered themselves into the hands of one of these protectors in order to be safe from the others. At other times patronage was more a wager on the future than a consequence of the status quo. During a civil war, Tacitus reports, the city of Fréjus supported the winning party, which was led by a local boy who had grown up to become an important personage; it did so out of "zeal for one of its own and in the hope that he would one day be a powerful man."

Actually "clientage" and "patronage" were terms that the Romans used indiscriminately to describe a wide range of relations. A protected nation was called the "client" of a more powerful state. An accused person was defended in court by his patron—or perhaps he recognized as his patron the person who was willing to defend him. Nothing is more misleading than studies of vocabulary. Sometimes a man offered protection because he already enjoyed power; at other times a man was chosen as patron to provide protection. The latter case

The Two Forms of Clientage

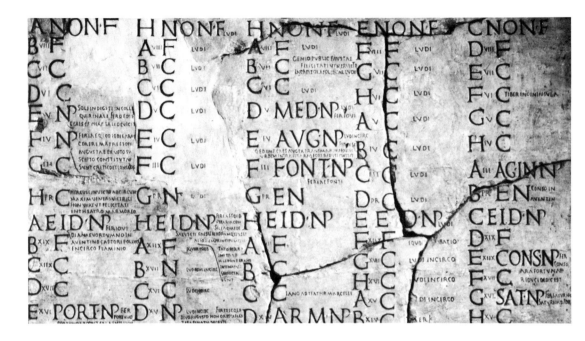

The pace of life: detail of a calendar ca. A.D. 25. Weeks did not exist; days of rest were religious feast days (a day of work was sacrificed to the gods), distributed throughout the year. On feast days magistrates, free men, students, slaves, and animals all ceased work. The word LVDI that appears in various places means "games" (such as chariot races) or theatrical spectacles. Gladiatorial combats were not religious and do not appear on the calendar. (Museum of the Aquila.)

was associated with the patronage of careers. An ambitious young man seeking promotion had little in common with the poor folk subject to a powerful neighbor and obliged to honor him, serve him, and rely on his support. The only problem the young man faced was which patron to choose. A compatriot? A well-placed old friend? A man who had supported him in the early stages of his career? Once selected, the protector would recommend the young man, possibly a stranger the day before, simply because the ambitious fellow had chosen him as protector, knowing that if he did not accept the proffered loyalty, it would be given to another. The Romans were in the habit of transforming generalized relations into personal ones, ritualizing them in the process. The younger generation divided itself into a thousand clienteles and went every morning to hail its patrons.

In return for his protection, the patron took pleasure in the knowledge that his peers' protégés did not outnumber his own. The circulation of political elites depended on personal connections. Oral promises, if not kept, resulted in charges of ingratitude. Patrons deluded themselves into thinking that they advanced the careers of young men out of pure friendship. They liked to give advice about careers. (Cicero adopts a condescending tone toward young Trebatius that he does not allow himself with other correspondents.) They wrote innumerable letters of recommendation, which, though usually quite devoid of content, became almost a distinctive literary genre. The essential thing was to inform one's peers of the name of some protégé. Each patron trusted his peers and used his influence in their behalf, as they used theirs in his. Some aspirants were no doubt omitted when recommendations were made. Only those likely to win the approval of the governing class could be recommended; otherwise the patron risked forfeiting his credibility. And credibility was everything. The man with many protégés and many places to distribute was hailed every morning by a small mob. By contrast, the man who turned his back on public life was abandoned: "He will have no more entourage, no escort for his sedan chair, no visitors in his antechamber." Neither in law nor in custom was there a clear dividing line between public life and private life. Certain philosophers urged such a division, but that was all. "Leave your clients, then, and come dine peacefully with me," said the wise Horace to a friend.

Given the vague distinction between public and private, in identifying a person it was customary to indicate his place in civic life, his political or municipal titles and dignities, if any. These became a part of a man's identity, much as an officer's rank or a noble's titles serve as identifying characteristics for us. When a historian or writer introduced a character, he specified whether he was a slave, a plebeian, a freedman, an equestrian, or a senator. If a senator, he could be either a praetorian or a consular senator, depending on whether the highest rank held in the course of his career was consul or merely praetor. If the man was a professional soldier, who chose to command a regiment in some province or on the borders of the Empire rather than return to Rome to take up one of these annual posts (a duty deferred until later in life), he was referred to as "young So-and-so" (*adulescens*), even if he carried forty years beneath his breastplate; his real career had yet to begin. So much for senatorial nobility. As for the notables in each Roman city, here is how Censorinus characterizes his protector (*amicus*), a man to whom he owes everything and dedicates his book: "Yours has been a distinguished municipal career. Of all the leading men of your city, you have been singled out for honor by being named priest of the emperors. And you even rise above your provincial rank,

Nobility of Office

thanks to your dignity as Roman equestrian." Thus, municipal life, too, had its hierarchy. A man who was not a plebeian and who belonged to the local council (*curia*) was a true luminary. He became a leading man, a "principal," after he had held all available annual posts, including the highest (which were also the costliest).

"Engaging in political life," which meant simply "holding public office," was not a specialized activity. It was something that any man worthy of the name, and member of the governing class, was expected to do—an ideal of private behavior. To be deprived of access to public office and hence to the city's political life was to be less than a man, a person of no account. Erotic poets seeking to elicit smiles from their readers with an amusing paradox used to say that they felt nothing but scorn for a political career, that the only campaign that interested them was that of love (*militia amoris*). Philosophers, experts on the subject, usually held that, if absolutely essential, political life (*bios politikos*) could be sacrificed, but only to philosophical life, that is, to full devotion to the study of wisdom. In practice, municipal offices and, a fortiori, senatorial offices were accessible only to wealthy families. But this privilege was also an ideal, almost a duty. Conformists, the Stoics held that the political life was life lived in accordance with Reason. A man could be as rich as he liked, but he did not count among the "first men of the city" unless he cut a figure on the public stage. Of course a wealthy man might not be allowed to live by himself, undisturbed. Others of his class might exhort him to become involved, or the people of his city might wrest him from his estates by gentle coercion, thrusting him into the political limelight. For the exercise of any office, which lasted only a year but conferred a rank for life, involved lavish expenditure on public pleasures, to which the people were addicted.

The individual who held public office paid dearly for his lifetime of honor. The lack of distinction between public and private funds was not a one-way affair. The curious institution of public benefaction by government officials has been called "evergetism." Any man named praetor or consul was expected to spend billions from his own pocket to pay for public spectacles, plays, chariot races at the Circus, and even ruinous gladiatorial battles in the Colosseum, to amuse the people of Rome. Afterward the newly appointed official went to the provinces to replenish his coffers. Such was the lot of families included in the senatorial aristocracy—one family out of every

Consul about to throw a handkerchief onto the track to signal the start of a chariot race, 4th century. (Rome, Museum of the Conservators.)

ten or twenty thousand. The true nature of evergetism, however, can be seen most clearly among the municipal notables: perhaps one family in twenty. For them there was no compensation for the financial sacrifices that evergetism obliged them to make.

In the least of the Empire's cities, whether Latin was spoken or Greek or even Celtic or Syriac, perhaps the majority of public buildings now explored by archaeologists and visited by thousands of tourists every year were built by local notables who bore the expense out of their own pockets. These same men paid for the public spectacles staged each year to the delight of the populace. Anyone who acceded to municipal office was expected to pay into the city treasury a sum of money, which went to finance spectacles during his tenure or else to construct public buildings. If an officeholder found himself in straitened circumstances, he was expected to make a written promise that he or his heirs would some day pay the expected sum. More than that, apart from the holding of public office, notables made spontaneous gifts of buildings, gladiator fights, public banquets, and festivals to their fellow citizens. Such endowments were even more common in Rome than in the United States today, with the difference that in Rome the gifts of the wealthy were almost exclusively intended to embellish the city and add to the pleasure of its citizens. By far the majority of amphitheaters, those stony monuments to wealth, were freely given by patrons, who thereby left a definitive mark on their city.

Were these gifts a product of private generosity or public duty? Both. The proportion varied from donor to donor and every case was special. What began as a desire on the part of the rich to make ostentatious display of their wealth increasingly came to be seen as a duty imposed upon wealthy citizens by their cities. Cities obliged wealthy men of rank to make a habit of what they might have been inclined to do from time to time. By their generous gifts notables demonstrated membership in the governing class. Satirical poets mocked the pretensions of the nouveaux riches, who hastened to provide fellow citizens with the desired spectacles. Cities became accustomed to a level of public luxury that they began to consider their due. The nomination of annual officials provided the occasion. Every year, in every city, little dramas took place, as new sources of wealth were found and milked. Every

Evergetism

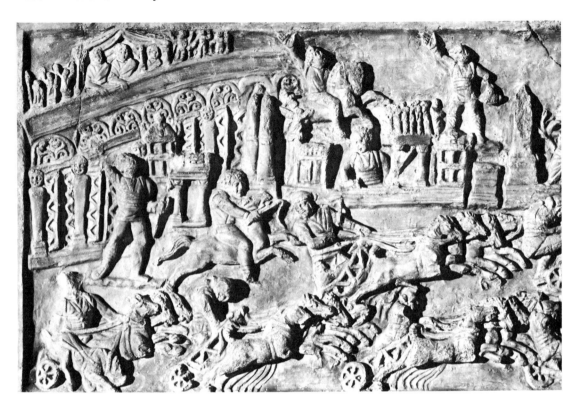

Chariot race (relief destroyed in 1944), 2nd or 3rd century. Statues of the gods are everywhere; the races were offerings to the gods, who took as much interest in the events as did men.

council member protested that he was poorer than his peers but that So-and-so was a fortunate and prosperous man and such a magnificent person that he would surely accept an office that required him, say, to pay for the cost of heating the water in the public baths. But the man designated might complain that he had already held this office. The more stubborn of the two would win the argument. In case of stalemate, the provincial governor might take a hand. Or the plebs of the city, fond of its hot water, might intervene peacefully by hailing the designated victim, extolling his spontaneous generosity, and electing him to office by unanimous acclamation. Or, again, an unexpected patron might come forward and spontaneously offer to help his city. The city would then show its gratitude by having the council name him to some high local office or by awarding a special title, such as "patron of the city," "father of the city," or "magnificent and spontaneous benefactor," a title that might be inscribed on the man's tombstone. Or the city might vote to erect a statue of its benefactor, the cost of which he would of course volunteer to bear.

These practices explain why local dignitaries gradually ceased to be elected by their fellow citizens and instead were designated by the council oligarchy, which chose officials from its own ranks. The problem was not too many candidates but too few. Since holding office was a matter more of disbursing funds than of governing, people were willing to allow the council to immolate one of its own members; the best candidate was the one who agreed to pay up. Notables enjoyed the dubious satisfaction of maintaining that the city belonged to them because they had paid for it. In return, this class had the privilege of assessing imperial taxes to its own advantage, shifting as much as possible of the tax burden onto the shoulders of the poor peasants. Every city was divided into two camps: the notables who gave and the plebs who received. A man was not a local luminary if he did not at least once in his life pay for a public building or banquet. This was the way the ruling oligarchy was formed. Was it also a hereditary oligarchy? The question is not easily answered. A father's dignities imposed a kind of moral obligation on his son, who was expected to make gifts simply because he was his father's heir. In seeking out victims cities always turned first to those whose fathers had held high office (*patrobouloi*), hoping that the sons would wish to emulate the generosity of their fathers. In case of a shortage of sons of officeholders, municipal councils resigned themselves to admitting into their ranks the scions of merchant families, say, to whom costly offices might then be assigned.

Fragment of sarcophagus, 4th century. An important man (he holds a scepter and is preceded by a lictor) travels by carriage; a secretary adds to his luster. An empty sedan chair follows. When the man reaches the city gates he will switch to the chair, being shrewd enough not to make an ostentatious entrance in his carriage. (Aquileia, Archaeological Museum.)

Notables put up with this system only because custom obliged them to. Protest was as common as silent submission. The central government also had doubts. Sometimes to ensure its own popularity it required notables to give the people pleasures that "will ward off unhappiness." Sometimes it sought the support of the notables by seeking to stem the tide of popular demands. Still other times it pursued its own interests and attempted to protect the rich from their penchant for ostentatious display: Did it not make more sense to provide a city with a new pier than to pay for a festival? The tendency was to give the populace whatever it found amusing, or to build buildings that flattered the vanity of the donor. It was only during times of famine that the plebs thought of asking its leaders to sell cheaply the grain held in their storehouses. The wealthy paid for the amusements of their fellow citizens out of civic spirit and for buildings out of ostentation. Civic spirit and ostentation—the twin roots of evergetism—again blurred the distinction between the public man and the private.

Aristocratic Civism

Ostentation meant spontaneity, civic spirit meant duty. The duty to give was paradoxical, in that it required the donor to give the city more than its due. The citizens of a modern state pay only the taxes they are required to pay, to the cent. But Greek cities, and the Roman cities patterned after them, held to a principle, or an ideal, that was far more exacting. When possible, they treated their citizens as a modern political party treats its militant activists: zeal is all or nothing and party members are expected to devote themselves fully to the cause. Ancient cities expected wealthy citizens to show similar devotion. It would take us too far afield to explain why this devotion went mainly to provide expensive amusements. (Briefly, officials found it most difficult to turn down requests to spend money on activities that were also acts of piety; when one of them honored the gods of the city by staging a festival or public spectacle, he always made a contribution to the public treasury.)

Besides civic duty, there was the ostentation of the nobility. The wealthy had always considered themselves public figures. They invited all fellow citizens to their daughters' weddings. If a rich man's father died, the entire city was invited to the funeral banquet or the gladiator fight in honor of the deceased. Such acts of generosity soon became obligatory. Throughout the Empire any notable whose adolescent son first donned adult garb or who took a new wife was expected to hold a public celebration or to donate money to the city. If he wished to avoid this obligation, he had to take refuge on one of his estates and celebrate the marriage there. But to do so was to forgo public life entirely and to moulder in oblivion. Nobles were proud men, who wanted their memories to endure, so rather than provide the citizens some fleeting amusement, they had buildings built with their names engraved on them. Or they established permanent foundations, another fashionable form of giving since every year on the founder's birthday the city celebrated his memory, paying for the celebration with the income from capital bequeathed for the purpose. Sometimes a festival named for a wealthy donor was celebrated in his honor.

All of these were ways in which wealthy men, living or dead, could confirm their status as local luminaries. A luminary is no longer a private person, however; stars are devoured by their fans. The relation between a benefactor and his city was a physical affair, a matter of face-to-face contact. In this it resembled the relation under the Roman Republic between ordinary citizens and political leaders, who made decisions from the rostrum before the eyes of the crowd, visible, like yesterday's generals, on the field of battle. Emperors, shut up in their palaces, wanted to continue this republican tradition by appearing personally in the amphitheater or circus, where the plebs could examine them and gauge their responsiveness to the wishes of the public, the one true judge.

The fate of municipal notables was similar. In a small town in Tunisia archaeologists have found a mosaic in which a powerful local figure named Magerius celebrated his own generosity. The mosaic, which had served as decoration in his antechamber, depicts a fight between four gladiators and four leopards; the name of each gladiator is recorded next to his portrait, as is the name of each animal. The mosaic is no mere decoration, but a truthful record of a spectacle which Magerius paid for out of his own pocket. It also records the acclamation of the public, which heaped praise upon its benefactor: "Magerius! Magerius! May your example serve to instruct those who come after you! May your predecessors also heed the lesson! When has anyone else done so much, and where? You offer a spectacle worthy of Rome, the capital! You pay from your own purse! Today is your great day! Magerius is the donor! That is true wealth! That is true power! The very thing! Now that it is over, give the gladiators something extra to

Rome, Villa Albani, between 177 and 180. The imperial government defended merchants against excessive customs duties. This decision was recorded in stone, because law enforcement was never automatic or assured.

CRISPINVS   HILARINVS

MAGERI

SPITTARA

The mosaic of Magerius
(overview with two details),
at Smirat (Tunisia).

send them on their way!" Magerius agreed to this last wish, and the mosaic shows the four bags of silver (each marked with an amount) that he sent to the gladiators in the arena.

The applause of the populace was normally followed by honorific titles and marks of honor awarded for life by the municipal council. Though obliged to bestow these honors, the city had the right to determine who deserved them. A notable could distinguish himself from his peers only by paying homage to his city. The honorific titles awarded to a benefactor, the public offices that he held, were no less important than, say, titles of nobility in prerevolutionary France, and they aroused just as much passion. The Roman Empire offers us the curious paradox of aristocratic civism. The hereditary presumption of the noble had to be confirmed by an ostentatious display of civic spirit, by a generous act that made the benefactor stand out but within a civic setting. Superior to the plebs of his town, the notable was an important man because he was worthy in the eyes of his fellow citizens, who benefited from his largesse. The city was both the beneficiary and the judge of its native son's devotion. The plebs was so keenly aware of this ambiguity that people often left the spectacle unsure whether they had been honored or humiliated by their benefactor. A phrase that Petronius imputes to one spectator captures this feeling well: "He gave me a spectacle, but I applauded it. We're even: one hand washes the other."

Thus, patriotic devotion cohabited with lust for personal glory (*ambitus*). Already, under the Roman Republic, members of the senatorial class sought popularity by staging public banquets and spectacles, more to please the plebs than to corrupt the electors. Even after election to high office had been eliminated, they carried on in the same tradition. Georges Ville said: "Behind self-interested ambition often lurked what one might call disinterested ambition, which sought the favor of the crowd for itself and was satisfied with that and nothing else."

Enough about the Roman "bourgeoisie." Like the clientele system, evergetism cannot be understood in terms of class interest. It was, rather, the consequence of an aristocratic mind-set, with its penchant for useless building and for erecting honorific statues to the glory of family dynasties. This heraldic art was fed by fantasies of nobility. To try to explain these in terms of Machiavellian strategy, redistribution of

The Uniqueness of Evergetism

This young Roman wears a toga, although he is not yet an adult (as is indicated by the *bulla* around his neck, which youths ceased to wear when they donned the toga of adulthood). Several copies of this statue have been found, which indicates that it was a widely reproduced official portrait. This young prince must be either the unfortunate Britannicus or the man who murdered him, Nero. But because effigies of Nero were destroyed after his death, and one of these statues was found in the Forum of Velleia, this is Britannicus. (Paris, Louvre.)

wealth, depoliticization, and a calculated effort to erect symbolic barriers between the classes is to oversimplify and rationalize a phenomenon whose cost and symbolic complexity went far beyond what was socially necessary. What confuses us is that this nobility, with its apparently civic symbolism, its "public" buildings and magistrate's titles, seems so different from the familiar European nobility of blood and landed titles. The Roman aristocracy was a unique historical entity, which, rather than extol the purity of its blood, sang its own praises in terms drawn from the vocabulary of the ancient city.

The group of curials did not coincide exactly with the class of the wealthy, if only because the number of seats available on the municipal council was generally limited to one hundred. The municipal council of a Roman city was an aristocratic club; not all the wealthy were admitted. Imperial laws insisted that, in case of financial need, wealthy merchants, however vulgar, should be admitted. But the wealthy nobles already in the club preferred to put pressure on one of their own, to force him to ruin himself for the sake of his city. Some nobles chose to flee the gentle violence of their peers. According to the last book of the *Digest,* they took refuge on their estates, with their farmers (*coloi praediorum*), for the power of the public authorities did not extend far outside the cities and into the countryside, where Christians like Saint Cyprian fled from their persecutors.

The official class was aristocratic in another sense: families that had attained prominent position tended to hold onto it for long periods. True, nouveau-riche dynasties were allowed to crash this exalted circle, but it is no less true that the leading families maintained their position for centuries, intermarrying and breeding among themselves. The marriage patterns of the few great families in one city have been studied by Philippe Moreau, who took Cicero's *Pro Cluentio* as his starting point. In Greece abundant epigraphic evidence has enabled scholars to trace the history of many a noble family over two or three centuries, in Sparta especially, as well as in Boeotia and elsewhere. Family trees fill entire folio-sized pages in our anthologies of Greek inscriptions of the imperial period. The time of the Empire was a time of stability for the aristocracy.

Evergetism was a point of honor among the aristocracy, whose caste pride was the driving force behind the various civic and liberal motives that historians have ably, but too exclusively, described: civic spirit, zeal in largesse, desire for distinction. But the historians are too subtle; the reality was far simpler. Noble pride was a fact, as was the existence of a patrimonial, indeed a hereditary, nobility. Every noble wanted to outdo his rivals so that he might claim to be the "first" or the "only" person ever to engage in some unheard-of act of generosity: previous officeholders may have distributed free bath oil to the populace, but along comes a new champion who prides himself on being the first to distribute perfumed bath oil.

"I want to make money," says one of Petronius' heroes, "and to have such a fine death that my funeral will become proverbial." No doubt he will order his heirs to stage a public banquet for the occasion. Bread and Circuses, or, rather, buildings and spectacles: authority was more often a matter of seizing the limelight than of obliging others to do one's bidding through the wielding of public or private power. It was monumentalization and theatricalization. Evergetism was not as virtuous as its most recent commentators believe. Nor was it as Machiavellian as some earlier commentators, imbued with vague Marxism, maintained. Nobility resided in a competition that was as irrational in a political and economic sense as ostentation was wasteful. Evergetism far exceeded what was needed to maintain one's rank or to mark class barriers, and there is no basis for reducing so fundamental a phenomenon as competition through waste to social terms, according to the modern taste in historical explanation. Nor does it make sense to rely on the explanations given by the ancients themselves: patriotism, festivals and banquets, generosity, and so forth. The phenomenon is as peculiar as the practice of potlatch that anthropologists have discovered among many "primitive" peoples. Among the Romans the passion to give was as all-consuming as the passions unleashed in "civilized" nations today by the desire for "political" power and "economic" wealth and nothing else, nothing more mysterious—or so we like to think.

View of the city of Alba Fucens (in the Abruzzi) ca. A.D. 50. It is difficult to interpret because it has been simplified. Instead of expansive, sumptuous villas or huge multistory apartment buildings, this may have been a city of tall, narrow houses. (Rome, Torlonia Collection.)

৵ "Work" and Leisure

S LAVERY was an important part of the Roman economy. Men could also be imprisoned for debt, sequestered by the creditor along with their wives and families and forced to work. And there was the state sector: condemned men, slaves of the innumerable imperial states, toiled under the whips of slavedrivers; many Christians suffered this fate. But for the most part Roman workers were legally free. Small independent farmers worked to pay taxes. As Peter Brown has written, the Roman Empire gave free sway to local oligarchies, to whom it delegated responsibility for administrative chores. Little was required of these local notables in the way of taxes, and imperial authorities refrained from exhibiting too much curiosity about the way in which taxes were extorted from the peasantry. (Unencumbering government of this kind has been the basis of much colonial rule in recent times.) Other peasants worked for these same notables as sharecroppers. Farm workers, laborers, and artisans hired to perform specific tasks reached agreements with their employers on the terms of employment, though this rarely took the form of written contracts (except when workers were accepted as apprentices). Just as the Napoleonic Code stipulated that the word of a master should be accepted in a dispute with a servant over wages, so did the Roman master mete out his own justice if robbed by an employee, as though the employee were a slave. Cities were essentially places where Roman notables (like the "urban nobility" of the Italian Renaissance) spent the money generated by land. The Roman Empire thus stands in sharp contrast to the France of the Middle Ages, where the nobility lived scattered about the countryside in fortified castles.

In the Roman city urban notables were surrounded by

Detail of mosaic from the Baths of Caracalla, 3rd or 4th century. In the 3rd century Rome rivaled Olympia as a center of athletic competitions in the Greek manner. This elderly gentleman trained professional athletes who came to Rome from all over the world to compete. (Rome, Lateran Museum.)

artisans and merchants who catered to the needs of the wealthy. Roman "cities" and modern cities have little in common but the name. A Roman city could be recognized by the presence of an idle class, made up of what I call "notables." Idleness was the cornerstone of "private life"; in fact, in the ancient world it was considered a virtue.

The urban nobility looked upon the countryside with disdain, and upon the cities, filled with workers, with suspicion. The imperial government did the same. In A.D. 215 an emperor decided to expel from Alexandria the Egyptian peasants who had gathered there in large numbers, because "their way of life proves that rural people are not suited to civic life." The Empire was really an empire only in its cities, where the notables in control of the municipal councils could regiment the working population. Romans were contemptuous of central Turkey whose cities were mere country towns inhabited by well-to-do farmers, wealthy enough to claim immortality by paying to have their epitaphs engraved.

Around 1820 an astrologer says to the young hero of Stendhal's *Charterhouse of Parma*: "In a century perhaps nobody will want idlers any more." He was right. It ill becomes anyone today to admit that he lives without working. Since Marx and Proudhon, labor has been universally accepted as a positive social value and a philosophical concept. As a result, the ancients' contempt for labor, their undisguised scorn for those who work with their hands, their exaltation of leisure as the sine qua non of a "liberal" life, the only life worthy of a man, shocks us deeply. Not only was the worker regarded as a social inferior; he was base, ignoble. It has often been held, therefore, that a society like the Roman, so mistaken about what we regard as proper values, must have been a deformed society, which inevitably paid the price of its deformity. The ancients' contempt for labor, the argument goes, explains their economic backwardness, their ignorance of technology. Or, according to another argument, the reason for one deformity must be sought in another: contempt for labor, we are told, had its roots in that other scandalous fact of Roman life, slavery.

And yet, if we are honest, we must admit that the key to this enigma lies within ourselves. True, we believe that work is respectable and would not dare to admit to idleness. Nevertheless, we are sensitive to class distinctions and, admit it or not, regard workers and shopkeepers as people of relatively little importance. We would not want ourselves or our children to sink to their station, even if we are a little ashamed of harboring such sentiments.

Therein lies the first of six keys to ancient attitudes toward labor: contempt for labor equals social contempt for laborers. This contempt persisted until about the time when the *Charterhouse of Parma* was written. Then, in order to maintain class hierarchy and discourage class conflict, it became necessary to recognize labor as a true value, shared by all. Social peace was bought at the price of hypocrisy. There is no mystery about the ancient contempt for labor; it is just that the social war had not yet reached the stage of a hypocritical and temporary armistice. A social class proud of its superiority sang hymns to its own glory (such is the nature of ideology).

---

1. The first key to ancient attitudes toward labor is that the source and character of a social group's wealth determined its value. In classical Athens, when comic poets characterized men by occupations (Eucrates the scrap dealer or Lysicles the seller of sheep), they had no intention of doing them honor; to be fully a man, one had to live in leisure. According to Plato, a well-organized city is one in which citizens are fed by the rural toil of their slaves and the trades are filled with people of no importance. The "virtuous" life, the life lived by a man of quality, is supposed to be one of "idleness." (As we shall see, this meant the life of a landowner, who did no "work" but spent his time overseeing his estates.) Aristotle failed to see how slaves, peasants, and shopkeepers could be expected to lead "happy" lives, meaning lives at once prosperous and noble. Such lives were the exclusive province of men who could afford to live as they pleased, according to their ideals. Only such men of leisure conformed to the ideal of humanity. Only they were worthy of full citizenship: "The perfection of the citizen cannot be predicated of the man who is merely free, but only of the man who is free from such necessary tasks as are performed by serfs, artisans, and manual laborers; the latter will not be citizens if the constitution awards public charges to virtue and merit, since no one who leads the life of a worker or laborer can practice virtue." Aristotle is not saying that a poor man has scant means and little opportunity to exhibit certain virtues, but that poverty is a defect, a kind of vice. For Metternich, mankind began at the rank of baron; for the Greeks and Romans, it began with the landowner. Greek and Roman notables did not consider themselves to be supe-

The Virtue of Wealth

Fragment of sarcophagus, 3rd century. A goatherd milks a goat in front of a reed hut. This sarcophagus was a popular model (the same shop produced a number of copies). The pastoral scene aestheticized death and dispelled sadness. (Rome, Museum of the Baths.)

rior to the average run of humanity. They believed purely and simply that they *were* humanity, hence that the poor were morally inferior. The poor did not live as men ought to live.

Wealth was virtue. Demosthenes, in a trial in which he stood as defendant and the Athenian mob as his judge, hurled the following insults in the teeth of his adversary: "I am worth more than Eschinus and I am better born than he; I do not wish to seem to insult poverty, but I am bound to say that it was my lot as a child to attend good schools and to have had sufficient wealth that I was not forced by need to engage in shameful labors. Whereas you, Eschinus, it was your lot as a child to sweep, as might a slave, the classroom in which your father served as teacher." Demosthenes won a decisive victory in this case.

Greek thinkers confirmed this natural conviction in the Romans. "The common arts, the sordid arts, are according to the philosopher Posidonius those practiced by manual laborers, who spend all their time earning their living. There is no beauty in such occupations, which bear little resemblance to the Good," writes Seneca. Cicero did not need to read the philosopher Panaetius, whose conformism he respected, to know that "wage labor is sordid and unworthy of a free man, for wages are the price of labor and not of some art; craft labor is sordid, as is the business of retailing [as opposed to large-scale wholesale trade]." No egalitarian, socialist, or Christian ideals existed to check this spontaneous contempt.

The ancients extolled the man who lived on unearned income as immoderately as the old French aristocracy accused commoners of beggary. A class of wealthy and more or less cultivated notables, determined to maintain exclusive control over the levers of power, exalted its idleness as the sine qua non of a liberal culture and a political career. Workers, Aristotle said, would not know how to govern; they cannot govern, he added, they should not govern, and, what is more, they scarcely even think of governing. In fact, according to Plato, all too many of the wealthy took no part in public affairs and concerned themselves solely with their pleasures and with increasing their wealth. The rich, wrote the mystic Plotinus, are all too often disappointing, but at least they have the merit of not having to work, hence "they constitute a species with some remembrance of virtue," whereas "the mass of manual laborers is a contemptible mob, whose purpose is to produce objects needed by men of virtue."

The rich of course had no need to work. The problem, according to Plato, was that many of them worked nevertheless, out of greed. Their love of wealth "leaves them no respite to concern themselves with anything other than their private property. The soul of the citizen today is entirely taken up with getting rich and with making sure that every day brings its share of profit. The citizen is ready to learn any technique, to engage in any kind of activity, so long as it is profitable. He thumbs his nose at the rest."

Rome, detail of butcher's tomb, 2nd century(?). The man cutting chops may have been a small shopkeeper or a major wholesaler. (Dresden Museum.)

Class Struggle

Historians have too often studied the ancients' ideas about labor as though these were doctrines elaborated by jurists and philosophers. In fact, they were confused collective notions, as well as class ideologies. The ancients laid down no principles. They did not say, for example, that "labor" existed only if one worked for another man or for a wage. But their representations were broadly applicable to inferior social

Tomb of mosaicist, 3rd or 4th century. Two seated workmen are cutting small cubes with large hammers. Two hod carriers bring colored stone or haul away the mosaic tiles. At top right, a figure invites spectators to admire the scene. (This sort of "deictic gesture" was to become very popular in medieval art.) (Ostia, Archaeological Museum.)

groups, whose members were reduced to earning their living by wage labor or by entering the service of others. The point was not to establish rules of conduct applicable to all, but to ascribe value to a social class in which some worked as servants, some as hired laborers. All were accused of "labor" so that the entire class might be held in contempt. Workers were reviled not because they worked, but because they belonged to this inferior class. Conversely, the class of notables, rich, cultivated, and powerful, was exalted because it possessed either the virtue of not having to work or that of ruling the city; it made no difference which. Thus, the "ancients' ideas about labor" were not so much ideas as evaluations, positive for the powerful, negative for the humble. Evaluation was the essential point; the details of their arguments are of no interest.

2. In making class evaluations, Romans used whatever argument came to hand. Xenophon explains that the manual trades feminized the men who worked in them, "because these men are forced to remain seated in the shade and sometimes even to spend entire days at fireside." Artisans, moreover,

"haven't time to be concerned with their friends and contribute to the safety of their city." By contrast, working in the fields accustoms a man to endure extremes of heat and cold and to get up early in the morning and encourages him to defend the land that feeds him.

If we are willing to concede that class interest plays a role in history, one historical mystery is easily solved: Why was commerce almost universally devalued until the industrial revolution? The key to the mystery lies in the fact that commercial wealth belonged to the newly rich, while old wealth was based on land. Inherited wealth defended itself against upstart merchants by imputing to them every conceivable vice: merchants are rootless, greedy, the source of all evil; they promote luxury and weakness; they distort nature by traveling to far-off lands, violating the natural barrier of the seas and bringing back what nature will not permit to grow at home. These ideas persisted from archaic Greece and India down to Benjamin Constant and Charles Maurras. In Rome citizens were divided, on the basis of wealth, into civic "orders" (simple citizens, decurions, equestrians, and senators). In establishing wealth, however, the census took account only of property in land. A wealthy trader could raise his status in civil society only by acquiring land. As Cicero wrote, if a merchant, tired of adding to his fortune, aspired to return to port and place his money in rural properties, he could shed his contemptible merchant's character and win high praise.

Sign for a shop that was undoubtedly called "Two Monkeys and a Snail," an allusion, I imagine, to the qualities of the clerks who sold fruit and game. The snail can be seen to the right of the women shown in profile.

The devaluing of nonlanded wealth amounted to a rejection of the parvenu. As long as cultivated land remained the principal form of wealth and agriculture the major source of income, to be wealthy meant to own land; it was the universal investment. Commerce was only a means to an end, a way to become rich. Landed property distinguished the heir from the parvenu. Commerce was a means of acquiring a desirable thing; land was the thing itself. This system of values had one peculiar consequence: a man who was already wealthy and who owned land was not disdained as a merchant if he decided to engage in trade. The important thing was not to begin in trade.

A Definition of Labor

Commerce is sordid, Cicero said, "if it is a small affair in which one buys only to resell immediately what one has bought. But if it is high trade, grand commerce, it no longer merits much scorn." He adds that, while all artisans' work is sordid, the liberal professions, such as architecture and medicine, are honorable. They might not suit persons of the highest rank, but anyone who did not belong to the cream of society could practice these professions without opprobrium.

3. But did practice of the liberal professions constitute "work"? What does the word mean? It has no exact equivalent in Latin or Greek. Was a writer a worker? A minister? A housewife? A slave did not "work": he obeyed, he did what his master ordered him to do. Similar questions may be asked in our own society. Is a soldier a "worker"? He follows orders. Plato, in *Laws*, establishes that a true citizen should not work; but two pages later he states that the same citizen should "spend several hours each night completing his political chores if he holds a public office or, if not, finishing off his business." By this Plato means the management of his estates, worked of course by his slaves. The physician and philosopher Galen mentions a teacher of his who was forced to give up the teaching of philosophy, "because his leisure was gone. His fellow citizens had induced him to take on various political tasks." This, however, was not work.

Consider the "philosophers, rhetors, musicians, and grammarians" mentioned by Lucian, "all those who feel they must accept a position in a household and receive a salary in return for giving lessons," because they are poor (that is, in the ancient meaning of the word, because their personal wealth is inadequate to their needs). Did they work? No. Some writ-

Coppersmith at work.
(Estonian Museum.)

Sign of a shop or dwelling called "The Four Sisters," three of whom were none other than the graces. (Berlin Museum.)

ers held that they practiced a profession truly worthy of a free man, a "liberal" dignity; others held that they were "friends" (the polite term) of the master who paid them. Still others held that these teachers were poor devils forced to earn their daily bread and to lead a life that was basically the life of a slave: their time was not their own; like household slaves, they heeded the bell that marked the beginning and end of the working day in all good houses. Strange "friendship, that speaks so much about labor and fatigue!" Tutors were not even allowed to become true freemen, because they were not allowed to acquire fortunes of their own. "Their wages, assuming they were paid, and paid in full, had to be spent down to the last cent. They could not put anything aside." Liberal profession, friendship, or wage labor? It is idle to ask how the Romans, or even their jurists, would have answered this question, for they had no answer. They held all three opinions at once, expressing astonishment at the paradox that an activity as "liberal" as scholarship (or "grammar") should fall to the lot of a poor devil with no money. Romans simultaneously felt respect and contempt for their domestic grammarian, their children's tutor. Friend or mercenary? In this society no one was a worker; all social relations were conceived in terms of friendship or authority.

Let us consider, finally, the activities that involved the holding of high office and personal dignity, namely, public functions. Here again we encounter an amalgam of prejudice

Gismondi model of Rome, near the Aracoeli, an apartment building from the 2nd century. This was a fairly large building of five stories divided into numerous apartments; the ground floor was occupied by shops.

A deceased merchant about to depart on a journey with his horse and slave; his son will be a worthy successor. One of Apuleius' heroes was such a merchant: he sold honey, cheese, and so forth to innkeepers and was always on the road, ready to go wherever he heard there was good cheese for sale at a reasonable price. (Aquileia, Archaeological Museum.)

and historical tradition. If a senator was sent to govern the province of Africa and received a fabulous salary for his work, there was no ambiguity. He held a glorious position, fully in keeping with the ideal that a noble should engage in political activity. Yet the man sent to govern the province of Egypt was not considered to hold high office. The difference was that Africa's governors were chosen from the ancient Senate, whereas Egypt's came from the corps of imperial "functionaries" created in the early days of the Empire.

Did these imperial functionaries serve the state and their prince? Their enemies charged that they were nothing more than slaves of their master, the emperor, who was supposed to use his servants to help him run the Empire much as he might use them to run his private estates. But one of these high functionaries, the writer Lucian, who served as high treasurer of Egypt, spoke for all when he said that there was no difference between an imperial functionary and a senator-governor. He was right, but collective judgments are not always based on reason. The physician Galen, who treated one imperial functionary, saw him as a kind of slave, since the man worked all day long for his master, the emperor, and "became himself once again, independent of his master, only at nightfall." The same ambiguity attached to another important role: steward for a great family. This post was generally entrusted to the scion of a ruined old family. Plutarch speaks of his steward in a tone of commiseration: he is an inferior brother.

---

4. What determined whether a governor of Egypt was a public man or a mere worker? Was it his position? No. Was it his "lifestyle," his lordly ways or submissive demeanor? No. What mattered was not what he was or did; judgment was imposed from outside. Ancient conceptions of labor contain quite an array of "outside judgments." Consider an analogy. How do we decide whether the powerful Medici family was a family of bankers or nobles? Were they bankers who lived like nobles or nobles who happened to be in the banking business? Is it their lifestyle that determines the answer, as Max Weber maintained? No. The judgment depends not on them, but on their contemporaries, who either agreed or did not agree to count the Medicis among the noble families of the day. And if they did agree to count them as noble, then their banking activities cease to be their profession and become a mere anecdotal detail. "Outside judgments" are a trap for unwary historians. Merely because the notables of the ancient world declared themselves to be men of leisure, it is wrong to conclude that they did not engage in banking and commerce.

In France today, a duke who runs a steel company remains a duke who happens to own some steel mills, while a steel

Outside Judgments

Below left: An oculist. Detail of sarcophagus, 2nd or 3rd century. Some eye diseases were endemic and were treated with lotions, cupping, bleeding, and washing. On the right and left hang two oversized cupping glasses. (Ravenna, Church of San Vittore.)

Below right: Tomb of Athenian physician, 1st century B.C. Patients were examined nude, so women often preferred female doctors or midwives. In the lower right corner is an oversized cupping glass. (London, British Museum.)

Gismondi model of Rome. The Tiber and two of the eight bridges, the larger of the two circuses, two of the eleven aqueducts, the Coliseum, and the rectangular park of the Temple of Claudius Apotheosized.

executive who is not a duke derives his whole identity from his position. In the ancient world a notable was not identified as a shipper or an estate owner; he was himself, a man. To speak anachronistically for a moment, his business card contained nothing but his name. Everyone regarded managing one's estates as a prosaic necessity and nothing more, no more characteristic of a man than the need to get dressed in the morning. If we could travel back in time to a Roman city and ask the man in the street what he thought of, say, a dynasty of shipowners who lorded it over his city, he would answer: "They are important people, powerful, wealthy men. They take part in public affairs and with their donations they've done the city a lot of good and paid for some magnificent games." Later in the conversation we would no doubt learn that they had also fitted out a great many ships, though that fact alone would not reduce them to the level of mere ship-owners. One historian recently showed that the ancients scorned commercial profits as the fruit of greed, yet considered it a merit for a noble to accumulate wealth by every possible means, including commerce. They held professional merchants in contempt, but regarded nobles as statesmen and men of leisure. Was their thinking contradictory? Logically, yes. But the Romans themselves were not aware of the contradiction. A notable who engaged in trade was not classed as a trader but as a notable, one of the most powerful of men. To be sure, the law forbade Roman senators to engage in maritime commerce. But senators violated the law without scruple, because what mattered was that one should not be *in business*. Senators *did* business but were not *in* business; appearances were preserved.

No notable or noble was ever defined by what he did. A poor man, on the other hand, *was* a cobbler or a laborer. In order to be himself and nothing else, he had to possess a patrimony. When, in his epitaph, a notable proclaimed himself a "good farmer," he meant that he had the talent necessary to ensure that his lands were well cultivated, not that he was a cultivator by trade. What facts did the epitaphs of notables mention? In the first place, the political offices they had held, and possibly liberal activities in which they engaged by predilection or "profession," much as nobles of a later age would make profession of a monastic vocation. Notables and nobles honored themselves by studying philosophy, eloquence, law, poetry, or medicine, and, in Greek parts of the Empire, by athletic prowess. Cities honored them with statues commemorating these achievements: "professions" were publicly honored. People defined themselves in terms of their professions; for example, one said, "former consul and philosopher." Now we understand the meaning of the title that Marcus Aurelius has claimed in posterity: "emperor and philosopher." With these words he signified that he had capped his political dignity with his philosophical profession.

---

5. To scorn working people socially is one thing, but every member of the ruling class knows that labor is useful to the state: It secures social peace. Isocrates writes that "in the good old days the lower orders were encouraged to go into farming and commerce, because people knew that idleness gives rise to indigence and indigence to crime." Ancient phi-

In Praise of Labor

losophy did not hold that a state is a "society" organized in such a way that each man works for the benefit of all the others. It maintained instead that a "city" is an institution imposed upon natural human society in order to allow men to live more nobly. According to this view, the poor work not to contribute to society but to keep out of mischief: crime and sedition. But there was one ancient thinker who believed that work, or at least commerce, benefited all citizens by securing necessary goods. Given the esteem for other activities that contributed to the common good, he was surprised by the contempt in which merchants were generally held. This was none other than Plato, the same thinker who freely expressed his disdain for people of low social rank. Even here Plato does not say that society is sustained by the labor of all, including tillers, artisans, and merchants. He mentions only commerce. For him, every citizen is sustained by his patrimony (cultivated by his slaves), a resource as "natural" as the air we breathe. Man begins to render service to his fellow man only when it becomes necessary to obtain goods not "naturally" available. Commerce complements inherited wealth.

Detail of sarcophagus, 2nd century or later. Visible are two barrels (which had replaced amphoras). On the left is a customer, purse in hand; on the right, the late merchant, holding a cup and tap. Since uninherited wealth bestowed no rank, this major wine wholesaler indicates only the most concrete details of his business, giving no idea of its size; he could be mistaken for a mere tavernkeeper. (Museum of Ancona.)

Work was, moreover, the only resource of the masses. The emperor knew this and, as the "conservator" of Italian society, attempted to preserve the traditional resources of every group. Caesar ordered that one-third of all shepherds be free men (because slave labor was putting free shepherds out of work). Augustus sought to protect the interests of peasants as well as traders. Vespasian refused to use machines in constructing the Colosseum, for fear of reducing the lower orders of Rome to famine. Roman policy had two aspects. It sought, first, to defend the state apparatus and augment its power in the face of internal and external threats. And then there was the *cura*. The emperor treated much if not all of Roman society as though he were its "curator," or guardian. He worked to ensure that society as traditionally constituted should prosper, much as a guardian is charged with overseeing a ward's affairs without disrupting whatever prior arrangements have been made.

6. I have been examining the opinion of labor current among notables and politicians, who held their inferiors in contempt or manipulated them. The inferiors themselves had a different view of things.

In Petronius' *Satyricon* the wealthy freedman Trimalchio makes a fortune speculating on maritime commerce and then retires, living as a notable on the income from his estates and on interest from loans. He is neither a notable nor a man of the people, but a man proud of having made a fortune according to the values of his own subgroup, through zeal, talent, and willingness to take risks. He orders the sculptor working on his tomb to depict the banquet he staged for his fellow citizens. The whole town attended. Richer than his peers, Trimalchio wants to be "recognized," if not by the upper class then at least by the civic corps of his city. Even if the notables despise him, and others, poorer than he, disparage him in private, all show him the outward signs of respect by coming to eat and drink at his expense.

Even more numerous were those who subscribed unreservedly to the values of their own class and enjoyed their work, prosperity, and good professional reputation without seeking recognition from their betters or the transient satisfaction of a momentary public glory. Archaeologists have unearthed hundreds of tombstones on which the dead had themselves sculpted as they appeared in their shops or workshops. Like most of Roman culture, these tradesmen's tombstones are Greek-inspired, for in Athens as early as the fifth century artisans had a "class consciousness" of their own.

A more positive idea of labor, which we should have suspected all along, has been revealed by documents of popular origin. This coexisted with the ideal of leisure cum political activity that scholars have long held to be typical of ancient society. In Pompeii some fine houses, filled with paintings and marble statues, were owned by bakers, fullers, and ceramics-makers, who proudly displayed the insignia of their trades; some of these men belonged to the municipal senate. In Africa a wealthy farmer asked a poet to prepare a verse epitaph, in which he tells how work made him wealthy. Those merchants and artisans and farmers who had epitaphs drawn up for themselves were wealthy men (epitaphs were expensive), and all made a point of indicating their occupation. One states that a man "worked hard"; another that he was a "well-known money changer"; still another that he was a "noted dealer in pork and beef." It should be mentioned that at this time a potter or baker stood higher in the social hierarchy than a potter or baker today (an oven represented a fairly large investment). In Petronius' *Satyricon* a young man of letters is put in his place by a freedman trader, who professes faith in himself and others of his kind: "I am a man among men. I walk with my head held high. I don't owe a cent to anyone. I've never received a summons, and no one has ever said to me from the forum, 'Pay me what you owe.' I've been able to buy some land and save some money, and I support twenty people, to say nothing of my dog. Come with me to the forum and ask for a loan. You'll quickly discover whether I have credit, despite my mere freedman's iron ring." We can understand why the tombstones of shopkeepers detailed their shops' interiors, showing merchandise, fine counters, beautiful women being handed fabric cuttings, and the tools or machines of the trade. Merchandise and tools were valuable capital: signs of wealth rather than insignia of a trade. Such funerary sculpture does more than just indicate the profession of the deceased, like a death certificate. It celebrates his position as the owner of a shop. But no one is ever shown working with his hands.

Properly understood, these images express the opposite of plebeian humility: they illustrate the wealth of a middle class determined to distinguish itself from the plebs by means of a costly display of bas-reliefs. I say "middle class," even though this was not a large group; in terms of percentage of the population it numbered in the single digits. Its situation, however, was intermediate and ambiguous. These bakers, butchers, and wine, clothing, and shoe merchants were not municipal notables. They did not belong to the privileged civic "order"—at least not yet. But they were as rich as many notables. And, like Saint Paul (an eminent representative of the middle class and the son of the owner of a shop that manufactured tents and surely employed a number of slaves), they knew how to read and write. They probably attended school until they reached the age of twelve.

In antiquity bakers, butchers, and shoe merchants were not poor shopkeepers but wealthy men. A baker, for instance, was also a miller, who owned grain mills and the slaves or animals needed to operate them. A butcher had to be wealthy enough to buy a whole steer. A shoe merchant was not just a cobbler working in a stall, or *taberna*, but a man who owned a number of slaves who both produced and sold footwear. For the sake of clarity, we should distinguish between three levels of economic status. (1) A plebeian owned nothing, simply earning his daily bread day after day. As in Ricardo's day, wages were set at the subsistence level. (2) A poor shopkeeper (a cobbler, say, or tavernkeeper) disposed of so little ready cash that every morning he had to buy the merchandise he would sell during the day. If a demanding client asked for a good bottle of wine, the tavernkeeper would have to go out and buy that wine from a wealthy wine merchant in his neighborhood. Even today in Greece or the Middle East a merchant's cash reserves often amount to no more than a single day's business. (3) A wealthy merchant was one who could afford to keep on hand several barrels of wine or sacks of flour or sides of beef. He was not a wholesaler but a merchant who

Blacksmith's tomb, 1st or 2nd century. The epitaph states that this smith kept a number of slaves and freedmen (or freedwomen). Center: the smith works at anvil; left: the furnace and bellows. (Aquileia, Archaeological Museum.)

sold to private individuals as well as to lesser merchants. A small butcher, for example, might buy a few chops from his wealthy neighbor to sell to his customers during that same day. Wealthy butchers, bakers, and clothing merchants lived in houses with patios, just like notables. They invested all their profits in these sumptuous dwellings, which set them apart from poorer merchants. The latter had only their stalls and slept above their shops, in attics accessible only by ladder.

In Pompeii the sumptuous homes with their patios and celebrated murals stand out quite clearly from the poor shops. But there are more sumptuous homes than there are shops. Were the rich in Pompeii more numerous than the poor? One has to assume, I think, that the richer homes were often rented out to a number of poorer families, each of which occupied several rooms.

Aesthetic Disdain

What about the four-fifths of the population who really worked? Theirs was a bitter struggle for survival, and no doubt they lived by the precept of Saint Paul: "He who does not work shall not eat." This was both a lesson to the industrious and a warning to the lazy, who might have hoped to share the meager pittance earned by others by the sweat of their brow.

Of this hard-working crowd of peasants, fishermen, and shepherds, some slaves, others free, we know very little. We know at least how the upper class viewed them: with the eye of the connoisseur. It was as a delightful exotic species that laborers were depicted in bucolic poetry (which has nothing but the name in common with modern pastoral) and Hellenistic genre sculpture.

Modern pastoral takes aristocrats and dresses them up as well-bred shepherds. But ancient bucolic was imbued with the ethics of the slave system, just as the blackface musicals attended by whites in the United States were imbued with racism. The bucolic poets took slaves, idealized them somewhat, polished them up, allowed them to speak their own language and tell their own jokes, but disguised them as lovers and poets. The point was to amuse "white" masters by making them imagine a naive and touching little world, so far beneath the real world that all is innocence: an idyll that survives no longer than a dream. The living is easy in this Garden of Eden—so, presumably, is the sex.

Genre sculpture, which decorated the homes and gardens

of the wealthy, depicted conventional types: the Old Fisherman, the Plowman, the Gardener, the Drunken Old Woman. These figures were represented with brutal, exaggerated naturalism. The veins and muscles of the Old Fisherman stand out with such relief that his desiccated body is reminiscent of an anatomical illustration; his face is so abstracted that for a long time this statue was thought to be of Seneca dying. This picturesque style is midway between expressionism and caricature. Old age and poverty are here nothing but a spectacle for the diversion of indifferent aesthetes; the onlooker does not penetrate beneath the surface, nor does he ever put aside his fundamental disdain. Physical deformity is an occasion for

Left: Old fisherman. The sculptor has realistically detailed the fish in the basket. (Rome, Museum of the Conservators.)

The so-called dying Seneca, a Roman copy of Hellenistic original. This is another elderly fisherman carrying his basket of fish. (Rome, Vatican Museums.)

smiles, like looking at midgets and giants at a carnival. Roman naturalism was full of condescension, without scruples. The philosopher Seneca was a scrupulous soul, who believed that harsh treatment of slaves was demeaning to a master. But this same Seneca one day happened to cast his eyes on the slave posted as a guard by his door and found him so unprepossessing that he turned to his majordomo, saying: "Where does this decrepit creature come from? You did well to post him at the door, for he seems on the verge of leaving this house for good and finding his final resting place! Where did you come up with this death's-head?" Whereupon the slave, hearing what Seneca had said, spoke up: "But Master, don't you recognize me? I am Felicio, with whom you used to play when you were little." Seneca then turned his gaze upon himself and wrote a meditation on the ravages that old age had wrought on his own person, from which he drew a lesson in wisdom and conclusions about the ontology of time.

To belong to the upper class, to the unmaimed, fully human part of humankind, it was necessary, first of all, to be wealthy enough to make a show of things that only money could buy, tokens of elite status. You also had to be master of your own time, at no one's beck and call, for only independent men were truly human. It was easier to meet these conditions by inheriting a fortune than by running a shop. With inherited wealth came standing, independence, and authority.

Rich and poor. What would seem striking to a modern observer transported back to the Roman Empire is the contrast between extremes of luxury and misery, not unlike what we might see in an underdeveloped country today. Ammianus Marcellinus wrote in substance that Aquitania was a prosperous province because the common people there did not go around in rags as they did elsewhere. When the poor get their clothing from the ragpicker (*centonarius*), luxury begins with new clothing.

The ancients did not scorn labor; they did scorn those who were compelled to work in order to live. It is wrong to imagine that ancient physicists neglected the technological applications of science because they disdained labor and idealized pure science. The error is threefold. First, it is hard to see what contemporary scientific discoveries would have lent themselves to technological application. Second, technology is in large part independent of science. (Ferrari, the automobile-maker, knew nothing about mathematics.) Finally, it is true that Greek engineers invented a kind of theodolith, which they used only for astronomical and never for geodesic purposes. This, however, was not because they were enamored of pure contemplation but because the vernier was not invented until the sixteenth century. Without a vernier a theodolith is precise only to within a half a degree (approximately the angle subtended by the moon in the sky), which is far too rough for surveying work. Greek mechanics invented amusing steam-operated automata but never developed the steam engine; the crankshaft and connecting rod were not invented until the Middle Ages, and without a crankshaft it is impossible to transform longitudinal into circular motion.

The ancients, nevertheless, did show great interest in practical and profitable activity. Disdain for the working poor has never prevented their being exploited.

Funerary relief, 2nd and 3rd century. A landowner checks his sharecroppers' accounts in a large account book or polyptych (consisting of five wooden tablets covered with wax). The so-called Saint Augustine's curtain is proof that the man was not easily accessible. (Trier, Landesmuseum.)

᪶ Patrimony

ALL men, even slaves, are equal in humanity, but those with a patrimony are more equal than others. Patrimony played as central a role in the ancient economy as the firm or corporation plays in the modern economy. But in order to understand it correctly, we must first shed notions more applicable to early modern Europe than to the Roman Empire. In Rome, to engage in business was no derogation of nobility. Usury and commerce were not the exclusive province of a specialized class or order, whether "bourgeoisie," freedmen, or equestrians. Not all nobles and notables were absentee landlords or "lazy aristocrats." Autarchy, that philosophers' myth, was in no way the aim of their management, and they did not limit exploitation of their estates so as to produce just what they needed to maintain their rank. Landowners sought to increase their wealth, to make money in any way they could. The key word is not autarchy or laziness or derogation, but business—noble business, to be sure. In ancient Rome the employer, the business executive, was the paterfamilias, the head of an extended household and master of a patrimony. Patrimony was the basis of all business dealings.

The economy, accordingly, was part of private life, in contrast to today's economy, which is based on publicly owned corporations. Today's economic actors are moral persons: firms or corporations. These moneymaking machines channel wealth into the pockets of individuals. By contrast, in Roman society the economic actors were private individuals, heads of families. In our economy an import-export firm does not change identity simply because some shareholders sell their stock to other individuals. With the Romans, a patrimony did not change its identity simply because its master decided to abandon ocean commerce and invest in land in-

Mosaic of Saint-Roman-en-Gal, 2nd–3rd century. Mosaics illustrating feasts or labors of the months are not unusual. September is apple-picking time; December is for olive-pressing, using a press with a horizontal screw. (Saint-Germain-en-Laye, Museum of National Antiquities.)

stead. It is wrong to conclude that the Roman family head sought only to secure the future of his household rather than to maximize his profit. The difference between the modern economy and the ancient one lies elsewhere.

"Let us behave as heads of family should," Seneca wrote Lucilius, repeating a proverb. "Let us increase what we have inherited. Let the estate that I pass on to my heirs be larger than the one I received." To squander one's patrimony was to wipe out the family dynasty and fall into the realm of the subhuman. Ruined nobles were potential malcontents and conspirators, accomplices of would-be Catilines, while the son of a parvenu or wealthy freedman might enter the equestrian order and dream of seeing his own son a senator. Acquisitive virtues were noble virtues. An upper-class child who was not a ne'er-do-well should choose a career in public service, said Cicero, for then at least he could help to increase the family patrimony. A neglected aspect of Roman education concerns the way in which young Romans learned to manage patrimonial interests. In 221 B.C. the Roman people heard a funeral eulogy for a very great lord named Cecilius Metellus, one of whose merits was to have "amassed a great fortune by honest means." Of course there was no dishonor in being "poor," as most people obviously were; some, like Horace, even made poverty a sign of wisdom.

The trouble is that the word "poor" does not mean the

same thing in Latin and English. For us "poor" establishes an implicit comparison between the majority who are poor and the handful who are rich; the whole of society is included in this comparison. For the Romans, however, the majority did not count, and the word "poor" took its meaning as a relative term within the minority that we would consider rich. The poor were the rich who were not very rich. Horace, who made a virtue of poverty, said he was prepared to see his ambitions come to nought, for his poverty would serve as his life raft. This "life raft" consisted of two estates, one at Tivoli and the other in Sabine, where the master's house covered some 6,000 square feet. Poverty in the Christian and modern sense was inconceivable.

Did the business of amassing wealth, or at least of tending to one's patrimony and affairs, mean forgoing leisure? No. Business activities were not an essential part of a person's identity (T. S. Eliot, to take a modern example, was a poet rather than a bank clerk). Managing a patrimony in land meant supervising the planting of estates, watching over a steward or slave overseer, and selling what the estate produced at the best possible price. Money had to be lent out at interest and never allowed to lie idle. All of these activities were implicit in the rights of ownership; indeed they constituted the exercise of those rights. Other ways of "amassing a great fortune," some honest, some not, involved the exercise or abuse of civil rights and civic honors: one could marry a dowry, seek out legacies and bequests, extort money by abuse of office, and pillage the public treasury.

Only common folk worked for a living. People of quality managed, that is, they engaged in the activity referred to as *cura* or *epimeleia*, which one might translate as "government," in the sense in which Olivier de Serres spoke of the "domestic government" of an estate. This was the only activity worthy of a free man, for it involved the exercise of authority. A family head's management of his patrimony, a public mission assigned to an individual, and even the government of the Empire were all instances of exercising authority, at least for those philosophers who liked to think of the emperor as a patriarchal sovereign. It hardly mattered that Scipio Africanus, in governing his estates, guided the plow with his own hand, like some latter-day Cincinnatus; he was nevertheless the master. As long as a man was master, it was a virtue to be "hard-

An Unclassable Class

Bronze scale, checked by the
authorities in A.D. 47. The pan
that hung from the chains has
disappeared. (Paris, Petit Palais,
Dutuit Collection.)

working," energetic. The adjective referred to a moral quality,
not an identity. When Virgil writes that with hard work one
can accomplish anything, he is not stating Holy Writ but
simply pointing out that with zealous application one can
overcome any obstacle. Not to be lazy was a virtue, born of
necessity. As Plutarch said, the man who never bestirred himself, who neglected his friends, his glory, and public affairs,
lived like an oyster. A high official was an energetic man who
from morning till night minutely examined the accounts of
the treasury, line by line. "Don't gather rust" was a maxim
of Cato, that truly great man.

It is clearly impossible to give a medieval or modern
equivalent for the class that I have been calling, for want of a
better term, the notables: nobles plus "middle class" or "gen-
try." These were men as proud as the nobles of prerevolutionary France, as universal in outlook and assiduous in business as the modern bourgeoisie, as dependent on the land for
their income as the European aristocracy in general, and,

though hard-working, convinced that they constituted a leisure class. And that is not all. In the Roman world we do not find the (to us) familiar connection between social class and economic activity. There was no Roman bourgeoisie, because the class that owned the land also engaged, without making a fuss about it, in more "bourgeois" activities. When we look for a class of traders, manufacturers, speculators, usurers, and tax farmers in Rome, we find it everywhere: freedmen, equestrians, municipal notables, and senators all took part in these activities. What determined whether Cato the Elder invested in maritime commerce, or whether a family of prominent municipal notables engaged in trade extending all the way to the Danube, was not social class but individual character and geographical location; there were considerable differences from person to person and region to region. As a matter of fact, Cato "invested his capital in solid and sure ventures. He bought lakes stocked with fish, thermal springs, land for fulling mills, starch factories, grazing land, and forests. He made maritime loans, the most reviled of all forms of usury. To that end he set up a company of fifty individuals and took a share of the capital through his freedman Quintio." Local traditions were also important. One city lived shut off from the outside world and was really no more than a peasant town of the kind that one sees today in southern Italy or Hungary. Not fifteen miles away, however, was the city of Aquileia, an ancient Venice or Genoa. Its notables were maritime traders who did business with the four corners of the world.

Left: Weighing balls of yarn with a similar type of scale. (Trier, Landesmuseum.)

Right: Shop interior, with wholesale trade indicated. In upper left corner is a scale, suspended at an oblique angle. (Rome, Museum of the Conservators.)

Rural scene, 3rd or 4th century. The hooded jacket was commonly worn. This is a simple and accurate image of rural labor. (Trier, Landesmuseum.)

Land ownership, individual investment, and family enterprises tell only part of the story. Keen for profit, Romans were quick to seize on business opportunities, particularly the wealthy, who were joined by some rather shady speculators. If a noble Roman learned from friends about a chance to make a killing, he was quick to act, even if he had no experience in that particular line of business and had to improvise as he went along. A piece of confidential information was too good a stroke of fortune to pass up; one could always put a freedman in charge of the business. The absence of an open market multiplied opportunities of this kind, as did the difficulty of obtaining information and the importance of political backing. The ruling and owning class connived with speculators who enjoyed access to information and influence over policy; these outweighed the laws of the market. The patrimonial economy was not exactly patriarchal, nor was it liberal.

The nature of Roman economic activity varied with the individual, the time, and the place. How do we know what a Roman fortune involved? Just because Juvenal speaks satirically of an ox driver and the young Virgil makes fun of mule drivers, it does not follow that the ox driver drove his own oxen or that the mule driver led his own mules. Reading on, we discover that the one headed a company that ran mule teams over the muddy roads of the Po Valley, while the other owned huge herds of livestock. Similarly, the Baron de Charlus [in Proust's *Remembrance of Things Past*] speaks contemptuously of Mrs. Singer [of the Singer Sewing Machine fortune] as though she were a woman who worked all day at a sewing machine. If the ox driver in question had owned only one or two oxen, the texts would never have mentioned him, at least not as an object of mockery.

Entrepreneurs

Suppose we have a text that refers to a Roman by name without indicating the man's occupation. How might we determine the nature and origin of his wealth? Since the patrimonial economy was not fully professionalized, this wealth could have come from many sources. A paterfamilias received part of his income from the earnings of certain of his freedmen and slaves, to whom he granted a measure of financial autonomy and legal rights, allowing them to do business as free men but for the master's benefit. This business "staff" worked to increase the master's fortune. They were the real businessmen of the Roman Empire, along with the steward, another

Sarcophagus, 2nd–3rd century. A moneychanger. (Rome, Palazzo Salviati.)

hero worthy of Balzac. More often a slave than a free man, the steward ran his master's estate and sold its produce, in some cases managing all of the master's affairs. The Roman economy rested on its stewards.

Many stewards were born free but sold themselves into slavery in order to further their careers. Masters trusted them. Accounting was not yet what it has become in our day. Stewards did not open books for inspection regularly; masters let their accounts run for years. The steward was expected to keep an accurate record of income and expenditures and to be ready to give an accounting whenever necessary—when the master died, perhaps, or the slave retired, or the estate was sold, or simply when the master was angry. Woe unto the steward who could not then come up with a sum of cash representing the difference between the total income and the total expenditures! The steward whose books balanced (*pariari*) earned the appellation *pariator,* an honor he might mention in his epitaph. Landlords also allowed their farmers to maintain open accounts for years on end. If the landlord died or sold his property, the amount of rent due (*reliqua colonorum*) was then calculated. Farmers were not systematically held in debt; it was just that accounts were not settled periodically. Such methods surely encouraged the idea that debt established a bond as between patron and client and that the debtor who sought to pay what he owed was a disloyal client who wished to renounce his benefactor.

Notables were ubiquitous throughout the economy. Some headed rural and commercial enterprises (not hesitating to transform, if need be, their private residences into shops for displaying their wares). As landlords, they sometimes acted as silent partners in businesses run by their stewards. Notables took shares in commercial companies and tax farms. The humbler of them occasionally did work themselves. Among Galen's patients was a man who cared little about the finer things and ran about town constantly on business: "He bought, sold, and often got into disputes, so that he perspired more than he should."

Noble Enterprise

The social and institutional character of the Roman economy was so different from that of our own that it is tempting to call it archaic. It sustained, nevertheless, a high level of production and was as dynamic and ruthless as capitalism. For, if Roman aristocrats distinguished themselves by their culture and their interest in philosophy, they were still avid for profit. The greatest nobles talked business. Pliny, a senator, in letters intended to be specimens of the finest in the genre, held up his behavior as a wealthy landlord as an example for others to follow. When a noble wished to get rid of old furniture or building materials, he held a public auction. (Auctions were the normal way for private individuals to sell their used belongings; the emperors themselves auctioned off unwanted palace furniture.) Money was not supposed to lie idle. Even loans to friends and relatives earned interest (not charging interest on such loans was considered a mark of special virtue). A woman's father had to pay interest to her husband

Christian sarcophagus. Possibly a scribe writing on parchment (with a tanned skin suspended overhead). The arch is somewhat flattened by license of the sculptor; no such arch was built before the Middle Ages. (Milan, Palace of the Sforza.)

if transfer of her dowry was delayed. Usury was a part of daily life; modern anti-Semites might have made ancient Rome the object of their obsession instead of the Jews. In Rome commerce and money-lending were not left exclusively to professionals or to any one class of society. Any toil, no matter how pleasurable, merited payment. One picturesque aspect of amorous customs among the Romans was that the female partner in a high-society affair was paid for her trouble. A matron who deceived her husband received a large sum or, in some cases, an annual income from her lover. Some cads reclaimed these gifts when affairs were broken off, and on occasion the courts became involved. The practice of accepting gifts from lovers was considered not prostitution but work for hire. The woman did not give herself because she was paid, the jurists held; she was rewarded for giving herself of her own free will. She who loved best was most handsomely paid. Women sought the wages of adultery as eagerly as men sought dowries.

This universal busyness effaced not only the boundaries between social classes (or civic "orders") but also the distinctions between economic categories. Men engaged in occasional business ventures in addition to their regular activities; they were speculators as well as professionals (whether they called themselves that or not). Men amassed wealth by the old-fashioned means of gaining control of established fortunes as well as by the modern means of creating wealth through investment. They made money by producing and selling goods as well as by extraeconomic means, some legal, some not: inheritances, dowries, bribes, violence, legal chicanery. They counted on the law of supply and demand as well as on political influence and contacts with other "men of the world." Apart from their involvement in business, notables were the major landowners. Ancient society therefore consisted of an immense and impoverished peasantry and a wealthy urban class engaged in a variety of business activities. It is this variety that makes the ancient world shine so brilliantly for us. Since medicine was a costly business in those days, Galen's clients were all notables, and males to boot. They lived in the cities, supervised the work of their stewards, sweated in business, practiced a profession (like Galen himself), helped run their cities, and at home read or copied out the philosophical works of their favorite sect. In old age they retired to their estates.

Ostia, 2nd–3rd century. A ship enters Rome's primary port, sailing in front of the lighthouse, where a flame is visible. Statues of gods are everywhere. The large eye on the right, a good-luck charm having no relation to the picture, countered the evil eye of the envious, who would have liked to cast a spell on the hero of this relief. The naked figure holding a horn of plenty who seems to be offering a wreath to the ship is Bonus Eventus, god of happy endings. (Rome, Torlonia Collection.)

When they died, their estates were held to consist of three principal parts: cultivated land (with its farming equipment), buildings (with their furniture), and notes of credit (*nomina debitorum*). Bank accounts, known to have existed during the Republic and early Empire, are not attested in the late Empire.

The usurers of the time were not bankers but notables and senators. Every family head kept a strongbox, or *kalendarium*, which contained a calendar of due dates on loans along with notes of hand and cash awaiting borrowers. The Roman expression for "setting aside money for loans" was "put it in the *kalendarium*." Every man had his own strategy when it came to money-lending: some lent only a small fraction of their wealth, others a much larger proportion; some lent small sums to many borrowers, others large sums to a few borrowers. Notes passed easily from creditor to creditor, either by formal dation or, more simply, by outright sale. They served as a means of liquefying debt and as an object of speculation: an expandable supply of currency. A man could bequeath his *kalendarium* and, with it, claims on his debtors and capital intended for usury to one of his heirs.

Other Ways of Acquiring Wealth

Usury was considered a noble means of acquiring wealth, the same as farming, dowries, and legacies. Among the Romans it was as common to court a wealthy old man in the hope of being remembered in his will as it is to flatter the boss today. Although such behavior was universally derided, everyone did it. It was customary for a testator to honor his friends and reward faithful clients with a bequest. Because of this custom wealthy men were surrounded by attentive courtiers; these became the sign that a man was of some importance.

A man or woman gained, Tacitus said, by not having children, for then he or she met with even greater consideration from others. Demographic research tells us that in prerevolutionary France an average family had four or five children, only two of whom lived to the age of twenty. The average Roman family had only three children. This suggests that not a few Romans outlived their children. Thus, quite a few inheritances must have been ripe for the taking, especially since under Roman law and custom testators enjoyed great freedom. With each new generation a considerable fraction of the national wealth was up for grabs. Who got what? Virtuosos when it came to chicanery, Romans knew what they were about. One divorced woman named her son as heir but, knowing that her ex-husband was of dubious reputation, stipulated that the son could receive his inheritance only if, when her will was opened, he was no longer under his father's power (for in that case the estate would have passed to the father). In other words, the son would inherit only if his father were dead. As it happened, the father was still living when the will was opened, but he hit upon a stratagem: he emancipated his son, who then inherited from his mother. Was the father a better man than his reputation suggested? The story is not yet over. The man set about courting his own son with gifts of toys and pets. In other words, he went fortune-hunting with his own son's inheritance as quarry, and he got what he wanted: the spoiled child died and left his estate to his father.

Public opinion did not condemn fortune-hunting, but some ways of going about it were considered more praiseworthy than others. "So-and-so, a man who in life had been surrounded by fortune hunters, died and left everything to his daughter and grandsons. Judgments varied: some called him a hypocrite and ingrate who neglected his friends, while others were delighted that this old man had frustrated the hopes of the self-seekers." Spoken by a senator, these words have the ring of truth.

Gismondi model of 2nd-century houses in Ostia. Even in Rome, not all apartment buildings were four or five stories tall. In Ostia apartment buildings were two to four stories, with shops at the street level and a mezzanine.

There were more ruthless ways of acquiring wealth. The Roman Empire had no real police force. Some imperial soldiers (such as the centurion Cornelius mentioned in the Bible) put down riots and tracked thieves, but they showed little concern about routine insecurity, which posed less of a threat to the image of sovereign authority that the Roman authorities wished to maintain. Daily life in the Roman Empire resembled daily life in the wild and wooly American West: no police in the streets, no deputies in the countryside, no public prosecutor. Every man had to defend himself and mete out his own justice, and the only practical solution for the powerless and the not-so-powerful was to place themselves under the protection of a strong patron. But who would protect these clients from their patrons, and these patrons from one another? Sequestrations, usurpations, and private prisons for debtors were commonplace. Cities lived in fear of local and regional tyrants, sometimes well enough ensconced to defy even so powerful a personage as the provincial governor. A powerful man did not hesitate to seize the property of one of his poorer neighbors, or even, riding at the head of an army of henchmen and slaves, to attack the "ranch" of another potentate. What could be done against such depredations? The chance of obtaining justice depended on the good will of a busy provincial governor, who for reasons of state was obliged to go easy on powerful landlords and who in any case would have been tied to them by bonds of friendship and common interest. His justice, if he chose to mete it out, would have been an episode in interfamilial warfare, an attempt to shift the balance of power among rival clans.

In addition to ordinary violence there was judicial violence. The Romans are reputed to have been the inventors of law. True, they wrote many remarkable lawbooks and took glory and pleasure from knowing and using the arcana of civil law. Law was a matter of culture, a sport, and a subject of national pride. It does not follow, however, that law actually governed daily life in Rome. Legalism merely introduced into the chaos of Roman affairs an additional complication, not to say a weapon: chicanery. In Greek regions of the Empire judicial blackmail and paralegal extortion went by the ancient name, "sycophancy" (from the Greek for "false accuser").

Suppose that a noble covets the estates of another noble who happens to be out of favor with the imperial family. The first man might then accuse the second of lese majesty. As accuser, he stood to receive a portion of the accused's estate if

Villas at the water's edge. Painting from the house of Lucretius Fronto in Pompeii. Architecture in a virgin landscape, and close to reality.

the latter were put to death. Or suppose that, far from Rome, a notable who had placed his hopes in a rich man's will was disappointed. He might claim that the man had not died of natural causes but had committed suicide or that he had been poisoned and that his heirs had failed to prosecute the murderer and avenge the death of their benefactor. The will might then be set aside and the estate confiscated by the imperial treasury, with a bonus paid to the informer. The imperial treasury was not so much a tax collection authority as it was a repository for estates confiscated by the emperor for want of an heir or because of some irregularity. The treasury had its own court, in which it sat as both judge and party. By this means the emperor soon became the greatest landowner in the

Empire. The treasury was therefore quite ready to believe denunciations by informers who provided opportunities to seize still more estates. This was common knowledge, so some testators, bent on frustrating their heirs, named the emperor as colegatee. The treasury then saw to it that the emperor received the entire estate. In short, the law served as a weapon in the struggle over patrimonies. No one could feel secure in the peaceful possession and transmission of his property. One newly wed fellow was even robbed of his wife's dowry: jealous relatives accused him of using black magic to seduce the woman.

The more industrious ways of getting rich suggest that the Empire was a chaotic place where anything was possible. One could obtain a government concession to exploit some resource, usually with monopoly rights, or take advantage of a disorganized economy by establishing, say, a needed transport service that nobody had yet undertaken to provide, some for want of capital, others for want of initiative. More than one Third World economy offers a similar spectacle today. In these circumstances, it is not surprising that many a notable found himself in charge of a host of unrelated businesses and other activities with which he had become associated simply because the opportunity was too good to pass up. One man might easily be involved in real estate, fabrics, dyeing, shipping on the Rhine and the Aegean, and farming, in addition to teaching rhetoric for a fee and importing merchandise from Egypt and Athens. It would be a mistake to think of an august Roman personage as resembling a simple country squire, living tranquilly amid fields and meadows. He led a more colorful life, more like that of a modern South American dignitary. In a society in which the contrast between rich and poor was stark, he carried himself like a noble, with nothing of the tradesman in his bearing.

Land

All of this varied business activity derived from ownership of land. A man's property might be scattered over many provinces, an estate here, a farm in some remote corner of the world. Every parcel, however, was recorded in the accounts (*rationes, libellus*) of the head of the family, which reflected the organization of the patrimony. Were the baths part of his household or a separate business? We need only consult the accounts, where the rent for the baths is recorded in a separate account, distinct from the household accounts per se. Were

Painting from Ostia. The name of the ship is *Isis of Geminus;* its captain and pilot is Pharnaces. This is a single-masted commercial boat called a *corbita.* The picture is a simplified representation of an ocean vessel, not a realistic image of a river boat (*caudicaria*). The passengers on board prayed to the goddess Isis for a good crossing. (Rome, Vatican Library.)

taxes paid by the landlord or his sharecroppers? What was the "law" or "custom" established by the landlord? The account books contain the answers. They also tell us whether tenants were farmers who sold their produce themselves or sharecroppers who paid the landlord in kind, leaving him to sell the crop personally or assign the job to his steward.

Landed property meant more than just agricultural estates. Buildings could be rented out in their entirety or divided into apartments. The land supported businesses of every kind. Notables may have owned not only the cultivated land but also the second great source of wealth: urban dwellings. On their property they constructed port facilities, taverns, brothels, and storehouses (that is, docks that were rented out for the storage of cargo and of precious objects and documents to be protected against damage by fire). They schemed to obtain that "princely boon," the right to hold a market on their property and collect a tax on all transactions. They exploited mines and quarries in conjunction with farming and industrial activities, such as brickmaking and the manufacture of pottery, which were done on the estate either under the landlord's control or by a concessionaire. Agricultural laborers were shifted to these activities during the off season. A contract recently discovered in Egypt tells of a potter who agreed to work for a period of two years for a landlord who had ovens on his estates. The potter was supposed to produce 15,000 jars per year, but the landlord was to provide the clay (it was customary to provide masons and artisans with needed materials).

We must be careful lest this diversity mislead us. Agriculture was still the primary form of production on which all other business depended. Crop yields were too low to allow land to be what it has become today in the developed countries: a resource so abundant that only a fraction of the population is employed on it. Today overproduction is a greater danger than famine. In antiquity agriculture yielded too little to permit much development of industry. The vast majority of the population had to work the soil to ensure their own survival and sustain the few noncultivators. This fact, as we shall see, greatly influenced the private strategies of the wealthy.

Each man who cultivated the land with his own hands fed no more than two or three others: his own family and the notable who owned the land. Yields were too low to sustain masses of industrial workers, though high enough to enable the wealthy to transform the surplus into monumental splendor, typical of class societies prior to the industrial revolution. Yet this feat depended on the ability to sell what the soil produced, that is, on a lively commerce. Wheat had to be exchanged for columns and statues. If the Roman world had been, as some have imagined, an empire without trade in foodstuffs, tourists and archaeologists would have far fewer ruins to explore. Agriculture and commerce were not antithetical but identical.

Land was at once a repository of wealth, a means of survival, and a source of trade goods. One ploy of the wealthy was speculation in essential commodities. Storehouses were filled with grain awaiting a bad harvest and higher prices: "They refuse to sell the products of the soil at their just price," wrote the jurist Ulpianus, "and, since they wait for the famine years, they are driving up the price." Regional specialization was also practiced. Archaeologists are convinced that certain regions of the Roman world (such as the Tunisian Sahel, then well-irrigated and fertile) produced, exclusively for export, one of the three principal riches of Mediterranean agriculture: wheat, wine, or oil. When the market was depressed or trade was interrupted, the patrimony survived; estates could fall back on a subsistence economy. Landlords were careful not to plant all their land in wheat or grapes, for these were speculative and costly crops. Part of every estate was left forested, for forests cost nothing to keep up and served as a kind of savings bank. One proverb described a fool who does everything backward by saying that he was "like a man in debt who sells his woods instead of his vineyards." The important thing was to own land, which would always maintain its value. It was not necessary to grow crops. Was there any need to waste time overseeing slaves, agricultural laborers, and sharecroppers, amusing as this activity may have been? Cato, according to Plutarch, came to "see farming as a diversion, as much as, if not more than, a source of income." Caring little for amusement, he preferred productive but uncultivated real estate, which did exist: "fish-stocked ponds, thermal springs, fulling mills, natural grazing land, forests." From these he "drew an income that was not subject to the hazards of the weather."

No matter how the patrimonial enterprise was organized, the important thing was to run it as a "good father" should.   *Investment*

This expression, less patriarchal than it may seem, survives in modern commercial law, where it is used to describe the sound management of publicly owned corporations. The paterfamilias was supposed to be "honest and diligent," according to Roman jurists, and Cicero and Seneca held that it was a merit for a man to increase his patrimony. The Romans devoted some thought to what they meant by "diligence" in this context: a paterfamilias worthy of the name could not rest on his laurels and merely pass on to his heirs an undiminished patrimony. He was advised to invest wisely, weighing the possible gains against the costs of investment.

In the final book of the *Digest* the jurist Paulus distinguishes among "necessary expenditures, which prevent a good from perishing or losing its values," expenditures on amenities such as gardens, paintings, and marble decorations, and "useful" expenditures (what we would call investments), which "might not have been made without causing the property to lose its value but which improve it by producing more income," such as "planting more vines than necessary to maintain a vineyard in good condition" or adding docks, a mill, or a bread oven to a property, or, again, "putting slaves out to apprentice." Paulus points out that the cost of these investments should not ultimately reduce the net income of an estate. For jurists, who frequently had to resolve questions of this kind, the problem was to determine who had the right to decide on an investment, and when. Justice required that such an important decision be taken by no one but the legal owner of the property. A guardian's only duty was to deliver to his ward an undiminished estate, but the duty of a paterfamilias was different, namely, to increase the size of the family patrimony.

A guardian was not supposed to show zeal. It was not his place to make investments whose risks would be borne by his ward; nor was he to offer generous gifts in his ward's name, even to enhance the child's reputation. The guardian's primary duty was to sell perishable goods (furnished houses, which could catch fire, and slaves, who might die) and invest the proceeds in sure properties: real estate and gold to be lent out at interest. (Hoarding was to be avoided at all cost, and for a guardian to ignore this dictum suggested, as for the servant of the Gospel, a lack of diligence.) Such a do-nothing attitude was to be avoided by the paterfamilias, however. Nothing could be further from the truth than to imagine that the paterfamilias simply served as guardian of the family for-

tune, which actually belonged to his posterity, or that he was merely the temporary beneficiary, the "usufructuary," of a property over which the family dynasty as a whole enjoyed eminent domain.

Under Roman law, moreover, the "beneficial occupant" of a property was entitled to make investments, to "improve" the property, as though he were the family head. The husband who administered his wife's dotal property enjoyed the same right. In Book XXIII of the *Digest* the jurist Javolenus tells of a man who had established marble quarries on his wife's dotal estates. He divorced and, as was customary, the woman reclaimed her dowry. Should she not be obliged to reimburse her ex-husband for the costs incurred in establishing the quarries, which increased the value of her property? Jurists of the old school answered no, because the expenditure was not "necessary," and, far from "improving" the estate, the husband had pillaged it of its underground supply of marble. But to this argument Javolenus retorts that merely "useful" expenditures are permissible, even on dotal property. He adds one proviso: that the quarry be one in which the supply of marble is not exhausted but "continues to grow." In that case the wife

A press for oil or wine, this time with a vertical shaft. The capstan was obviously known; the crank was not invented until the Middle Ages. (Aquileia, Archaeological Museum.)

would not have lost anything, since the husband did nothing but harvest the quarry's fruits. (The notion that marble and gold grow like plants is common to many peoples; it forms the basis of Roman law on mines and quarries.)

Reading between the lines, we can interpret what the usufructuary was allowed to do as a clue to what every good paterfamilias was required to do if he wished to be considered a good administrator of his estates. Unlike the paterfamilias, the usufructuary was certainly not allowed to alter the use to which an estate, or part of an estate, was put. He could not replace ornamental gardens with productive plantations, for example. This restriction aside, he was allowed, as Ulpianus observes in Book VII, "to improve the situation of the property," by establishing stone, sand, or chalk quarries (chalk was used to starch clothing and give it luster), or by extracting gold, silver, sulfur, and iron from mines "that the paterfamilias had dug or might have dug." Certain conditions had to be met, however. The mines had to bring in more than the vineyards or olive trees they replaced. The underground resources must not be depleted during the period of beneficial occupancy. Finally, the new investment must not be so costly as to ruin the estate, and overall income, allowing for the cost of additional labor, must not be diminished.

The Business Mentality

These revealing texts show that the contrast often drawn between capitalist rationality, which allegedly seeks to maximize profits, and "patrimonial rationality," which allegedly aims simply to transmit wealth undiminished from generation to generation, is beside the point. The Romans sought to increase their patrimony wherever possible and put themselves ahead of their posterity. To say that a capitalist firm has no strategy other than to maximize profits is like saying that politics is the art of acquiring new territory. In reality, the policies of a modern corporation are as complex as those of a modern state and as variable from one company to another as the foreign policy of Sweden is different from the foreign policy of a great empire. Just about as worthless is the academic claim that the Romans were a nation of peasants. Roman notables were entrepreneurs who aimed to get rich. They did not amass acres as misers amass gold. They invested, took risks, and speculated. Their penchant for profit was an ethnic feature that distinguished them from many other nations. Nations with similar economic structures and class interests may still exhibit quite different drives, just as some ethnic groups are more hard-working, more artistic, or more bellicose than others. The facts are the facts; such different "mentalities" cannot be manufactured or produced at will. Economists who have tried to develop certain Third World economies have learned to their sorrow that knowledge of econometrics is not enough, and that simply creating economic opportunities cannot ensure that people will actually avail themselves of those opportunities. Attitudes cannot be shaped at will. Roman economic attitudes were very aggressive. To know what a Roman paterfamilias was really like we should look not at economic structures or obvious class interests but at attitudes, the real independent variable in this equation. A wealthy Roman had the soul of a businessman and knew a great deal about making money. Obviously this had positive consequences for the level of production. As for the distribution of wealth, that is another question.

To conclude, let me say simply that this Roman talent for business was strengthened by a rather surprising circumstance. Like the Jews, the Greeks, and the Chinese, the Romans were not just farmers, generals, and soldiers, but also the people of a *diaspora*. In the last two centuries before Christ and even earlier they fanned out through the Greek Orient, into Africa, and out to the very limits of the civilized world as traders and bankers as well as planters. Taking advantage of their political influence, they seized the good land of Africa and central Turkey and soaked up the profits of Greek commerce. The city of Rome sheltered numerous Greek intellectuals of whom their Roman counterparts were jealous, while Mytilene and Smyrna were full of Italian businessmen, whom the Greeks had excellent reasons to hate.

Death scene, ca. A.D. 100. Weeping women beat their breasts. The torches were kept burning even during the day. At the feet of the deceased are three tablets containing his will. Seated, at right, slaves freed by the dead man's will wear the Phrygian cap as a sign of freedom. (Rome, Vatican Museums.)

✑ Public Opinion and Utopia

THERE we have it—a composite portrait of the ideal Roman: a male, free and born that way, wealthy but not newly wealthy, well-bred, even cultivated, a businessman, proud of having held political office, and yet fundamentally a man of leisure. Like the various details of his fine clothing, each of our specimen individual's features is a legacy of the Greek and Roman past. There was no need to coerce people to accept this ideal; it was taken for granted.

Funerary art, less concerned with the hereafter than with what a man had been on earth, cast this imposing image in terms comprehensible to all. Depending on the whim of the stonecutter and the preference of the buyer, tombs emphasized varied aspects of men's lives. Opulence was represented by showing the deceased poring over his accounts or accepting the homage of his farmers or tending his shop or cutting wheat with that recent marvel of human ingenuity, the mechanical reaper. On a woman's tomb luxury might be symbolized by picturing the noble lady seated in a high-backed chair or in front of a mirror held by one slave while selecting jewels from a casket held by another. Images were often little more than emblems: an umbrella sculpted on the side of a tombstone told passersby that the woman buried there had had a slave to hold her umbrella and the leisure to go strolling. Or a woman making her toilette might raise her hand in homage to a statue of Venus, symbol of marriage, presented to her by a maid, who had taken it from the household repository of pious images (*lararium*). Senators' sarcophagi juxtaposed images of private and public life. In the center of one, we might see the late senator taking his wife's hand. On the sides, in a general's armor, he could be shown seated on a dignitary's low folding chair, accepting the surrender of barbarian chieftains he had

Detail of sarcophagus, 2nd century(?). The woman honors the religious statue of Venus with a gesture of her hand. This sculpture comes close to the reality of Roman religion. (Arezzo Museum.)

Physician, seated, examines his patient, a naked child who stands before him, 2nd–3rd century. In the background are the doctor's two assistants or pupils. Though slaves, they will succeed him if he emancipates them. (Rome, Vatican Museums.)

vanquished (or might have vanquished, given his high office). Other tombal reliefs depict money being distributed to his fellow citizens at his behest or a gladiator fight paid for by the late dignitary. The dead man's rank is suggested by the number of fasces carried by the lictors, those apparitors and executioners who preceded him everywhere during his year of public life. Rome had no penal law, so every important dignitary had the right to use force as he saw fit.

Every person had his or her role. On the left face (the most honorable) of the tombstone the husband is shown practicing his profession: he examines his patient, who stands naked and at attention before the physician. On the right face, the wife exhibits the feminine virtue of piety: followed by slaves, she goes to raise her hand before the image of some god in gratitude for a favor granted; a slave holds up a sign on which her mistress has had a description of this favor inscribed. In other words, some tombs commemorated not the opulence, leisure, rank, or profession of the deceased but finer aspects of character such as piety (for women) or cultivation (for men). A woman burns a few grains of incense in homage to a god, say, or a man seated in his armchair reads a book (a scroll) or holds a rolled scroll in his hand as proof that he has completed the studies that capped preparations for entry into good society.

Little about these images was egalitarian or individualistic. Originality, pride, cheerfulness, grace, and lightness of touch are not conspicuous among Roman traits. Their funerary art underscores this in a ponderous way. Roman society was unequal in fact and inegalitarian in its distinction of "orders" (akin to the "three estates" convoked by Louis XVI just prior to the French Revolution). People were constantly and visibly reminded of the differences between individuals. One showed laudable "frankness" (*parrhesia*) by speaking insultingly to people of the lower orders. The "friends" of great personages were categorized into distinct, and unequal, groups. (This was true even of the "friends" of the Gracchi, two celebrated social reformers of the old Republic.) No great man ever went out without a cortege. When he visited a town that had named him its "patron" because of some public benefaction, he made a formal public entry. "Yesterday I had to dinner people of higher rank than you," Trimalchio proclaims to his guests. He can be faulted only because, coming from a vulgar freedman like himself, his words are an outrage; he has invited above his station. Simple folk were especially susceptible to the "simplicity" that a few of the powerful had the knack of affecting. "That most respectable dignitary returned our greeting," said one. Commoners were expected to address their betters with humility. Every gesture contributed to what Ramsay MacMullen has called the "explicit expression of status."

These obvious signs of status were confirmed by no less explicit moral ideas, which now reinforced, now mitigated, status differences. People might, for example, praise their governor for his "mildness." Everyone was judged by his scrupulousness in performing public and private duties. "The tyranny of opinion—and what opinion!—is as beastly in the small towns of France as in the United States," wrote the individualist Stendhal, who had in mind the puritanical America of his day. Pagan civism was perhaps no less harsh in its judgment of private behavior than the small-town puritanism reviled by Stendhal.

Rome, reputed to be the mother of law, is supposed to have been a government of laws, a state where no one could be obliged to do what was not prescribed by law and where public justice supplanted arbitrary private justice. Roman law can fairly be called individualistic. Both sexes enjoyed the same freedom to divorce, property could be freely alienated, and testators enjoyed a large measure of freedom. No religious belief was enforced; each city had its preferred gods, and each individual had his or hers. The secular arm left it to the gods themselves to avenge any insults—if they could—and the only respect the citizens of a city were required to show its gods was to observe their holidays by not working. The right to change place of residence or line of work was uncontested. An easygoing indulgence of sexual sins, even when committed by women, was erected into doctrine by the Senate itself. Yet, as Bleicken has remarked, this liberalism was a "tacit consequence of an aristocratic idea of private life," and Rome, like Greece, never incorporated formal guarantees of freedom into its law. The law in fact was regarded as a mere codification of the duties imposed by family piety, loyalty, wealth, and status.

"Private" (the antonym of "public") was a common Latin adjective, but its meaning was negative: it characterized those things that an individual might do without failing of the duties required of a man holding public office. There was no rec-

The Individualism of the Law

Physician's wife carrying a basket of flowers to a god. The slave, carrying a sign, raises his hand to his forehead in a salute to the god.

Silver coin from time of
Domitian. Diameter: 19 mm.
With this coin one could enjoy
an entire day of modest luxury.
Gold coins were used for major
purchases and international
trade.

ognized sanctuary in private law; there were boundaries which
the law did not transgress, but it was under no obligation not
to transgress them. Am I making a mountain out of a historical
molehill? No doubt, but the fact remains that the absence of
guarantees left the door open to all kinds of dangers. Like
storms, these dangers descended briefly on Rome, the blood-
iest episodes being the persecution of the Christians and
Manichaeans.

In addition, certain emperors attempted to enforce their
own notions of moral order. Roman sovereigns, unlike their
Chinese and Japanese counterparts, did not have what Maurice
Pinguet has called "the old Confucian habit of measuring
power by moral order." Some, such as Augustus, Domitian,
the Severi, and Constantine, did try to correct morals by
decree. Augustus instituted severe measures against adultery
by women (severe in appearance, at any rate). Domitian compelled men to marry their mistresses, had buried alive one
vestal virgin who violated her vow of chastity, and forbade
satirical poets to use obscene language. The Severi made adultery by the husband a crime and abortion an offense against
both husband and fatherland. Constantine's legislation swept
away a lax aristocratic ethic and substituted strict moral laws,

Sarcophagus, 2nd century. The three virtues of a nobleman. Left: Clemency. As a general, he conquers and pardons barbarians (behind him are the Fatherland and, with bare leg and breast, Courage). Center: Piety. He sacrifices an ox. Right: Concord between man and wife (dressed as a bride), in the presence of Venus and Cupid (with torch). A Grace, with bared shoulder, touches the bride's hand. (Mantua, Ducal Palace.)

more popular than truly Christian in origin. This moralism was quite unusual. Greek and Roman lawgivers could attempt to revolutionize society by decree. Imprudent, they were not always careful to avoid lagging too far behind or moving too far ahead of actual mores. The ancients did not regard the city as a product of natural social forces, but rather held that it was an institution created by law, which could decay if not protected by the lawgiver against its natural enemies. The citizen, they believed, is a reprobate in need of discipline. Thus, the main purpose of moral reform was to prove that the reigning emperor was indeed a master, who, not content to establish public order, which private vice scarcely threatened, sought also to regulate the moral conscience of each individual. Once this idea had been driven home, the revolutionary new laws ceased to be enforced and were forgotten under the next emperor. Only the code of Constantine endured, leaving its mark upon the Middle Ages.

These brief tempests may be safely forgotten. In normal times civil law accurately reflected Roman mores. Law and morality were linked by an umbilical cord that was never

Did Roman Law Exist?

Bronze coin with head of Severus. Diameter: 28 mm. With this coin a slave could buy his daily bread and escape death by starvation.

Reverse of same coin: each of the three figures (gold, silver, bronze) holds a horn of plenty and a pair of scales.

really cut. Although technically complex, Roman civil law was more verbal than conceptual, and scarcely deductive. It afforded professional students plenty of opportunity to demonstrate their virtuosity. Did it enable ordinary people to obtain justice, however? Did it enforce respect for the rules when people violated them and oppressed their neighbors? In a society as unequal and inegalitarian as the Roman, it is obvious that formal rights, however clear, had no reality, and that a weak man had little to gain by going to court against powerful enemies. But even when the law was not simply violated, did it provide means of enforcing people's rights? One example will suffice, I think, to show that the public authorities did not so much supplant private vendettas as organize them.

Suppose I lend money to someone who decides not to pay me back. Or, better still, suppose that all I own in the world is a small farm, to which I am attached because my ancestors lived there and the country is pleasant. A powerful neighbor covets my property. Leading an army of slaves, he invades my land, kills those of my slaves who try to defend me, beats me with clubs, drives me from my land, and seizes my farm. What can I do? A modern citizen might say, go to court (*litis denuntiatio*) to obtain justice and persuade the authorities to restore my property (*manu militari*). And this was indeed what would have happened toward the end of antiquity, when provincial governors finally succeeded in imposing their ideal of public coercion. But in Italy in the first two centuries A.D. events would have taken a different turn.

For one thing, the aggression against me by my powerful neighbor would have been considered a strictly civil offense; it would not have been covered by a penal code. It would have been up to me, as plaintiff, to see to it that the defendant appeared in court. In other words, I would have had to snatch the defendant from the midst of his private army, arrest him, and hold him in chains in my private prison until the day of judgment. Had this been beyond my power, the case could never have been heard (*litis contestatio*). But suppose that I did manage to bring the defendant into court and, thanks to the intervention of a powerful man who had taken me on as client, succeeded in obtaining justice, meaning that the court declared the law to be on my side. It then would have been up to me to enforce that judgment, if I could. Was I obliged to recapture my ancestral farm by myself? No. By an inexplicable twist in the law, a judge could not sentence a defendant simply to restore what he had taken. Leaving my farm to its fate, the judge would authorize me to seize my adversary's chattels real and personal and sell them at auction, keeping a sum equal to the value placed on my farm by the court (*aestimatio*) and returning the surplus to my enemy.

Who would have considered recourse to a system of justice so little interested in punishing social transgressions? Most likely two types of people. When powerful, stubborn men quarreled over a piece of land, both parties wished to be judged to have the better case by the many Romans who followed trials in the courts because they found chicanery or legal eloquence to their taste. Such men would have settled their dispute in the courts, as they might have settled it at other times in history in a duel before witnesses. Or a creditor might bring suit against a debtor in default, who was scarcely in a position to put up a fight. The creditor would already have seized the debtor, who might at first have attempted to hide. Ulpian tells of one debtor who stayed away from the public market in order to avoid running into his creditor. When he saw him, he quickly hid behind the columns of the courtyard or one of the many kiosks in the marketplace. Recourse to the law was therefore just one of many possible moves in the social game,

Painting of a dispute before a judge. This is the work of a talented artisan, whose hand captured the movement and tension of the figures. At issue in this lawsuit is a large amphora of oil that has been broken; the two pieces of the amphora can be seen at the orators' feet. (Ostia, Archaeological Museum.)

and some people begged that it never be used against them: *Juris consultis abesto,* "No lawyers in this business!"

Apart from its strategic uses, the law formed part of the substance of the old Roman culture. To have recourse to law, to make learned use of the ins and outs of civil law, was sophisticated behavior. Consider the following example. In

Tomb of the Haterii, ca. A.D. 100. The family tomb, which resembles an overdecorated temple, celebrates its own construction. Above the temple the sculptor has represented another scene, for which he could find no other place. The machine on the left is a marvel of human ingenuity, which the family was proud to display on its tomb. (Rome, Vatican Museums.)

theory, no Roman woman could take a case to court without a male representative (although this rule of law was honored mainly in the breach). A non-Roman inhabitant of the Empire, a Greek or Egyptian woman, say, had even less right to take her case to court. Yet the papyri tell us that many such women went to court anyway. What was the rule? We are obliged to admit that there was none. And we discover, too, that many Roman women chose male representatives even though it was not strictly necessary. Although there was no rule, there were elegant, or perhaps pedantic, ways of going about things.

Obscurely baffling, Roman law was marked by survivals of popular and private justice. Even under the Empire it was not unusual to see justice meted out in the streets. The simplest way to force a debtor to pay up was to surprise him at home and provide him with an "escort" (*convicium*). The man was heaped with ridicule, and mocking songs were sung, with choruses demanding that the debt be paid. The jurists required only that the debtor not be stripped naked and that the words of the songs not be obscene. The sensibilities of the community, called to witness, had to be respected. The debtor, for his part, sought to win the public's pity. He dressed in mourning garb and stopped cutting his hair as a sign of dereliction.

Fear of public opinion played a large role in private life, of which the public considered itself a legitimate judge. In small towns anyone who braved public opinion was hounded and mocked. He was seized, placed in a kind of hearse, and followed by a laughing and crying crowd of "mourners" before being allowed to escape. Even the dead were insulted in this way if their wills did not meet with public approval. Such greetings were also in store for stingy heirs who offended the crowd by not footing the bill for the gladiator fights expected when a notable died. In one Ligurian town the plebs halted the funeral cortege of a former officer in the town square. His family was able to take his body to the pyre only after promising to pay for a memorial spectacle.

View upon leaving Pompeii, just outside the city gates, on the road to Herculanum. The first of a row of tombs, all in the form of altars, is decorated with the image of a ship.

The many, in other words, arrogated to themselves the right to judge the conduct of each individual. Whether notable, plebeian, or senator, no Roman was allowed an intimate life all his own. Anyone could address anyone else and judge anyone else. The least important citizen could address the "public," which after all consisted of other citizens like himself. Any man willing to play the fool, for instance, could play

The Publicity of the Tomb

A deceased couple depicted as Mars and Venus, after A.D. 120. Since the dead, like gods, were venerable and invisible, funerary art often immortalized them as gods in an act of hyperbole that only archaeologists have taken literally. The husband, who must have been a good senator, was prouder of his military functions than of his civic ones. Just as many a contemporary of Napoleon III contrived to resemble the emperor, this senator resembled his emperor, Hadrian. His wife refused to play Venus in the nude; other women were bolder. (Paris, Louvre.)

to the gallery. Nowadays of course we have subway graffiti, a forum anybody can use to tell everyone else what's on his mind or whom he loves or simply to record his name and the fact that he exists. It was no different with the citizens of Pompeii. The walls of that small city, like so many others, are covered with graffiti left by strollers for the amusement of other strollers.

Oddly enough, a similar kind of publicity was fashionable in the ancient equivalent of our modern cemeteries: the roadside. The land abutting the Roman highways belonged to no one, and it was here that the Romans placed their tombs, on the outskirts of their cities. No sooner did a traveler pass through the city gates than his eyes were drawn to tombs flanking the road. A tomb was meant to be viewed not by a person's family and close friends but by everyone. The grave, underground, was one thing, and was honored each year by family memorial services. The tombstone with the epitaph was something else again; it addressed itself to passersby. We must not imagine that Roman epitaphs resemble modern ones, which speak to heaven alone. A typical Roman epitaph was cast in the following pattern: "Read, passing friend, what role I played in this world . . . And now that you have read, have a pleasant journey." And the passing reader inscribed his reply on the tomb: "You take care, too." We know for a fact that when a Roman felt like reading a little, he took a walk outside the city. Epitaphs were easier to read than the cursive script of books. Nothing will be said here about two later developments: the necropolis and the pagan catacomb.

The roads leading out of Roman cities, with their double rows of memorial billboards, were like some Broadway of the beyond. Certain epitaphs sought to captivate the traveler's attention, to distract his eyes from neighboring monuments. They offered rest and recreation within the cemetery walls. None spoke of the suffering of the bereaved; all mentioned the social role of the deceased and his faithful discharge of duties toward family and friends. To make dinner conversation about one's host's tombstone was not a social gaffe likely to bring morbid thoughts to his mind. He would have been reassured, rather, that his dignity and virtues would remain in the public eye after he was gone. Some men were not averse, after a few drinks, to reading their own epitaphs, composed by themselves as carefully as they composed their wills. There was no better way for a city to show gratitude to a benefactor than to detail the official honors that would grace his funeral.

One lady was delighted to learn that her fellow citizens planned to donate saffron (then valued as a perfume) to scent the pyre on which she was to be cremated.

Archaeologists have recovered some 100,000 Roman epitaphs, and MacMullen has noted that they became all the rage around the first century A.D. and began slowly to die out in the third century. This is not surprising, for Roman epitaphs reflected not some fundamental idea of death but the reign of public rhetoric. Epitaphs were not limited to the great. Simple private individuals may not have been public figures, but they did live in the public eye, watched by their peers. Some therefore left the public a message in their epitaphs as well as their wills: "I lived meanly so long as it was given me to live, and I advise you to enjoy yourself more than I did. That's life: you get this far and no farther. I never heeded the advice of any philosopher. Beware of the doctors: they are the ones who killed me." The deceased draws from his life a moral for the living. The hereafter, rarely mentioned in these epitaphs, has been the object of too much attention from historians influenced by Christianity, who fail to recognize the public function of ancient tombs. In some cases epitaphs were used to censure. From the grave people castigated those who had done them wrong. One patron damned an ungrateful freedman, calling him a highway robber. A father announced to all the world that he had disinherited an unworthy daughter. A mother accused another woman of poisoning her son. For us, to engrave such words on a tombstone would be an affront to the majesty of death. But the Romans washed their dirty linen in public. In Pompeii, on the Nocera road, one epitaph expresses the hope that a wicked friend will feel the wrath of the gods of heaven and hell.

Public Censure

Public censure of private conduct was heard everywhere, and reminders of the rules of conduct were ubiquitous. The air was heavy with calls to order, with an insistence on respect for the rules. One notable in Pompeii had the following maxim painted on the wall of his dining room: "Kindly restrain your quarrelsome words, if possible. If not, get up and go home. Keep your sweet eyes and lewd looks from straying to other men's wives and let chastity shine in your face." The guests did not consider these admonitions insulting. They felt, rather, that virtuous mottoes graced their respectable company. The Romans burned enough incense to virtue to kill an ox. Ovid, a delicate poet forced to endure the tragedy of exile, paid tearful homage to the devoted wife he left behind in Rome; she did not betray him. Eulogizing himself, Horace lays his cards on the table: as a young man, thanks to his father's admonitions, he had been no one's catamite. Statius, in praising the late wife of his patron, says that she was so modest that she never would have betrayed him for anything in the world, not even a large sum of money. It was a compliment to praise a woman for not selling herself or an adolescent for not having been kept. The same Statius congratulates one adolescent for not participating, though an orphan, in ephebic loves. However vigilant the censors, the praise was crude.

Skeletons were eagerly let out of closets. When it came to countering vice with virtue, the slogan was, "anything goes." Statius, continuing his panegyric, tells us that the same adolescent, his protector, ran into some difficulties; his mother tried to poison him, but the emperor had sent her to prison. If the poet passed judgment in public so clumsily, it was only because public opinion had preceded him. The collective conscience commented, as shamelessly as it pleased, on anyone's life. This was considered not gossip but legitimate censure, *reprehensio*. Every marriage, divorce, and will was weighed in the balance, as Cicero's letters show and as Pliny's, written only in order to be published, show even more. Pliny's correspondence, in fact, was intended to serve as a manual for the compleat Roman senator, with the author as prime example. Whenever Pliny mentions a will or a divorce, he carefully details what people thought, and, if public opinion was divided, he decides which side was correct. The ruling class felt it had the right to govern the private lives of its members, in the interest of all. Those who braved public opinion faced ridicule. Insulting songs (*carmen famosum*) were quietly circulated, and pamphlets (*libelli*) passed from hand to hand, heaping obscene insults and sarcasm upon the deviant in order to demonstrate that public opinion was more powerful than any man. When one senator decided to marry his mistress, Statius, his protégé, dotted the i's: "Let the lying insinuations in the pamphlets be silenced. This illicit love has just submitted to the laws of Rome, whose citizens have now seen with their own eyes the kisses they used to jabber about." There was a great deal of cant in this civic puritanism, which was quick to denounce anyone who did not conform. An entire literary genre, satire, has its roots here.

No one was exempt from justifying his private life before the bar of public opinion, not even the emperors, or at any rate not the "good" emperors. When Claudius learned of Messalina's misconduct, he harangued the imperial guard, detailed his wife's infidelities, and promised the guardsmen that "he would never remarry, for marriage had turned out so badly for him." When Augustus learned of his daughter's and then of his granddaughter's mischief (both pretended to live as great ladies rather than as exemplary members of the reigning family), he listed their offenses in a message to the Senate and a manifesto (*edictum*) to the people. The "bad" emperors turned this public censure upside down: they paraded their mistresses and catamites to show that a potentate stands above public opinion.

A paterfamilias worthy of the name avoided criticism by soliciting advice from friends and peers, seeking their approval in advance for any important private decision, whether it be to punish a son in accordance with paternal authority or to free a young slave or to marry or to repudiate a wicked wife or to remarry or to commit suicide (for otherwise a suicide might be accused of cowardice). To the same council of friends men laid out insults they had suffered. One man, unjustly disinherited by his brother, publicly read his brother's will along with his own; the contrast between the two aroused general indignation. The council of friends had something of a formal quality, and in old families when one quarreled with a friend and no longer wanted his presence on the council, it was necessary to notify him officially of that fact (*renuntiare amicitiam*).

There was no conspiracy of silence within the governing class. Public and private wrongs were set forth for all to see. Pliny, who held himself up as a model of sophisticated virtue, denounced his peers' foolishness or, rather, their flaws (no one in Rome was mortified by being made to look a fool) and published passages from private letters that led to the downfall of one overly greedy governor. In senatorial tones Seneca detailed the sexual perversions that prevented one of his peers from being named consul. Members of the governing class did not hesitate to slander their peers because they never spoke as private individuals. Every citizen was to some degree a public man, an activist. The legitimacy accorded to public opinion resulted in a rather odd "freedom of the [oral] press." People were permitted to accuse a late emperor of tyranny and of wanting to suppress the frankness (*parrhesia, libertas*) of noble opinion, provided that they were careful to add that the reigning emperor was anything but a tyrant. Hence reigning emperors were praised as freely as their predecessors were damned.

Moral Authority

A senator was not a man like other men. Whatever he said was public and was supposed to be believed. He judged the public and private actions of his peers, in much the same way that our generals and diplomats award merits and demerits in their memoirs to fellow generals and statesmen. The governing class ruled legitimately, not so much by virtue of the official titles held by its members as in the name of a class "authority" (*auctoritas*) that was "naturally" theirs: that was the way things were. This authority pertained to private morals as well as public life. A senator was entitled to say how any citizen worthy of the name ought to live. If the senator was also a historian or philosopher, his books were not read in the same way as the books of mere mortals. If a historian, he would have been expected to say what people ought to think about the Roman past, in order to drive home the political, moral, and patriotic verities of which the Senate was the conservatory or academy. Historians of more humble origin would loyally repeat this edifying version of history. Or, being themselves insignificant, they would, with all due respect, content themselves with a valet's view of great affairs, regaling their readers with anecdotes about the private lives of the great. A senator who was also a philosopher, like Cicero or Seneca, had the exclusive right to explain how philosophy applied to politics and to scour the books of wisdom for traces of old Roman principles, which it was the duty of the senator to uphold.

Every noble was expected to be a man of gravity, since he was already a man who carried weight (*gravis*). He was not supposed to make jokes in public; to have done so would have been a travesty. Still, there was a time for seriousness and a time to let oneself go (*non intempestive lascivire*). A senator who knew how to make jokes and be simple in private was especially praiseworthy. Private life was the proper place for humor. Scipio, so rigid in public, showed himself quite "civil" with his intimates. Rome had a long tradition of aristocratic sophistication; censure had long since ceased to be mordant and become needlingly ironic. The satires of the noble Lucilius retain something of the esoteric quality of works addressed to "insiders." His mocking allusions are delicate without sacrificing any of their bite. This same Lucilius laughed along with Scipio and other peers. When they were together in their rural villas, the stiffness imposed by the rigid aristocratic code of behavior was no longer necessary, and these august personages indulged in one of the children's games of the time: chasing one another around the dinner beds. Their notion of private civility allowed them to behave much like overgrown children (*repuerascere*).

In doing so these nobles behaved, however briefly, much as the common folk behaved all the time. Ordinary people could sing in public as they harvested grapes or did the mending. Seneca said, "A poor man laughs more often and more heartily." The Romans did not share the haughty elegance of the Greeks, for whom distinction of manners was an important basis of public life and private attitudes. Two centuries before the birth of Christ, Rome, which had always been a semi-Hellenized city, entered for the first time into diplomatic relations with the Hellenistic kingdoms, at that time still the world's leading power. A Roman ambassador who found himself in the presence of Antiochus the Great, the most famous man of his day, could express his high conception of his Roman fatherland in no other way than by holding himself stiffly, in consequence of which his words were deemed offensive. The king made the ambassador understand how little he was impressed by such haughty, half-barbarian manners, but added that he forgave him because he was so young—and handsome.

Rome, whatever has been said about it, was a state that obeyed not laws but orders from its governing class—*pace* the many sociologists who will find this assertion difficult to accept. Roman public law itself becomes clearer as soon as one ceases to look for rules and accepts the fact that everything depended on the relative strength of the various parties in contention. What is even more curious is that Rome was in no sense a traditionalist state, governed in the English manner by respect for custom. Roman institutions were a jumble and remained remarkably fluid throughout Roman history. Rome was an authoritarian state unconstrained by rules. Much has been made of Roman "good faith," but Roman loyalty was to a man, not to a pact. Much has also been made, and still is made, of "ancestral customs" (*more majorum*), but the claim is specious: custom enjoyed no authority in Rome. Custom was invoked only in connection with public institutions. Only the

This Roman bronze is a copy, one-third scale, of an ancient Greek statue of an athlete. But the copyist has added a horn of plenty in the left hand and what may have been a wreath in the right, thus turning the idle beauty of the nude into a Bonus Eventus. (Paris, Petit Palais, Dutuit Collection.)

great, alone authorized to talk politics, mentioned it. And it was invoked only as an objection, that is, only when it was about to be violated. Ancestral custom was adduced in order to prevent a rival from introducing an innovation advantageous to himself or as grounds for doing something unusual. (One could always argue that the new was really a return to some forgotten custom.) In any case, current custom was explicitly cited in opposition to ancestral custom; the one was no less worthy of mention than the other. Whether ancient or recent, custom served only as an argument. It could be used to justify whatever one pleased.

Popular Wisdom

Public life was ruled by the will of the governing class, and private life by fear of what the governing class would say. Public opinion was internalized in the form of self-restraint and occasionally revealed itself in public outbursts of shame. Such shame was considered honorable. As we saw earlier, one wicked master, ashamed of having mistreated his slaves, begged Galen to whip him. In Sparta when the sage Apollonius accused a wealthy shipowner of neglecting public affairs and thinking only of enriching himself, he burst into tears and immediately changed his ways.

People were as obsessed with superstitions as we are with Freudian slips. In the ancient world, astrology, considered a scientific doctrine, was part of high culture and enjoyed the same respect among the cultivated as does psychoanalysis today. Maecenas and Tiberius never did anything without consulting their astrologers. Dreams, too, were taken as omens. The issue was very controversial. One high official, a most learned man, had a dream one day that seemed to presage his losing a case in court. He begged a senator with whom he was friendly to postpone the hearing. The senator asked him to think it over: dreams could no doubt be meaningful, but their meaning was often ambiguous. Another high official experienced what was not a dream but a true apparition: he was walking in a courtyard when a giant figure appeared before him. It was Africa, with the feminine features ascribed to her by painters and sculptors, and she revealed that one day he would enjoy the good fortune of being named governor of the province Africa. This came to pass. Another fashionable topic concerned the existence of ghosts. When the philosophers were consulted, they said that this came down to the problem of the immortality of the soul: if the soul is immortal, ghosts are possible.

The "evil eye" was widely feared. To protect against its spell people placed a painting or sculpture of a phallus, scorpion, or some other penetrating creature in their doorways; these were supposed to put out the evil eye. Fear of the evil eye was essentially fear of the jealousy of neighbors or hatred of rivals: *Rumpere, invidia!* is the legend found alongside one phallic charm.

Such were the shames, fears, and phobias of the rich. The private life of the common folk was governed by custom, which had been erected into a kind of philosophy, a popular oral doctrine comparable to that of the Old Testament's Book of Proverbs.

Senatorial opinion reminded people at every opportunity of what they ought to do. Popular wisdom, on the other hand, taught that "the wise man does this, the madman that." The man of the people instructed his children by expounding the faults of others and painting a diptych of good and evil, or prudence and imprudence in private dealings. Aristocratic behavior did not claim to be based on any philosophy; it was a law unto itself. Proverbs were good for the common folk. The wealthy freedman who was father to the poet Horace sent his son to school to obtain the liberal education that he, the father, lacked; personally he instructed the boy in the teachings of popular wisdom. In order to encourage his son to shun vice and adultery, he cited the case of a man who had been caught red-handed and lost his reputation. To teach the principles of prudent management he told of another man who had ended his days in poverty. The common man had as much to fear from imprudence as from immorality. "How can you fail to see that an action is either immoral or unprofitable when the man who commits it gains nothing but condemnation for his efforts?" As a positive example, Horace's father cites a great man who, having been named to a jury, is officially recognized as good: "There is an authority." When he grew up to become a poet and thinker, Horace sensed a kinship between the oral but explicit doctrine he had heard from his father and the express, written lessons of philosophy. Many others sensed the same kinship. An epitaph such as "He never took lessons from any philosopher" or "He learned the venerable truths on his own" expresses not disdain for culture but the claim that popular culture and high culture are equal. The man buried here, the epitaph claims, needed no philosophy to live as a philosopher, to know what was good and useful.

Softness   Apart from this proverbial wisdom of the people, Rome had an oral tradition of common sense, a tradition shared by all classes of society and pertinent to every sort of problem. It was a veritable philosophy, like Marxism or psychoanalysis, the two varieties of common sense most prevalent in the West today. Like Marxism and psychoanalysis, Roman oral doctrines could explain and demystify anything. They demonstrated that the reality in which people lived was radically distorted, that it should have been other than what it was, and that all ills, public and private, stemmed from this state of affairs. The fault lay not with class society but with some fundamental defect shared by virtually all men: softness, perhaps, or extravagance. Everyone took these facts for granted, and philosophers claimed to derive them from their doctrines or, in perfect good faith, bolstered their doctrines with the teachings of common sense. For at least half a millennium the Greeks and the Romans lived convinced that their society was decadent; "Roman decadence" was a familiar topos. Oral philosophies are accidents of the history of ideas, not some sort of immutable functional reflection of reality. They are free creations, and each stands in a different relation to reality. Some are conformist, others demystifying.

Softness destroys individuals and dooms societies, which are mere aggregates of individuals. But what is softness? Not so much a specific defect as a symptom, a clue to analysis of the psyche. At first sight it seems to be but one defect among others, perhaps no more than a set of not very virile traits: an effeminate way of speaking, affected gestures, a slow way of walking, and so on. But the Greeks and Romans subjected these details to puritanical scrutiny and attached undue importance to them. They held that this visible softness was a symptom of a more deep-seated softness, a profound weakness of character. Like a weakened organism unable to resist infection, a character that lacked resistance was in danger of succumbing to every vice, even, and perhaps primarily, those vices bearing the least resemblance to the soft character. Thus, softness was the cause of luxury and lasciviousness, for which there was a single word (*luxuria*) and which consisted in denying oneself nothing and believing that "anything goes." In the Roman Empire a man who loved women too much, who made love too often, gave proof that he was effeminate. How could one combat softness? By struggling against its root cause: indolence. Not that the Romans believed that "the Devil finds work for idle hands"; nor did they share the modern notion that man has an excess of energy, which he will expend in sex if he does not invest it in work. The Romans held that indolence is the grandmother of vice, because an idle character will lose its muscle tone, will "break training," so to speak, and become vulnerable to the diseases of the soul. The Greeks and the Romans subscribed to a kind of machismo, condemning pleasure, dancing, and passion with clerical strictness and casting a pall of suspicion over solitary pursuits. During brief periods, whenever an emperor or public opinion succumbed to an excess of moral fervor, certain types of private behavior were not tolerated.

Another philosophical anthropology hinged on the notion of extravagance, or excess, rather than softness. This enabled the Romans to condemn man as he was and the world as it was, in their very principle. Man may be a creature of reason, but all men are mad. Delusions of grandeur drive men to want more than they can ever use. Excess is thus the root cause of ambition and greed, which in turn are the causes of luxury, conflict, and decadence. This idea was central to the philosophy of Horace, which consisted not, as some have said, in recommending that the wise stick to the happy medium in all things, but in deploring the fact that such obvious advice is never heeded, that fate has arranged things so that there is a radical flaw at the heart of every man. Against this universal flaw, a highly systematic philosophy fought with energy born of despair.

Excess

Proponents of this philosophy sought to show in a new light the most widespread form of excess: greed, the desire for wealth. It is enough, they argued, for a man to be comfortable. What is the good of a man's wanting more than he needs in order to live without working? But humans are foolish enough not to be content with what they have, and to want to live like millionaires. Clearly the conception of poverty invoked here is one that seems rather peculiar to us. What was the point, Galen asked, of owning fifteen pairs of shoes? Two were enough. With a house, a few slaves, and suitable furniture, one could live happily. From Prodicos to Musonius and beyond, all the philosophers delighted in making paradoxical praise of "poverty." Pleasure in this paradox was quite widely shared. We find it in the theater, a popular pastime, where the public expressed its approval. Seneca tells us that

ΛΕ ΡΕΝΝΙο   ΣΕΚΟΥΝΛ
ΚΑΙΛΕΚΡΙΑΠΟΜΠΩΝΙΑΣ ΛΕΡΕΝΝΙΩΠΡΑ
ΚΑΙΕΑΥΤΟΙΣ   ΖΩΝΤΕΣ

Banquet on a Greek tomb. A Roman epitaph explains the meaning of such images: the deceased, sorry to have led a mean life, wished to be depicted at least on his tomb at a feast. "But what good is it to the dead to be shown feasting? They would have done better to have lived that way." (Avignon, Calvet Museum.)

audiences applauded tirades against the miserly and greedy, who harm themselves with their passion for more. Greek economists taught that the real goal of production ought to be autarchy, which involved reducing needs to the point where one was no longer dependent on the economy. This ideology has persuaded some recent historians of the ancient world that the ancients did not care about production and that therefore the economies of Greece and Rome must not have been very highly developed. Such a view reflects a fundamental misunderstanding of the oral philosophy of excess, which did not describe reality but condemned it.

We must know how to make do with little, said Epicurus. But, he added, if need be. Whether condemning wealth or softness, the oral traditions of the ancients had but one goal: to protect the individual by censuring those weaknesses and appetites that left him vulnerable to life's tempests. The ancients were critical of anyone who hoisted too much sail in heavy weather. They used philosophy as a tranquilizer. If excess makes an individual vulnerable, religion, proverbs, and eschatological speculation bring tranquillity. And if theory condemns softness, reality offers an abundance of pleasures.

The common people condemned avarice above all, avarice being defined as the accumulation of wealth without enjoyment. But if a wealthy man—a prince or object of public adulation—indulged himself ostentatiously and made a great show of banquets, mistresses, and favorites, people regarded him with a fair degree of sympathy; the simple pleasures of the bed and dinner table everyone could understand. Reassured plebeians consoled themselves with the belief that the powerful were made of the same stuff as themselves.

Hercules and Bacchus, second half of 1st century. These colossal statues, carved from very hard stone (whence their smooth finish) were found in the imperial palace in Rome. The old satyr who grabs Bacchus is larger than life. Hercules represents virtuous, civilizing power; Bacchus, whose face would not be out of place on a statue of Venus, represents pleasure and wild abandon. (Museum of Parma.)

⚘ Pleasures and Excesses

'**B**ATHING, wine, and Venus wear out the body but are the real stuff of life," a proverb warns. In Sparta—yes, Sparta—the following epitaph commented on an erotic relief that graced one tombstone (such things were not unknown):

> This is what is called a temple.
> This is where your mysteries lie.
> This is what a mortal must do
> When he sees where life ends up.

To everything there was a season, and pleasure was no less legitimate than virtue. One picture is worth a thousand words: the ancients liked to show Hercules in moments of weakness, spinning at the feet of his mistress Omphale or drunk on wine, barely able to stand, his eyes distracted and face alight. Besides pleasures, there were marvels: spectacles, the grandeur of public buildings, the size of a city. People also marveled at the miracles of technology; in the theater scenic machinery enchanted spectators with its ingenuity. Geographic maps and plans of cities and buildings were quite common, less cause for astonishment than home computers today. The engineer's art was held in high esteem by civilian and military authorities and admired by the people. Major projects such as canals and roads struck the imagination as grand exploits; Nero's engineers undertook to cut off the isthmus of Corinth by digging a canal. Technology in this period did not pretend to dominate and revolutionize nature, as it does today, but in isolated areas the ancients were capable of amazing feats—miracles, as astonishing as the feats of nature. Among them were the siphon (which enabled aqueducts to span valleys) and the sundial. In the first century B.C. the sundial was all the rage; every city wanted one. Emperor Nero, well aware of the value of amazement, contrived to reign as, much later, the princes of the Renaissance would

A fragment of an official plan of Rome, engraved on marble ca. 210. Part of what filled the space between the monuments: a street lined with shops and multistory buildings and, side by side, three houses with patios (the three dotted rectangles). The plan, which shows domestic interiors as well as outside walls, celebrated the immensity of the city and human domination of space thanks to the surveyor's art.

do—as *artifex,* a word meaning both "artist who creates spectacles" and "engineer." He was unfortunately overthrown, because the notables and the nobility preferred urbanity, at least in an emperor.

Urbanity required savoir-vivre. A well-bred man (*pepaideumenos*) exhibited neither baseness nor presumptuousness in the company of his peers, and every noble, every notable, was well-bred by definition. Respect for others was to be shown with liberal ease; the deference due a superior was to be offered with familiar simplicity, the mark of the free man's civic pride. Let "barbarians stand petrified before kings" and the superstitious tremble before the gods like slaves before their masters. In the eyes of the governing class "liberty" reigned, and the reigning sovereign was a "good emperor" so long as he adopted a liberal tone with citizens of the upper class, gave orders as though speaking to equals, avoided acting like a living god or barbarian potentate, and refused to take seriously his own divinization, a concession to the religious enthusiasms of the masses. The political style of the High Empire was one of conviviality. Public men, it was felt, should be as free and easy with one another as the participants in Cicero's philosophical dialogues, and religious life should be conducted in the same liberal atmosphere. Nothing could be farther removed from Christian relations with the divine, based as they were on the model of the family. Filial love for the Father must have struck the pagans as distastefully intimate and servilely humble. It probably seemed plebeian.

Sarcophagus. Couple banqueting, their children at their feet. The lady, who is interested in music, sits in a handsome armchair, but her lord and master is entitled to a dining couch. Slaves serve an abundance of dishes. (Rome, Vatican Museums.)

Even in politics, the style of interpersonal relations between the emperor and his subjects was frequently much more important than actual political or economic decisions or the manner in which power was shared. Here again it is hard to differentiate between public and private life. Emperors were toppled because of private immorality or because of what they thought privately about the people they governed. The prince's private misconduct obviously did no harm to political or material interests, but it was humiliating to Roman notables to think that their emperor entertained megalomanic or immoral ideas, which offended their sense of honor.

Our impression of the ancient world prior to the "decadence" of the late imperial period—an impression of classicism, humanism, clarity, reason, and liberty—comes from the thin veneer of style that graced private relations within the governing class. The style of private letters and prose generally, including epitaphs, reflects the same values. Our impression is also shaped by Roman art, with its taste for realism. As Ernst Gombrich has written, the catacomb painters and medieval sculptors who recreated the "Bible in images" represented the elements and content of legend in a conventional montage. By contrast, classical pagan art consisted of momentary images—snapshots—of legends that presumably everyone knew: man and the real stood on a footing of equality. Portraits of the emperors from late antiquity depict the sovereign with the traits of a mystic or a Mussolinian hierarch. But imperial portraits from the period of High Empire show the prince with the head of a handsome young man, an intellectual, or a respectable gentleman. His features are individualized; his head is that of a man like other men. There is nothing ideological or didactic about these busts.

For those who subscribed to the liberal ideal, friendship rather than passion epitomized the desirable qualities of reciprocity and inward freedom. Love is slavery, but friendship is freedom and equality. This despite the fact that in reality the word "friendship" often (though not always) meant "clientage." Did people really have more friends then than they do now? I don't know. But friendship was talked about far more often than we talk about it today. Frequently, though, a culture speaks not of what really exists but of imaginary solutions to its real contradictions. (The Japanese do not commit suicide more often than Westerners, but they talk about it much more.)

In late antiquity everything changes. Rhetoric turns dark and expressionistic, and the style of politics becomes author-

Gold coin. Weight: 8 grams. Depicted is Emperor Augustus, given the profile of a young god by a Greek engraver.

itarian and sublime. The exaggerated tone of the Late Empire, so extreme that it is almost a caricature, is responsible for the period's reputation as "decadent." For a long time historians, misled by this, believed that the population of the Empire, urban life, production, the monetary economy, and the authority of the government all suffered a serious decline. Such is the power of style to deceive.

The Urban Ideal

The style of the first two or three centuries of the Empire was one of urbanity and urbanism. The notables, as we know, were a nobility of the cities, who visited their rural estates only during the heat of summer. As for nature, these city folk appreciated only its agreeable aspects (*amoenitas*). They explored its wild depths in cumbrous hunting parties only to prove their *virtu,* or courage. The nature they loved was "humanized" with parks and gardens; a landscape made a better composition if the site's possibilities were exploited by, say, placing a small sanctuary on a hilltop or at the end of a spit of land. Men were fully themselves only in the city, and a city was not so much a place of familiar streets and bustling, anonymous crowds as an array of material conveniences (*commoda*) such as public baths and buildings, which lifted the spirits of residents and travelers alike and made the city much more than just a place where numbers of people lived. Pausanias asks: "Can one call 'city' a place that has neither public buildings nor gymnasium nor theater nor square nor water to supply a single fountain, and where the people live in huts, small shacks (*kalybai*) perched on the edge of a ravine?" Romans did not really feel at home in the country. To feel at home they needed a city, in particular a city surrounded by ramparts. This is a trait of the Roman psychology: walls were a city's finest ornament, defining the space of the communal home. Nowadays, even if we do not live in fear of thieves, most of us lock our doors at night. Similarly, walled cities locked their doors at nightfall, and nocturnal comings and goings were suspect. Would-be miscreants did not dare apply to the night watch for the keys to the city gates and were forced to enlist the aid of accomplices, who might lower them in baskets from atop some poorly guarded section of the city wall.

Banquets

Walls were a sign of civility, banquets a ceremony of civility. The moment Horace arrived at his beloved country retreat he invited a woman friend to join him for dinner, most likely a freedwoman, a well-known singer or actress. Banquets were occasions for the private man to savor his accomplishments and show off to his peers. The banquet was as important to the Romans as the salon to the eighteenth-century French aristocracy, as important even as the court of Versailles to the seventeenth-century nobility. The emperors kept no court. They lived in their "palace," on the Palatine Hill, much as the nobles of Rome lived in their private villas, with only slaves and freedmen for company (which of course meant that the palace housed the various ministries of government). When night came, however, the emperor dined with his guests, senators and others whose company he relished. The time of public "honors" and "government" of the patrimony was over. Now the private man could relax at table. Even the poor people (*hoi penetes*), nine-tenths of the population, had their nights of revelry. During a banquet the private man forgot everything but his "profession," if he had one. Those who had vowed to devote their lives to the pursuit of wisdom celebrated not as the profane did but as philosophers.

There was an art to banqueting. Roman table manners were apparently less elaborate and formalized than ours, however. People dined with clients and friends of all ranks, and

Silver pieces, found at Boscoreale, before A.D. 79. Rarely has the average of any art reached as high a level of good taste as in Late Empire embossing. (Paris, Louvre.)

Banquet on a Syrian tomb, 2nd century. (Museum of Beirut.)

protocol was strictly observed in the assignment of "dining couches" around the pedestal table that held the platters of different dishes. Without couches there could be no real feast, even among the poor. Romans sat up to eat only at ordinary meals (with simple folk, the mother stood and served the father seated at table). Roman cooking strikes us as a mixture of oriental and medieval. The food was quite spicy and covered with complicated sauces. Meat was boiled more often than it was braised or roasted, so that it was bloodless, and served sugared. Romans preferred their food in the sweet-and-sour range. As for drink, there was a choice between wine with a flavor something like marsala and a resiny wine such as one might drink in Greece today, both diluted with water. "Make it stronger!" the suffering erotic poet orders his cupbearer. The trickiest part of the evening, and the longest, was that set aside for drinking. Early in the dinner people ate without drinking. Later they drank without eating: this was the banquet in the strict sense of the word (*comissatio*). More than a feast, the banquet was a festival, and each man was expected to hold his own. As a token of festivity guests wore hats with flowers, or "wreaths," and were perfumed, that is, anointed with fragrant oil (alcohol was unknown, so oil was used as a solvent for perfumes). Banquets were unctuous and brilliant, as were nights of love.

The banquet was more than just a meal. Guests were expected to express their views on general topics and noble

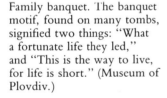

Family banquet. The banquet motif, found on many tombs, signified two things: "What a fortunate life they led," and "This is the way to live, for life is short." (Museum of Plovdiv.)

subjects or to give summaries of their lives. If the host had a domestic philosopher or tutor on his staff, he would be asked to speak. Between dishes there might be music (with dancing and singing), by professional musicians hired for the occasion. At least as much a social manifestation as an occasion for eating and drinking, the classical banquet gave rise to a literary genre, the "symposium," in which men of culture, philosophers, and scholars (*grammatici*) held elevated discussions. Ideally the banquet hall was supposed to resemble not a dining room but a literary salon; when this happened, confusion with popular merrymaking was no longer possible. "Drinking," then, meant the pleasures of good company, culture, and in some cases the charms of friendship. Thinkers and poets found it perfectly possible to philosophize about wine.

Confraternities

Ordinary folk enjoyed one another's company in less ostentatious ways. They had taverns and "colleges," or confraternities. As in Moslem countries today, men met friends at the barber, the baths, or the tavern. In Pompeii taverns (*cauponae*) were numerous. There one met travelers, had food warmed (not all the poor had ovens at home), and flirted with bejeweled waitresses. Amorous taunts are recorded on the walls. These popular customs were considered bad form by the nobility, and a notable seen lunching in a tavern risked tarnishing his reputation. Street life was disreputable. One old philosopher was so immoderate in his desires that he never went out without money, people said, so that he could buy any pleasure that he happened upon. The imperial government waged war for four centuries against the taverns to keep them from serving as restaurants (*thermopolium*), for it was considered morally healthier to eat at home.

As for the *collegia*, or confraternities, the emperors were suspicious of them, since they were places where numbers of men gathered for purposes that were hard to define. Rightly or wrongly, government feared their potential power. In principle, the collegia were free, private associations, whose members were free men and slaves who practiced a common trade or worshiped a common god. Nearly every city boasted one or more. In one town, for example, there was a weavers' association and a college of worshipers of Hercules. A neighboring town was home to a blacksmith's confraternity and an association of clothing merchants who worshiped Mercury. Each confraternity was confined to a single city. Members

Funerary relief. The deceased, who served drinks in life, is shown with two customers seated at a table. (Ostia, Archaeological Museum.)

lived in the town and knew one another. All were men; no women were admitted. Finally, all the collegia, whether religious or professional, were organized along the same lines as the city itself. Each had a council, magistrates who held office for a year at a time, and benefactors, who were honored with handsome declarations patterned after the honorary edicts issued by the city council. In sum, the collegia were make-believe cities. They served religious and professional purposes, and their members were common people from a particular city or town.

Why did people join such groups? Why did the carpenters in one town or the worshipers of Hercules in another feel the need to band together? One thing is certain: the colleges were nothing like modern trade unions, nor were they workers' mutual aid societies. They offered men a place to meet and to enjoy one another's company, away from women. If a college was religious in character, honoring its god provided a pretext for staging a banquet. If professional, it brought together men working in similar trades; cobblers liked to talk to other cobblers, carpenters to other carpenters. Each new member paid an entry fee. Coupled with gifts from benefactors, these dues enabled college members to stage joyous banquets and buy members decent burials (which were also followed by banquets). Slaves joined colleges to ensure that they would not be buried like dogs. In this there is a strict parallel with the workers' and religious confraternities of early modern Europe. In Florence, Davidsohn tells us, religious and craft confraternities were associated with worship of the Virgin or a saint. Members' funerals were celebrated with much pomp, and a cortege followed the deceased member's body to the collective tomb the confraternity had built at its own expense. Early modern confraternities were renowned for their immoderate love of banquets, often held to honor founding members who had donated money for toasts to be drunk in their memory; Roman collegia seem to have been no different. The two things that interest the collegia, Saint Cyprian wrote, are banquets and burials. In a few cases the zeal for banqueting required no pretext; at Fano on the Adriatic there was a confraternity of "*bons vivants* who dine together."

Collegia proliferated to the point where they became the center of plebeian private life. Not surprisingly, the imperial government viewed them with suspicion. And not without reason, for any association tends to acquire purposes beyond its officially stated aims, beyond even its unconscious desires.

When men come together for whatever reason, their conversation will quite naturally range over matters of common interest. At the end of the Republic, candidates for election sought the support of colleges as well as cities. Later, in the politically troubled city of Alexandria, religious colleges met and, "under the guise of taking part in some sacrifice, people drank and in their drunkenness talked nonsense about the political situation." After "talking nonsense" long enough they took to the streets, egged on by a notable who defended the privileges of the city's Greeks against the Roman governor and who, by means of generous donations, had secured for himself the position of president of these religious groups, the ancient equivalent of our political clubs.

More numerous, however, were the clubs where people went merely to drink with friends. The need for association was so great that groups formed even within households and, under the guise of piety, in the finest society. The slaves and freedmen of one household, or the sharecroppers and slaves of an estate, might band together in a college, pay dues to cover members' burial costs, and show devotion to the master's family by erecting a small domestic sanctuary in honor of the protective deities of the household or estate. These colleges also mimicked the political organization of the cities.

Bacchic Ideology

In the cities themselves, as we saw earlier, wealthy benefactors paid for public feasts. Banquets were important occasions, rituals of conviviality and drink. Some were held at fixed intervals, others on special occasions; eagerly anticipated, they added solemnity to pleasure. Funerals, too, were important occasions for which people prepared diligently. The worship of Bacchus symbolized and glorified Roman attitudes toward both feasting and death. "Worship" may be too strong a word. Even if people naively believed in the existence of Bacchus, they never worshiped this god, who was famous mainly from his legends. Certain mystical sects held that he was a truly great god, but most Romans, when they felt the need of divine protection, worshiped deities considered more authentic than Bacchus, to whom no shrines were erected. Yet the legend of Bacchus was more than a legend. Bacchic imagery was ubiquitous, and its meaning was obvious. Images of Bacchus are found in mosaics, in paintings that hung on the walls of houses and taverns, on dishes, and on household objects of all sorts, to say nothing of sarcophagi. No other

Mausoleum of Igel, near Trier, ca. A.D. 200. Servants of the Secundini family, which owned land and engaged in wholesale trade, prepare drinks for their masters.

A servant prepares drinks for his masters. Note the style of the furniture; the table leg features a lion's head.

image was as widely disseminated, not even that of Venus. Bacchic imagery was appropriate anywhere because it evoked only pleasant associations. The god of pleasure and sociability, Bacchus was always accompanied by a train of tipsy friends and ecstatic female admirers; pleasant excesses of all sorts lay in store for them. A benevolent, civilizing god who soothed the mind, Bacchus won peaceful victories in every corner of the world. He was clever enough to calm the fiercest tigers, who hitched themselves like lambs to his chariot. His admirers were as beautiful, and as lightly clad, as his lovely mistress, Ariadne. Bacchic imagery certainly had no religious or mystical significance, but it was not merely decorative, either. It affirmed the importance of sociability and pleasure, on which it bestowed the blessings of the supernatural. It was an ideology, an affirmation of principle. Against this was set the image of Hercules, symbol of civic and philosophical "virtue."

Bacchus, emblematic of a principle, was one god the people did not doubt. His worshipers banded together in popular confraternities, whose chief concern (proved by their regulations) was to drink toasts in honor of this amiable deity. In the Middle Ages people no less joyously worshiped certain

Triumph of Bacchus, mosaic from Susa, 2nd–3rd century. Victory crowns the god on his chariot, as *putti* ride lions. In contemporary theater the triumph of Bacchus was a subject of (pyrrhic) dance, as were Venus and the Graces, Nymphs, and Seasons, according to Philostratus and Athenaeus. Only rarely did mosaics depict pious images; the gods most often represented were Venus and Bacchus, and their style was mythological. (Tunis, Bardo Museum.)

Funerary relief, 1st–3rd century. Young woman idealized as bacchante. Crowned with ivy, the plant of her god, the seated bacchante or maenad dreamily teases a goat, which strains against her restraint. She supports herself with one arm, whose tension reveals the energy dormant within her. This melancholy masterpiece poeticizes death; it does not suggest that hope was vested in the hereafter. (Rome, Museum of the Baths.)

saints from the *Golden Legend*. To the cultivated, the Bacchus legend was a pleasant fancy; the god might exist, or he might be one of the many names of the godhead, or he might be a superhuman individual who had lived in the distant past and whose legend was based on authentic exploits. These beliefs were enough to encourage speculation about the god, and a few sects formed for the purpose of worshiping him: small, isolated groups in which exalted piety and authentic religious fervor coexisted with more worldly attitudes. To understand this mixture of snobbery and salon mysticism, we need only think of the early days of Freemasonry, in the time of *The Magic Flute*. Like Freemasonry, the Bacchic sects had secret rites, initiation rituals (or "mysteries"), and a hierarchy from which women were not excluded. Archaeologists have happened upon the actual site used by one of these mystery sects only once or twice. Nevertheless, I feel I ought to say a word about them, because sects, popular and otherwise, were a feature of the age, and religious fervor was no less important than the need for sociability. The speculations of these mystery sects contributed to the spiritual revolution of late antiquity.

Festival and Religion

Feasting and piety could coexist in sects and confraternities because festival was an integral part of pagan religion. A cult was nothing more than a festival, which pleased the gods as much as it pleased the men and women who took part. All religions are likely to confound spiritual emotion with formal ritual; untroubled by the confusion, the faithful find sustenance in both. Was wearing a wreath in antiquity a sign of feasting or religious ceremony? How can we tell? Piety meant honoring the gods as they deserved. Religious festivals yielded a twofold pleasure: besides enjoying oneself, one did one's duty. The pagans never asked the faithful how they "really" felt; hence we have no way of knowing. Paying homage to the gods was a solemn way of enjoying yourself. Fortunate were those who, more than others, felt the presence of divinity and whose souls were moved.

The principal rite of every cult was of course the rite of sacrifice, which people attended in a contemplative mood. It is important to bear in mind, however, that in a Greek or Latin text the word "sacrifice" always implies "feast." Every sacrifice was followed by a dinner in which the immolated victim was cooked on the altar and eaten. (Great temples had kitchens and offered the services of their cooks to worshipers

who came to sacrifice.) The flesh of the victim went to the participants in the ritual, the smoke to the gods. Scraps from the meal were left on the altar, and beggars (*bomolochoi*) spirited them away. When sacrifice was made not on a household altar but at a temple, the custom was to pay for the priests' services by leaving them a set portion of the sacrificial animal; temples earned money by selling this meat to butchers. (When Pliny the Younger wishes to inform the emperor that he has eradicated Christianity in the province of which he is governor, he writes: "The meat of sacrificial animals is on sale once more," proving that sacrifices have resumed.) Which was it: Did people eat sacrificial victims or did they sacrifice animals they wanted to eat? That depends. The word for a man who made frequent sacrifice (*philothytes*) came to mean not a devout person but a host who gave good dinners, an Amphitryon.

The religious calendar, which varied from city to city, was filled with festivals, days when no one was required to work. These occurred at irregular intervals throughout the

Ornamental relief. The driving rhythms of the double oboe and tambourine set the pace of the march. The panther skin and long cane topped with pine cone are the insignia of Bacchus. (Madrid, Prado.)

year. (Incidentally, the week, a period of astrological rather than Judeo-Christian origin, did not come into common use until the end of antiquity.) On feast days people invited their friends to sacrifices in their homes; such invitations were considered a greater honor than mere dinner invitations. Vapors of incense spewed forth from many houses on these great occasions, according to Tertullian. Among the important holidays were the national feasts of the emperors, the festivals of certain gods, New Year's Day, and the first day of each month. A custom cherished by Romans wealthy enough to practice it was that of sacrificing a piglet on the first of the month in honor of the household gods, the Lares or Penates. Once a year the birthday of the paterfamilias was celebrated with genuine fervor. On that day the family feasted in honor of its protective deity, or *genius*. (Each individual had, as it were, a divine double, or genius, whose existence had little consequence other than to allow people to say "May my genius protect me!" or "I swear by your genius that I have carried out your orders.") The poor sacrificed less costly animals. If Aesculapius cured them of some malady, they sacrificed a chicken at his temple, and then returned home to eat it. Or they might place a simple wheat cake on the family altar (*far pium*).

A simpler means of sanctifying a meal was what Artemidorus, I think, called "theoxenies"; one invited the gods (*in-*

Sacrifice of a bull, a ram, and a boar, first half of 1st century. Officiating at the altar is a veiled figure, probably an emperor. The animals are ready, and the scene will soon resemble a slaughterhouse, a butchershop, or a barbecue. (Paris, Louvre.)

Diana the archer. Hellenistic art. Common women prayed to the mother of Diana to give them daughters just as beautiful. (London, British Museum.)

vitare deos) to dinner by removing their statuettes from the house's sacred niche and placing them in the dining room during the meal, as platters of food were heaped in front of them. After dinner the slaves feasted on these untouched dishes. This custom probably explains the following lines from Horace: "O nights, O dinners of the gods at which my friends and I ate before the household genius, and I gave my excited slaves consecrated dishes to eat." If the slaves were excited, it was the feast that excited them, and this was as it should be. Peasants, too, celebrated seasonal festivals according to a rustic calendar. With gifts formally offered by share-croppers, the great landlord of a district used to sacrifice a tithe of the soil's produce to the gods of the fields, after which everyone ate, drank, and danced. Then, at nightfall, as Horace states explicitly and Tibullus implies, people had the right, even the duty, to make love as a fitting end to a day in which they had enjoyed themselves while honoring the gods. Someone once reproached Aristippus, a philosopher and theoretician of pleasure, for leading a life of indolence. "If it is wrong to live like this," he replied, "why do people do it for the gods' feasts?"

The Baths

In addition to the enthusiasms and delights of the religious calendar, there were other pleasures with nothing sacred about them that could be had only in the cities. These were among the benefits (*commoda*) of urban life, the product of public benefaction, or evergetism, and included public baths, theaters, chariot races at the Circus, and fights between gladiators or hunters and wild animals in the arena of the amphitheater (or theater in Greek areas). Baths and public spectacles cost money, in Rome at any rate (we know little about the subject, and it seems likely that generosity of benefactors had some influence on the price of admission), but the cost was in any case modest. Free seats were reserved at every show, and lines began forming the night before. Free men, slaves, women, children—everyone had access to the baths, even foreigners. When gladiators were on display, people flocked to the cities from great distances. The better part of private life was spent in public establishments of one kind or another.

The baths were not for cleanliness. They offered an array of pleasures, rather like our beaches. Christians and philosophers denied themselves these pleasures. Not so soft as to lust after cleanliness, they bathed only once or twice a month. A philosopher's dirty beard was proof of the austerity on which he prided himself. No rich man's house (*domus*) was without a bath, which occupied several specially prepared rooms, with heating under the floor. And no city was without at least one public bath, supplied, if necessary, by an aqueduct, which also carried water to the public fountains. (Door-to-door water delivery was still a corrupt business monopolized by criminals.) The gong (*discus*) that announced the opening of the public baths each day was a sweeter sound, Cicero says, than the voices of the philosophers in their school.

For a few coins the poor people could spend several hours a day in a luxurious setting provided by the authorities, the emperor, or the city notables. Along with complex installations, including hot and cold baths, there were promenades and fields for sports and games. (The Greco-Roman bath was also a gymnasium and in Greek regions was still called by that name.) The two sexes were separated, at least as a general rule. Excavations at Olympia allow us to follow the evolution of the baths over more than seven centuries. Originally modest, functional buildings, with a cold pool, hot slipper baths, and a steam bath, the "therms" eventually developed into pleasure palaces. A well-known quip calls them, along with the amphitheaters, "cathedrals of paganism." Beginning in the Hellenistic era, their role expanded from one of facilitating cleanliness to one of making life as pleasant as possible. The great novelty (which dates from around 100 B.C. in Olympia and earlier still at Gortys in Arcadia) was the heating of the basement and even the walls of the building. Large numbers of people were offered an enclosed place that was always warm. At a time when, no matter how cold it became, people had no source of heat at home other than braziers and wore overcoats in the house as well as in the street, the baths were a place to keep warm. Ultimately in the baths of Caracalla the Romans introduced "climate control" throughout the building by means of convection. There was another kind of evolution in the baths: from functional edifice to dream palace, with sculptures, mosaics, painted decor, and sumptuous architecture making the splendor of a royal residence accessible to all. Life at the baths was like life at the beach in summertime; the greatest pleasure was to mix with the crowd, to shout, to meet people, to listen to conversations, to spot and tell stories about odd characters, and to show off.

The wind of musical abandon effaces differences and stirs the most splendid drapery. (Rome, Vatican Museums.)

Spectacles

Passion for the races at the Circus and the fights at the arena, Tacitus complained, rivaled the study of eloquence among young men of good family. These spectacles were of interest to everyone, including senators and philosophers. Gladiators and chariots were not pleasures for the plebs alone. Criticism of them, usually by Platonic philosophers, smacked of that conventional utopian wisdom that we have learned to recognize. In the theater the plays known as pantomimes (a kind of opera; the word has since changed its meaning) were attacked for encouraging "softness" and occasionally prohibited. The gladiator shows were different. Infamous as they were, they at least had the merit of fortifying their spectators' courage by inuring them to the sight of blood. But even gladiator fights and chariot races had critics, who charged that such spectacles typified the human tendency to complicate life unnecessarily and waste time with frivolities. In Greek parts of the Empire intellectuals condemned athletic competitions for the same reason; to which other intellectuals responded that athletes offered lessons in endurance, moral strength, and beauty.

Intellectuals, along with everyone else, attended these spectacles. Cicero, who liked to say that he spent show days writing books, was one of the crowd and reported the events to his noble correspondents. When Seneca felt the shadow of melancholy steal across his soul, he headed for the amphitheater to cheer himself up. Maecenas, a sophisticated Epicurean noble, inquired of his client Horace about the program of the fights. But Marcus Aurelius, good philosopher that he was, found one fight pretty much like another and went to see the gladiators only to fulfill his duty as emperor. The passions of the public were engaged, however, and wealthy youths and honest yeomen divided into rival factions backing one actor or racing team or group of gladiators against another. The enthusiasm sometimes spilled over, but the ensuing riots concealed no ulterior political motives or class divisions. Occasionally it was necessary to exile an actor or chariot racer who had stirred the passions of the crowd for or against him.

In Rome and other Italian cities spectacles were the great drawing card. In Greek areas, by contrast, athletic competitions were. Greeks flocked not only to great games (*isolympicoi, periodicoi*) and lesser games (*stephanitai*), which were associated with fairs, but also to minor games (*themides*). The Greeks enthusiastically borrowed gladiatorial combats from

Rome. 3rd century(?). This *bestiarius*, or animal-fighter, defended himself against bears with pick and whip. (Copenhagen, Ny Carlsberg Glypotek.)

the Romans. Athletes, actors, racers, and gladiators were stars. The theater set fashion, and many popular songs were first heard on the stage.

The role of spectacles and competition in ancient life at first seems surprising. The most distinguished individuals, even public officials, confess a passionate interest in these events without the slightest embarrassment. Rather than build dams or docks, cities and their benefactors ruined themselves building aqueducts (to supply water to the public baths), theaters, and gigantic amphitheaters. This passion can be understood. Public spectacles were not dependent on individual tastes (as opposed to policy), nor were they leisure activities (as opposed to the more serious and laborious parts of life). Hence it is wrong to draw a parallel with our Olympic Games or World Cup Soccer or World Series. The ancients did not distinguish between popular and elite sports, and spectacles were public institutions, organized (and sometimes financed) by government authorities. In a period in which idleness was an ideal, no contrast was drawn between pleasure and work; nobles and plebeians alike took public spectacles seriously.

Philosophers charged that the passions aroused by these spectacles were excessive, and Christians agreed: "The theater is lasciviousness, the Circus, suspense, and the arena, cruelty." As critics saw it, the cruelty belonged to the gladiators themselves, who volunteered to commit murder and suicide. All were volunteers; otherwise they would have put on a poor show. The criticism that occurs to us—that the spectators must have been sadists—never occurred to any Roman, philosopher or not. The gladiators brought Rome a strong dose of sadistic pleasure of which people fully approved: pleasure at the sight of bodies and at the sight of men dying. Gladiator fights were not mere fencing matches with actual risks. The whole point was to witness the death of one of the combatants or, better still, the decision whether to slit the throat or spare the life of a fallen gladiator who, exhausted and frightened for his life, was reduced to begging for quarter. The best fights were those that ended in exhaustion, with the life-or-death decision made by the patron who had paid for the show, in conjunction with the public. Innumerable images on lamps, plates, and household objects reproduced this great moment. And the patron boasted of having decided a man's fate: the cutting of the gladiator's throat was depicted in mosaic, painting, or sculpture and placed in his antechamber or on his tomb. If the patron had purchased from the imperial treasury men sen-

Detail of sarcophagus, 2nd century(?). Boxers: an evocation more literary than biographical of Greek athletic competition and educational methods. (Rome, Torlonia Collection.)

tenced to death in order to have them executed during the intermissions in the fights, he also had the artists show these prisoners being thrown to wild beasts. After all, he had paid for them. In Greek regions the death of a boxer during a match was not a "sports accident." It was a glory for the athlete to die in the arena, just as if he had died on the field of battle. The public praised his courage, his steadfastness, his will to win.

It would be wrong to conclude that Greco-Roman culture was sadistic. People were not convinced that watching suffering was pleasurable; they were critical of those, such as Emperor Claudius, who took obvious delight in viewing the slaughter, rather than adopting an objective attitude as if witnessing an exhibition of courage. Greek and Roman literature and imagery are not generally sadistic. In fact the contrary is true, and when the Romans colonized a barbarian nation their first concern was to prohibit human sacrifice. A culture is a tissue of exceptions, whose incoherence goes unnoticed by those involved in it, and in Rome spectacles were such exceptions. Images of victims occur in Roman art only because the victims died in spectacles that were sacred institutions. In our own time sadistic images, justified on patriotic grounds, occur in war films but are condemned elsewhere. Our pleasure in such things must be unwitting. The Christians were more critical of the pleasure than of the atrocity of the institution.

Desire and Passion

Similar incoherences and baffling limitations are found in every century. In Greco-Roman culture we find them associated with another pleasure: love. If any aspect of ancient life has been distorted by legend, this is it. It is widely but mistakenly believed that antiquity was a Garden of Eden from which repression was banished, Christianity having yet to insinuate the worm of sin into the forbidden fruit. Actually, the pagans were paralyzed by prohibitions. The legend of pagan sensuality stems from a number of traditional misinterpretations. The famous tale of the debauches of Emperor Heliogabalus is nothing but a hoax perpetrated by the literati who authored that late forgery, the *Historia Augusta*. The legend also stems from the crudeness of the interdictions: "Latin words are an affront to decency," people used to say. For such naive souls, merely uttering a "bad word" provoked a shiver of perverse imagination or a gale of embarrassed laughter. Schoolboy daring.

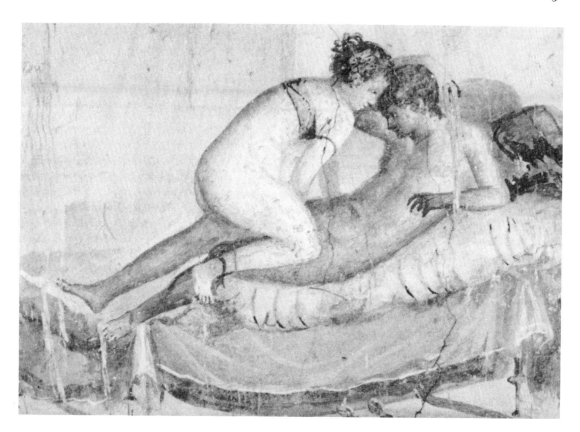

What were the marks of the true libertine? A libertine was a man who violated three taboos: he made love before nightfall (daytime lovemaking was a privilege accorded to newlyweds on the day after the wedding); he made love without first darkening the room (the erotic poets called to witness the lamp that had shone on their pleasures); and he made love to a woman from whom he had removed every stitch of clothing (only fallen women made love without their brassieres, and paintings in Pompeii's bordellos showed even prostitutes wearing this ultimate veil). Libertines permitted themselves to touch rather than caress, though with the left hand only. The one chance a decent man had of seeing a little of his beloved's naked skin was if the moon happened to fall upon the open window at just the right moment. About libertine tyrants such as Heliogabalus, Nero, Caligula, and Domitian it was whispered that they had violated other taboos and made love with married women, well-bred maidens, freeborn adolescents, vestal virgins, or even their own sisters.

Pompeii, so-called Centenary House. Painting found in an out-of-the-way room of a house whose decoration ranks among the finest in Pompeii. For reasons of modesty the servant has not removed her final layer of clothing. (Naples, Archaeological Museum.)

This puritanism went hand in hand with an attitude of superiority toward the love object, who was often treated like a slave. The attitude emblematic of the Roman lover was not holding his beloved by the hand or around the waist or, as in the Middle Ages, putting his arm around her neck; the woman was a servant, and the lover sprawled on top of her as though she were a sofa. The Roman way was the way of the seraglio. A small amount of sadism was permissible: a slave, for example, could be beaten in her bed, on the pretext of making her obey. The woman served her lord's pleasure and, if necessary, did all the work herself. If she straddled her passive lover, it was to serve him.

Machismo was a factor. Young men challenged one another in a macho fashion. To be active was to be a male, regardless of the sex of the passive partner. Hence there were two supreme forms of infamy: to use one's mouth to give a woman pleasure was considered servile and weak, and to allow oneself to be buggered was, for a free man, the height of passivity (*impudicitia*) and lack of self-respect. Pederasty was a minor sin so long as it involved relations between a free man and a slave or person of no account. Jokes about it were common among the people and in the theater, and people boasted of it in good society. Nearly anyone can enjoy sensual pleasure with a member of the same sex, and pederasty was not at all uncommon in tolerant antiquity. Many men of basically heterosexual bent used boys for sexual purposes. It was proverbially held that sex with boys procures a tranquil pleasure unruffling to the soul, whereas passion for a woman plunges a free man into unendurable slavery.

Thus, Roman love was defined by macho domination and refusal to become a slave of passion. The amorous excesses attributed to various tyrants were excesses of domination, described with misleading Sadian boldness. Nero, a tyrant who was weak more than cruel, kept a harem to serve his passive needs. Tiberius arranged for young slave boys to indulge his whims, and Messalina staged a pantomime of her own servility, usurping the male privilege of equating strength with frequency of intercourse. These acts were not so much violations as distortions of the taboos. They reflect a dreadful weakness, a need for planned pleasure. Like alcohol, lust is dangerous to virility and must not be abused. But gastronomy scarcely encourages moderation at table.

Amorous passion, the Romans believed, was particularly

Nymph attacked by satyr, 1st–2nd century. Decorative excess was well suited to scenes in which creatures of fancy made love, drank, or listened to music with Edenic ease. (Venice, Archaeological Museum.)

to be feared because it could make a free man the slave of a woman. He will call her "mistress" and, like a servant, hold her mirror or her parasol. Love was not the playground of individualists, the would-be refuge from society that it is today. Rome rejected the Greek tradition of "courtly love" of ephebes, which Romans saw as an exaltation of pure passion (in both senses of "pure," for the Greeks pretended to believe that a man's love for a freeborn ephebe was Platonic). When a Roman fell madly in love, his friends and he himself believed either that he had lost his head from overindulgence in sensuality or that he had fallen into a state of moral slavery. The lover, like a good slave, docilely offered to die if his mistress wished it. Such excesses bore the dark magnificence of shame, and even erotic poets did not dare to glorify them openly. They chose the roundabout means of describing such behavior as an amusing reversal of the normal state of affairs, a humorous paradox.

Petrarch's praise of passion would have scandalized the ancients or made them smile. The Romans were strangers to the medieval exaltation of the beloved, an object so sublime that it remained inaccessible. They were strangers, too, to modern subjectivism, to our thirst for experience. Standing apart from the world, we choose to experience something in order to see what effect it has, not because it is intrinsically valuable or required by duty. Finally, the Romans were strangers to the real paganism, the at times graceful and beautiful paganism of the Renaissance. Tender indulgence in pleasures of the senses that became, also, delights of the soul was not the way of the ancients. The most Bacchic scenes of the Romans have nothing of the audacity of some modern writers. The Romans knew but one variety of individualism, which confirmed the rule by seeming to contradict it: energetic indolence. With secret delight they discussed senators such as Scipio, Sulla, Caesar, Petronius, and even Catiline, men scandalously indolent in private yet extraordinarily energetic in public. It was an open secret among insiders that these men were privately lazy, and such knowledge gave the senatorial elite an air of royalty and of being above the common law while confirming its authentic spirit. Although the charge of energetic indolence was a reproach, it was also somehow a compliment. Romans found this compliment reassuring. Their brand of individualism sought not real experience, self-indulgence, or private devotion, but tranquilization.

Stucco roof of a large villa, which probably dates from slightly before the birth of Christ. Slimly elegant figures perform ambiguous rites. In the unarticulated spaces of an idealized landscape we count fewer trees than buildings of uncertain purpose, whose design is a fanciful extension of the exoticism of Alexandrian palaces. (Rome, Museum of the Baths.)

✒ Tranquilizers

HOW can individual anxieties about life be alleviated? This was the primary question for the various forms of wisdom that we call "ancient philosophy," as it was for religion, which generally did not aim to secure salvation in the hereafter. Indeed, the very existence of a hereafter was often denied, or else the other world was such a vague concept that it implied little more than the peacefulness of death, the tranquillity of the grave. Philosophy, religion, and the afterlife aroused precious little anxiety. What is more, the boundaries of their respective provinces were so unlike what they are today that the three words meant something quite different from what we imagine. Who am I? What should I do? Where am I headed, and have I any reason for hope? There is nothing natural about these modern questions; they derive from their Christian answers. Ancient philosophy and religion managed to get along without asking them. The problem of the ancients, with its various subdivisions, was different.

For us, philosophy is an academic subject and a part of our culture. Students study it and educated people are curious about it. Our religion is an amalgam of spiritual practices, moral precepts, and thoughts about the afterlife. The notion that after life there is nothing strikes us as eminently irreligious. For the ancients, however, moral precepts and spiritual practices were an essential part of "philosophy," rather than religion, which had very little to do with ideas about death and the hereafter. Sects existed, but they were philosophical sects, which furnished disciples with credos and rules of good behavior. One became a Stoic or an Epicurean and lived more or less faithfully, according to the convictions of one's sect—much as one might become a Christian or a Marxist today (thereby incurring a moral duty to live the faith or engage in active political work). Ancient China offers a useful parallel. There Confucianism and Taoism, doctrinal sects, offered theories and ethical systems to anyone who cared for such things. Another parallel is with modern Japan, where a man can take an interest in a Buddhist sect, yet still observe, like everyone else, Shinto religious practices. He may marry according to the Shinto rite but die and be buried according to Buddhist rite, implicitly accepting consoling Buddhist beliefs about the afterlife to which he devoted scarcely any thought during his lifetime.

The Nature of Divinity

The paganism of the Greeks and Romans, though a religion without salvation or afterlife, was not necessarily indifferent to man's moral behavior. What has misled some historians is that this religion, without theology or church, was, if I may put it this way, more an à la carte religion than a religion with a fixed menu. If an established church is a "one-party state," then paganism was "free enterprise". Each man was free to found his own temple and preach whatever god he liked, just as he might open an inn or peddle a new product. And each man made himself the client of whichever god he chose, not necessarily his city's favorite deity: the choice was free.

Such freedom was possible because between what the pagans meant by "god" and what Jews, Christians, and Moslems mean, there is little in common but the name. For the three religions of the Book, God is infinitely greater than the world which he created. He exists solely as an actor in a cosmic drama in which the salvation of humankind is played out. The pagan gods, by contrast, live their lives and are not confined to a metaphysical role. They are part of this world, one of three races that populate the earth: animals, which are neither immortal nor gifted with reason; humans, who are mortal but reasonable; and gods, who are immortal and reasonable. So true is it that the divine race is an animal genus that every god is either male or female. From this it follows that the gods of all peoples are true gods. Other nations might worship gods unknown to the Greeks and Romans, or they might worship the same gods under different names. Jupiter was Jupiter the world over, just as a lion is a lion, but he happened to be called Zeus in Greek, Taranis in Gallic, and Yao in Hebrew. The names of the gods could be translated from one language to another, just like the names of planets and other material

Mosaic, Pompeii. Enjoy life while there is still time. The measuring instrument (a square with level) indicates that death is the great leveler and gives the true measure of all things. (Naples, Archaeological Museum.)

things. Belief in alien gods foundered only where it was the product of an absurd superstition, something that smacked of a fantastic bestiary. The Romans laughed at the gods with animal bodies worshiped by the Egyptians. In the ancient world religious people were as tolerant of one another as are Hindu sects. To take a special interest in one god was not to deny the others.

This fact was not without consequence for man's idea of his own place in the natural order. Imagine a circle, which represents the world according to the religions of the Book. Given man's importance in the cosmic drama, he occupies at least half the circle. What about God? He is so exalted, so awesome, that he remains far above the circle. To represent Him, draw an arrow, pointing upward from the center of the circle and mark it with the sign of infinity. Now consider the pagan world. Imagine a sort of staircase with three steps. On the lowest step stand the animals; on the next step, humans; and on the third step, the gods. In order to become a god, one did not need to rise very far. The gods stood just above humans, so that it often makes sense to translate the Latin and Greek words for "divine" as "superhuman." Epicurus, according to one of his followers, "was a god, yes, a god," by which he meant a superhuman genius. This explains why the cosmos was characterized as "divine"; things occurred that were superhuman, that no human could cause to occur. This also explains why it was possible to apotheosize kings and emperors. The practice was ideological hyperbole, perhaps, but not absurd. The emperor simply moved up a notch; he did not go soaring off toward infinity. Given this conception of divinity, the Stoics and Epicureans were able to ask disciples to aspire to become sages, that is, mortal equals of the gods, "supermen."

Human beings entered into relations with both the lower fauna and the divine fauna. Because the gods were superior to men, men were obliged to pay them homage, to offer the same respect (*colere, timan*) offered to superior men, to sovereigns. The gods had their own ways and their own shortcomings; it was not amiss to smile respectfully at them, much as one might be amused by the behavior of some foreign potentate, wealthy enough to indulge his every desire. People joked about the innumerable loves of the great Jupiter much as the subjects of libertine kings joked about the royal loves, while showing proper fear of and respect for the throne. Joking about the sacred requires simple faith. Relations between

The "great cameo of France," probably A.D. 17. This is neither the most beautiful nor the least boring of ancient cameos, but it is the largest (12 inches). Depicted are members of the dynasty founded by Augustus, apotheosized or in glory. The piece traveled from the imperial treasury of Rome to that of Byzantium and finally to the Sainte-Chapelle in Paris, where it was brought by pillaging crusaders. (Paris, Bibliothèque Nationale, Cabinet des Médailles.)

Ephesus. One of two temples to the apotheosized Hadrian, donated by a public benefactor in A.D. 118, with graceful and sumptuous floral decoration. The prettiness of the facade results from the violation of a rule to which our eyes are unwittingly accustomed: rather than a straight lintel supported by two round columns or an arcade supported by two rectangular pillars, we have here an arcade on columns, imitating eastern models.

men and gods were reciprocal. A believer who promised Aesculapius a cock in return for a cure hoped that the divine race would honor its contracts as faithfully as men of good faith honored theirs. Sometimes they were disappointed: "Is that what you call honest dealings, O Jupiter!" When men were disappointed in the gods, they criticized them, just as we criticize the government: "Jupiter, have pity on this sick girl. If you let her die, you'll be blamed." When the beloved prince Germanicus died, the Roman mob demolished temples, as demonstrators today might stone an embassy. People could turn their backs on the gods: "Since the gods did not spare me, I will not spare them either," wrote one furious unfortunate.

Relations with the Gods

Relations between men and deities resembled relations between ordinary men and such powerful brethren as kings or patrons. A man's first duty to a god was to salute the god's image. The most common form of prayer involved flattering the god's power: "Help me, Jupiter, because it is in your power." If the god did not help, he risked incurring suspicion that he was less powerful than he seemed. Some people sought to wear the gods down (*fatigare deos*), to overcome their haughty indifference with endless prayers. They "frequented their temples" and went every morning to hail the gods, as clients hailed their patrons. Special homage was paid to the god of the temple near one's home, for a powerful neighbor was the best and most natural protector a person could have. With liberal grace and serene naiveté, the pagans modeled relations with the gods on political and social relations among themselves. It was the Christians who substituted the paternal model, basing relations with God on relations within the family, which is why Christianity, unlike paganism, would be a religion of obedience and love. The genius of Saint Augustine, the sublimity of Saint Theresa—these were extraordinary elaborations of the familial model. And so was Luther's anguish over the arbitrariness of the all-powerful Father. Pagans of sound mind rejected still another model of divine relations: the servile model. The man who constantly trembled with fear at the thought of the gods, as though they were capricious and cruel masters, projected an image unworthy of the gods and unworthy of a free man. Such fear of the gods (*deisidaimonia*) was what the Romans meant by "superstition." They left it to the Oriental masses, accustomed to bow down to potentates, to conceive of piety as a matter of declaring oneself the slave or servant of a god. At bottom the classical relation between man and god was noble and free, one of admiration.

True piety meant thinking of the gods as benevolent, just, and providential, like good supermen. Not all men achieved this, because every man's character affects his behavior with the gods. Some held that a god is only as good as his word; they offered a contract—"Cure me and I'll give you an offering"—and paid up only if their prayers were granted. Others believed that the gods were as unscrupulous as themselves: "Make me richer than my neighbor," they asked. They did not dare to utter such a wish out loud, in front of other worshipers, so they wrote it down and left the sealed document on the altar. The truly devout were more scrupulous, knowing that the gods have always preferred a humble cake offered by a pure heart to the costliest of sacrifices. If they multiplied their solemn vows and turned to the gods whenever they were in difficulty, it was out of love, not self-interest. A pious man liked to be in contact with divinity as often as possible: prayers, pilgrimages, apparitions of the gods in dreams all served. Piety lay not in faith, works, or contemplation but in a whole range of practices that seem self-interested only because the beloved god-patron was a protector.

Two serpents, symbols of the Lares, and an altar, indicating that they were worshiped. These symbols were borrowed from Greece, where many homes had live but quite harmless serpents as tutelary deities. (Ostia, Archaeological Museum.)

Illness, travel, and childbirth were occasions to prove one's loyal confidence in one's protector.

Some of these practices were consecrated by tradition. What was the mark of an impious man? A little-known passage in Apuleius tells us: "He never made solemn vow to any god, never went to temple. When he passed a chapel, he would have thought it a sin to bring his hand to his lips to signify adoration. Not once did he offer the gods of his estates, who fed and clothed him, first choice of the harvest and of the increase of his flocks. On the grounds of his country seat there is no chapel, no place consecrated to the gods, no sacred wood." A pious man behaves quite differently. When traveling, he "stops when he passes a chapel or sacred wood and composes a vow, places a piece of fruit on the altar, and sits for a moment with the gods." The gift and the vow, the exchange of divine protection for man's gift, are as important as prayer. If God is a father, there is little to do but pray to him. But if the gods are patrons, one can offer them gifts and receive gifts in return, symbolizing a friendship between unequal partners, each with a life of his own; indeed, there would be no reason for men and gods to enter into relations at all were such relations not in the interest of both parties. If the human partner behaved any more humbly, he would not be acting like a free man. People smiled when women went to temple and told the goddess Isis their troubles. Such intimacy with the gods was plebeian. A free man knew how to maintain a proper distance between himself and other men and between himself and the gods. He did not abase himself before his deity. Leave it to the common people to spend all day in the temples waiting on their gods like slaves, behaving like valets and hairdressers before the statues of their deities.

These private religious practices, reminiscent of the popular cults of the saints in the Middle Ages, were reassuring in two ways. People with little or no religious disposition, who in another society would have been nonbelievers, sought in relations with the gods a sort of magic tranquilizer for the dangers and sorrows of real life; for them pious practices were the equivalent of a good-luck charm or amulet. For those of religious bent, these practices facilitated contact with "another" reality. The divine devalued the real by suggesting the existence of another realm. The closer one came to this other world, the smaller reality seemed; the real ceased to be man's only concern. In private letters, numerous examples of which have been found in Egypt, there was much talk of the gods

Bronze statuette. Not an exhibitionist but the god Priapus himself, quite male despite his feminine hair style and clothing. His divinity was limited to his power to chase away thieves, whom he frightened by his obscenity. This statuette was intended to make people laugh and to ward off the evil eye by means of indecency. (Paris, Petit Palais, Dutuit Collection.)

(although the divinity of the emperor is never mentioned). Detailed and complex, religious rites were performed with great care in a meditative spirit. Innumerable bas-reliefs depict worshipers, both male and female, making offerings to the gods. If we knew nothing of the pleasure that pagans took in performing these rites, we could no more understand these sculptures than an asexual being can understand an erotic film.

The tranquilizer of magic was hardly distinguishable from the tranquilizer of religion. Magical and religious acts and symbols were commonly confounded. ("Religion" is one of those paradoxical things whose essence is confusion.) A country chapel evoked the possibility of supernatural aid. The simplest religious act, such as pouring onto the household altar the first drops from a cup one was about to drink from (*libatio*), proved that the utilitarian was not everything. The emperor himself was worshiped in private and had his place in every household's niche of sacred images. Was this because

Left: Pompeii: bacchante sacrificing on an altar before a statue of Bacchus. Most Bacchic images are of no religious significance, but some embellished the sacred meeting place of a sect or the private home of a Bacchic priest. (Naples, Archaeological Museum.)

Right: Small bronze: tutelary deity of city, or City apotheosized. An authentic pious image, as opposed to an image of fantasy or myth. This image of the City wears a crown in the form of a rampart. The goddess prepares a libation. (Paris, Petit Palais, Dutuit Collection.)

people considered him a god? No. Nobody made vows to him and no one imagined that this mortal had the power to cure illness or recover lost objects. Was it mere religious camouflage for patriotic obedience? No. Was it a cult of personality for a charismatic dictator? Not that either. In drinking a toast to the emperor's sacred image after dinner, a man raised himself to the level of that ineffable otherness, proof of whose existence lay in the fact of its veneration.

"The Gods"

Small bronze. Female worshiper pouring a libation. Another authentic pious image, with little to satisfy the fancy or the taste for art. The woman's left arm hangs submissively at her side. (Paris, Petit Palais, Dutuit Collection.)

Private religion played a third role (although not as well as philosophy or, later, Christianity): it was the impartial guarantor of a system of ethics and of interests that wished to appear disinterested. Thus far we have considered religion only in relation to the various individual gods of the pantheon—Jupiter, Mercury, Ceres, and so on. Yet the Greeks and Romans referred just as often to "the gods" as a group. Or, rather than use the plural, they sometimes spoke of the "divine" in the neuter or even of "god," that is, of god in general (just as a philosopher might say "man") or even "Jupiter." The plural "gods" and these various synonyms meant something quite different from the sum of all the individual gods. "The gods" had a function, and virtues, that each single god lacked, or at least did not always have. Only individual gods were honored by cults; "the gods" were not. But their will was cited; it was hoped that "the gods" would not fail to be providential, reward their friends, and avenge themselves against their enemies. "The gods" loved virtuous men and would ensure the victory of the just cause. They will punish my persecutor, said one oppressed man; they will punish that scoundrel in the afterlife, they will not allow such crimes to go unpunished. "The gods" will protect our city. "The gods" were Providence to every hope. It was commonly said that "the gods" governed events or that they had arranged the world for man. In truth, no one had any very clear idea how they went about doing these things, but there was no need to wonder about it. The gods' intervention was recognized and anticipated only where laudable and desirable, and no attention was paid to anything else. To say that an event had been brought about by the hand of the gods was just a way of saying that it was undeniably praiseworthy and that Heaven itself ratified this objective judgment. With "the gods" in the plural, paganism had its Providence, which it adduced but did not worship.

What is more, not only "the gods" (or Providence) but also those good supermen, the individual gods of the pantheon, promoted good morals. They were for virtue and against crime. To be sure, the divine race existed for its own sake and was not defined in terms of its role as lawgiver or avenger. But gods were like good men: they approved virtue and hated vice, and the wicked, who imputed to the gods an immorality all their own, would one day learn this lesson, to their sorrow. There is my considered answer to the highly controversial but ill-posed question, Was paganism an ethical religion in the same sense as Christianity? The gods liked men to behave piously toward them. Because they profited from what men offered them? No, but because piety is a virtue and gods like virtue, just as men do. "I alone survived," says a man who survived a shipwreck, "because I am a pious man." A little later he rectifies this: "I alone was saved because never in all my life did I do anything wrong." The gods, as I said earlier, were a divine species of fauna, males and females whose genealogies and adventures formed the subject of myths set in an imaginary time, prior to and different from our own. In the present, however, time has come to a halt for them; they do not age any more than the characters in our comic strips. These fictional beings also played the role of metaphysical divinities, of Providence and the Good, and had done so since the time of the Homeric poems. Here popular religion, which I have been describing, and the religion of the cultivated class, the wealthy elite, had come to a parting of the ways several centuries earlier. The elite could believe in a metaphysical divine but not in the gods of the mythological pantheon, from which, however, they found it impossible to divorce themselves entirely.

Irreligion was unknown among the Roman populace. The people never ceased to believe and to pray. But what might a cultivated Roman, a Cicero, a Horace, an emperor, a senator, a notable, have thought about the phantasmagoria of the ancestral gods? My answer is categorical: he did not believe in them at all. He had read Plato and Aristotle, who four centuries earlier had already ceased to believe. Virgil, an exquisitely religious soul, believed in Providence but not in the gods of his own poems—Venus, Juno, or Apollo. Cicero and the solemn encyclopedist Pliny could not find enough sarcasms to heap upon the gods. These ethereal beings, they

The Religion of the Educated

Pompeii. Because inlaying was considered a minor art, the artist felt free to portray this touchingly familiar scene. Despite the difficulty of cutting marble, Hellenistic craftsmen produced remarkably fluid images. At least seventy other examples of this Venus undoing her sandal have survived. (Naples, Archaeological Museum.)

wrote, have human figures, if the sculptors and naive believers are to be trusted. Are we to believe, then, that inside their bodies we find a stomach, intestines, and sexual parts? What, pray tell, do the blessed immortals do with these organs? The beliefs of the governing class deserve a separate chapter in every history of Roman religion. Such a chapter would treat not Mercury or Juno but perhaps "Providence, Chance, or Fate"—not a bad title. For that was the crux of the religious problem. Should one believe in Providence, as did many pious and cultivated souls and followers of the Stoics? Should one believe in Fate, as did those who studied physics and astronomy (which included astrology)? Or was there nothing in the confusion of this world but Chance, as many impious people held, thereby denying the existence of any kind of Providence? But all educated people smiled at the women of the lower orders who worshiped the goddess Latona in her temple, believed that she looked as the sculptor depicted her, found her happy to have a daughter as beautiful as Diana, and wished that their own daughters were as pretty. In the senatorial order, guardian of the public religion and breeding ground of its priests, the consecrated doctrine was one of amused skepticism regarding official religious ceremonies and naive popular beliefs.

Yet if it was impossible to believe in the strict letter of the old religion, it was just as impossible to dispense with it entirely, not because it was the official creed, believed in by the populace, but because it contained a kernel of truth. Polytheism gravitated not so much toward monotheism (which historical accident would later bring to the fore) as toward the simplicity of abstraction (and it is of the essence of abstract words that they are used only in the singular). Providence and the Good were subjects about which philosophers discoursed at length. A cultivated man might have stated his beliefs more or less as follows: "Providence exists, as I want to believe. The kernel of truth in all these fables about the gods must lie therein. But is there any other reality to Apollo or Venus? Are these names of the one God? Emanations of the Godhead? Names for his virtues? An abstract principle, yet at the same time a living thing? Or nothing but a meaningless fable?" There was certainty on the essential point, divine Providence, but doubt about everything else. It was therefore permissible to participate in popular religion, partly out of condescension, for the fables tell the truth in a naive, thus false, language, and partly out of intellectual prudence, for who knows if

Apollo, despite the legends that surround him, is not just a name but an Emanation. It was possible to use the language of the old religion without seeming ridiculous. When the skeptic Horace just missed being crushed by a falling tree, he thanked the gods of the pantheon according to the traditional forms. Though sure that he owed his salvation to the God-head, he did not know how to thank that abstraction by other than the venerable ceremonial means. When he saw his maid offer a cake to the protective geniuses of his house, he understood that she dimly sensed the conclusion to which he eventually came: atheists notwithstanding, the Hazards of the World are also a Providence whose will it is that we conform to the Good.

The Second Paganism

We have seen what the common people, on the one hand, and the cultivated class, on the other, thought about the gods. But around A.D. 100, speaking very roughly, there occurred a transformation similar to that which we have witnessed in other areas. The old paganism was internalized and modernized and ceased to be beneath the notice of cultivated men and women. Do not confuse this development with the more recent conflict between Catholicism and the Enlightenment. Antique irreligion was not an episode in the allegedly eternal wars between enlightenment and obscurantism, or between freedom of thought and the authority of the church. It hinged on the question of whether religion was or was not culturally respectable. Pagan religion oppressed no one. The question was whether, for an educated person, it was ridiculous, beneath contempt.

I am using the word "culture" in a very simple sense: "to be cultivated" meant "not to think like the common folk." Culture was a privilege, along with wealth and power. This is not true in all societies. In Homer's day leaders talked, thought, prayed, danced, and even dressed like their followers, whose beliefs they shared. But Hellenistic and Roman society was quite different from Homeric society: it was riven by a cultural divide. For Cicero, religion was an amalgam of foolish superstitions, good for the uneducated. How could anyone believe, naively, that Castor and Pollux had manifested themselves to a citizen in the Via Salaria, or that Apollo hovered in the heavens with a silver bow?

That is not all. A cultivated man usually attaches too much importance to words. He expresses his opinion and imagines that his words correspond exactly to his actions (just as sociologists take the answers that people give to their questionnaires as an authentic representation of their thinking). The religion of the common people was not easily expressed in words, however. A common man who prayed fervently to Apollo rarely thought, while praying, of the god's silver bow or the puerile myths about his loves and exploits. If questioned, however, he would speak of those legends, docilely repeating what he had been told. The educated judged the uneducated on the basis of these naive responses, attaching greater importance to words than to the secrets of the heart.

When paganism began spontaneously to modernize itself around A.D. 100, it ceased to be a mythological religion and began to prefigure the Christian relation to God. Relations between men and gods ceased to be those between two living species, two kinds of fauna each with a life of its own, and became those between a monarch and his subjects. This monarch was either a single, providential god or a collection of providential gods, all of which resembled one another and may have been nothing more than several names for one god. These gods were interchangeable, and all wore the providential uniform. They lost their mythological biography and personal traits. All fulfilled the same function: to govern, counsel, and protect men and rescue them from the grip of blind Fortune or Fate. It was not ridiculous to believe in such gods.

The gods no longer existed in a realm of their own; their existence corresponded to the function of governing individual human beings. And individuals began to count docile obedience to the sovereign gods as a virtue. I do not think that this docility was adopted from the ancient Orient, long habituated to humbling itself before potentates. There is nothing servile about it. The believer did not seek to abase himself but to exalt the sovereignty of the divine. There was nothing capricious or venal about the providence of the gods, which became one with justice and reason. People no longer curried favor with the gods by promising sacrifices. In the old paganism the worshiper took the initiative and offered the god a bargain: "If you see to it that I have a good journey to Alexandria, I'll make you a sacrifice." In the new paganism the initiative belonged to the gods themselves, who gave orders (called "oracles") to the faithful for their own good: "Go to Alexandria without fear, then offer me a sacrifice." People felt happy and reassured because they lived under the protection of a sovereign deity.

Pompeii, tomb of a woman. The ship of life has arrived at its destination, and the sailors furl the sail.

Finally the new paganism ceased to be institutionalized. It was much more informal than the old paganism. Each person could shape religion as he pleased. In the past, when someone wished to know the will of the gods, he sought out a priest or oracle: a legitimate institution. Now, the orders of the gods were conveyed to individuals in all sorts of ways, outside official channels. They came in dreams, in ominous incidents, in vague presentiments, and so on. Divine commandments were seen everywhere. The boundary between ordinary life and the divine became fluid. The gods traveled everywhere, without stopping at the official customs stations. In addition, a whole literature of popular piety made its appearance. Some of these books were best-sellers that helped to modernize and "spiritualize" popular religious practices.

One concern is curiously absent from these musings on religion: the afterlife, the immortality of the soul. The Romans devoted little more thought to this subject than do most of our contemporaries. The Epicureans did not believe in the immortality of the soul, Stoics did not believe in it much, and the official religion for the most part avoided the question. Beliefs about the afterlife were a subject separate from religion. The most widely held opinion, even among the lower orders, was that death is nothingness, eternal sleep. The vague notion that Shades survived somewhere after death was, it was often repeated, nothing more than a fable. To be sure, numerous philosophers had speculated in great detail about the survival of the soul and its fate in the hereafter, but these speculations remained the property of small sects. No generally accepted doctrine taught that there is anything after death other than a cadaver. Lacking a common doctrine, Romans did not know what to think; consequently they assumed nothing and believed nothing.

By contrast, funeral rites and funerary art made all sorts of affirmations to allay the anxieties that attend the anticipation of death. Even if people did not strictly believe these affirmations, they appreciated the consolation they contained. A sarcophagus found at Simpelveld, extensively carved on the inside, showed nothing less than a domestic interior in which the deceased lay on her bed, propped on one elbow. The Fates cut the thread of life, but the tomb, this tomb in particular, spun it out indefinitely, embroidering on the metaphor of eternal rest: everything continues after everything has ceased,

The Afterlife

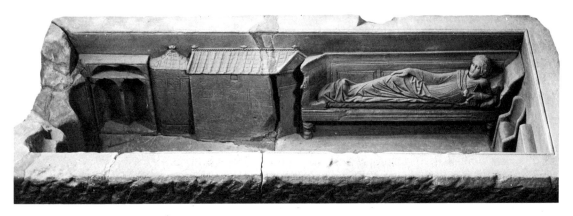

Sarcophagus found at Simpelveld. Note the furniture. (Leyden, Museum of Antiquities.)

and nothingness assumes the comforting form of monotony. On many children's tombs a sleeping *putto* equivocates between sleep and death. Images of ships or of travelers on horseback or in carriages, which appeared on many tombs, illustrated not some voyage in the hereafter but the voyage that is life in this world. The natural end of that voyage is the port or roadside marker that is death. It was consoling to think of death as a time of rest after a long journey. A more resigned attitude was that life is after all but a brief voyage. On some sarcophagi in fact a comparison was made between life and the Circus races: the chariots race seven laps around the course and then are gone.

The Romans had their feast of the dead, which lasted from February 13 to 21. During this period they left offerings at the graves of their loved ones. But they no more believed that the dead ate these offerings than we believe that the dead admire or smell the flowers that we place on their graves. In

Greece people had long placed in graves terra-cotta figurines, tanagras, representing Cupids, Victories, or Sirens. Everyday religion had little to say about these funerary geniuses, so special beliefs pertaining particularly to funerals were created. Distinct from other beliefs, these were viewed, in the absence of more substantive teachings, as circumstantial rather than universal truths. By the time of the Roman Empire they had fallen into oblivion. Greek tombs, like their Roman counterparts, now contained only small objects of homage such as lamps, mirrors, and vials of perfume. Consoling ideas about the afterlife stemmed from the desire to believe, not from the authority of an established religion; they therefore lacked the coherence of dogma. As Rohde has observed, a single epitaph could simultaneously exhibit perfect incredulity and sublime hope. A problem of interpretation confronts anyone who would move from ancient images to ancient mentalities, however. What an image represents often matters less than the sphere to which it belongs. A Bacchic bas-relief on a tomb indicates not so much belief in Bacchus as the existence of a sphere of religious ideas—nothing more precise. Consider a modern analogy. Many sixteenth- and seventeenth-century religious paintings exhibit quite secular attractions: saints who are too pretty by far, sometimes depicted in a state of seminudity. Yet any viewer, even a *philosophe* or libertine, would have recognized these as religious paintings and assigned them to a sphere higher than that reserved for Boucher's nudes.

Bacchus, that happy deity and marginal character who lent himself to every innovation, a god who belonged primarily to mythology and was ignored by common religion

Life is a circuit of the track. (Naples, Archaeological Museum.)

and whom imagination could bend as it pleased, was the favorite god of graveside theology. His legend and rites were depicted on numerous sarcophagi, and especially on the tombs of children. The death of a youngster called for consoling poetization. One adolescent's epitaph reads: "He was kidnaped by Bacchus to become his initiate and companion." Only occasionally are these the sarcophagi of initiates of some Bacchic sect, and their decoration does not reflect the convictions peculiar to such sects. Nor do they illustrate, as some have alleged, the existence of a widespread Bacchic religion. Yet these figures are not just decorative. People were never sure just how much truth there might be in any of these fables or sectarian doctrines. Bacchus, god of the hereafter, was a consoling "maybe" about whom everyone had heard.[2]

Epitaphs and funerary art tactfully suggested none but consoling ideas. But Plato, Epicurus, Lucretius, and others repeatedly tell that the souls of the dying were often troubled by memories of their sins and crimes and anguished at the thought of soon having to appear before the gods, who would punish them. To us, such statements seem comprehensible. What dying people feared was not punishment in the underworld, a mythological fantasy that no one took literally. It was "the gods" who frightened them, for everyone knew that the gods were just, providential, and vengeful, even if they did not ask exactly how these qualities manifested themselves. The gods were there to avenge human conscience. Valerius Maximus writes: "That scoundrel died with thoughts of his perfidy and ingratitude on his mind. His soul was torn apart

A child died so young that his life's journey ends (left) as it began (right), on his mother's knees. (Rome, Museum of the Baths.)

as by a torturer, for he knew that he was passing from the gods of heaven, who hated him, to the gods of the underworld, who execrated him."

I do not believe that Lucretius, an Epicurean, exaggerated the torment of the dying in order to make his sect's tranquilizing philosophy seem more essential. He simply told the truth: paganism, a religion of festival, had an ethical component, which aroused anxieties that it could not allay because it was not a soteriological religion that could reassure the faithful by organizing their lives in this world on the pretext of securing salvation in the next. Those seeking to learn how to live in this world had to turn to the philosophical sects: the Stoics, the Epicureans, and others. The wisdom these sects offered promised to free individuals from anxiety and make them happy—that is, tranquil.

Philosophical Sects

In a famous book, more learned than perceptive, Max Pohlenz expressed astonishment that the philosophy of the ancients, unlike that of the moderns, based moral obligation on the self-interested grounds of happiness. In this he displayed an odd lack of historical sense. It is hard to see how the ancients could have done otherwise, for what they meant by philosophy did not take for its aim, as Kant took for his, establishing the possible grounds of morality. The aim of ancient philosophy was to provide individuals with a method for obtaining happiness. A sect was not a school where people came to learn general ideas; they came looking for rational means of achieving tranquillity. Morality was among the remedies prescribed by certain sects, who gave reasoned justifications for their prescriptions. This has confused modern students of the subject.

The Epicurean and Stoic sects offered adherents a formula based on the nature of the universe (that is, philosophically grounded), whose purpose was to enable them to live without fear of men, gods, chance, or death, to make individual happiness independent of accidents of fate. In summing up their aims, both sects declared that they wished to make men as tranquil as the gods, their mortal equals. The differences between the two sects lay in subtleties, and in the metaphysics used to justify their remedies. Stoicism (not to be confused with what Vigny calls by that name) prescribed mental exercises by means of which a man might maintain his mind in a state where nothing could harm it. Epicureanism held that

Tomb of a physician, 3rd–4th century. He is not, as was once thought, reading a medical treatise but rather his classics; however narrow his profession, he is a cultivated man. (New York, Metropolitan.)

man's chief need was to free himself of illusory anxieties. Both sects were contemptuous not only of death but also of vain desires, desires for money and honors, perishable goods that cannot promise unbreachable security. The Epicureans taught that man should liberate himself from false needs; they recommended living on friendship and cold water. The Stoics argued that their method was based on reason and Providence, while the Epicureans, with their atomism, allayed fears born of superstition. The Stoics believed that human beings feel innate affection for their families and cities, so that if duties toward these are neglected, feelings of incompleteness and unhappiness result. The Epicureans, on the other hand, held that human happiness requires us to abide by only those pacts that we ourselves have ratified out of deliberate, self-interested calculation. Both sects held that a man who, because of illness or persecution, found it impossible to lead a humane life in his body or his city could reasonably resort to suicide; indeed, suicide was the recommended remedy in such situations.

The sects did not barrage their members with moral precepts; they promised happiness. Would a literate man have made a free choice to join a sect had he not been seeking personal advantage? Stoicism and Epicureanism were intellectual faiths. They asked how man might be made heroic, how he might be delivered from his anxieties and vain desires. And

Sarcophagus, traces of poly-chrome, 2nd century. Bac-chantes and musicians. Silenus and Pan precede Bacchus, left, in chariot drawn by centaur. The human figures are over-come by rapture or ecstasy; the animals, similarly over-whelmed, lie on the ground. (Rome, Museum of the Con-servators.)

they answered: by intellectual persuasion. If a man's intellect is supplied with good reasons, his will will follow. It is hard to see what authority a "director of conscience" might have exercised in the ancient world other than that of persuasion, for his followers were not subject to his discipline.

There was a clear difference between the sects and the schools. All people of good society had been to school in their youth and studied rhetoric. A few, at some point in their lives, "converted" (this was the word they used) to the doctrine of some sect. Besides a handful of wealthy converts who lived lives of leisure, sects also included a handful of converts of more modest station. These men had little income and were obliged to supplement their meager resources by accepting positions as tutors in noble households, becoming clients of powerful lords, or making careers as itinerant lecturers. They took vows of devotion to philosophy, proof of which could be seen in their austere clothing—almost the uniform of the philosopher. For the rich, who did not earn their daily bread from their devotion, the degree of commitment to the sect varied. Only the truly convinced carried the consequences of their profession of faith to the point of wearing philosophical garb and long, ill-kempt beards. Most well-to-do converts were content to change a few symbolic details in the way they lived, to read the works of their sects' authors, and to keep a philosophy tutor around to teach them the dogma of the faith and advertise the spiritual elevation of the household.

Why did these wealthy converts hesitate to commit themselves fully to the wisdom of their sect? They frequently claimed that they did not have the time, that managing their property or tending to the duties of office demanded too much of them. In any case, as Seneca pointed out, the important thing was that they should devote their thoughts to the sects' teachings, surround themselves with friends who were philosophers, and spend their leisure hours in conversation with the philosopher they kept on call. To one high official attracted to Stoicism, Seneca recommended simply reading and doing mental exercises, avoiding practices that he, Seneca, considered more ostentatious than sincere, such as wearing the philosopher's garb and beard, refusing to eat from silver plates, and sleeping on a mattress on the floor. Nevertheless, many people were quite serious about changing their lives, and some even succeeded in doing so.

The Influence of Philosophy

Simple people made fun of the converts and noted the contrast between their avowed convictions and the way they lived—their opulence, their groaning tables, and their mistresses. These jibes were dictated by envy, for philosophers as a human type enjoyed a considerable measure of admiration and authority. A senator could, without losing caste, dress and write as a philosopher, and so could an emperor. No Roman writer, poet, or scholar played the role of public conscience, which was reserved for the philosophers, provided only that the way they lived, their exterior trappings, proved that they lived in accordance with their teachings. Philosophers were permitted to administer public rebukes and to give advice; one of their functions was to give high moral counsel to the cities they visited. When Saint Paul preached in the Areopagus of Athens, he was following their example. In essence, the philosophers constituted a lay clergy, and the mockers told merry tales about them similar to those told about the ways of the clergy in the Middle Ages. One senator, condemned to death, went to meet his fate in the company of his domestic philosopher, who continued to exhort him right to the very end. Another, on his deathbed, engaged in learned conversation with a philosopher of the Cynical sect. Still another great personage, gravely ill, heeding the advice of a Stoic that he commit suicide, let himself die of hunger.

Every convert to a doctrine became a propagandist for the faith and sought to attract new members. One prospect might prove refractory, but another was not hopeless, there was still a chance of winning him over. The words "conversion," "dogma," and "heresy" were borrowed from the philosophical sects by the Christians. Stoicism, Epicureanism, Platonism, Cynicism, Pythagoreanism: each sect continued the doctrine of its founder and remained, or believed that it remained, faithful to his dogmas. The idea of an unfettered search for the truth was anathema. The doctrine was passed on from generation to generation as a sacred treasure, and each sect engaged in ardent polemic with its rivals. The sometimes considerable modifications these doctrines incurred over the course of centuries were introduced unwittingly. The sects were associations of believers who entered into them freely; although there was no hierarchy or organization, nonetheless they were "sectarian" in their beliefs. Besides being unorganized, these sects differed from the Christian churches and sects in one major respect: they did not assume that one day their truth would or could impose itself on all mankind. They believed that only a handful of the fortunate would ever see the light. They did not seek to save mankind in spite of itself. In other words, their universalism was not imperialistic.

The dogmas of the sects served as rules of life for the

Sarcophagus said to be of Plotinus, late 3rd–4th century. The deceased, a man of letters, who must have been a celebrity, sits in the center, a bundle of books at his feet. Around him are relatives or disciples. At either end a Sage stands guard, setting this uncommon family or group of disciples apart from the common run of mankind. Chronological objections have been raised to the identification of this tomb as that of Plotinus. Every age boasted more than one celebrated man of letters. (Rome, Vatican Museums.)

handful of believers who considered themselves members. As Pierre Hadot has shown, an ancient philosophy was not constructed to be interesting or true but to be put into practice, to change lives, and to be profoundly assimilated through intellectual exercises, which would serve as the model for the spiritual exercises of Christianity. These exercises were to be practiced every day: "Remind yourself constantly of the truths that you have often heard and even taught yourself." Members were supposed to meditate upon the sect's dogmas and apply them to everyday events; they were supposed to look for occasions to think about these dogmas, to recapitulate the verities, to repeat them silently in the presence of others and aloud to themselves; and they were supposed to attend public lectures and to give lectures themselves. Spiritual exercises were also supposed to be recorded in writing. According to Hadot, the *Meditations* of Marcus Aurelius are not, as was long believed, the emperor's intimate diary, a collection of random thoughts and free speculation, but the product of methodically following a typical three-point plan of meditation.

The influence of sectarian doctrine was not limited to members of the sect. It extended to many different aspects of social, to say nothing of political, life, although the significance of many points of doctrine changed as its scope of application widened. Stoicism became an ideology of right-thinking people, universally respected. The Stoics were such vigorous conformists that people mistook them for original thinkers. More generally, philosophy ceased to be a method for living and became an object of intellectual curiosity among cultivated people. It was little more than culture and ideology to a man like Cicero, who lived as a lettered senator rather than a philosopher. Philosophy played a considerable role in his intellectual life and almost no role at all in his personal life. No man could claim to be educated without some knowledge of sectarian dogma. Physicians and architects were divided over the question whether their arts should be philosophical or strictly empirical. Above all, the philosophical doctrines provided the raw material of rhetoric. A student or amateur of rhetorical art could shine by decking his argument out in philosophical dress. Teachers of eloquence taught apprentice orators which doctrines were most useful to study. Philosophy ended up as part of cultural life, incorporated into its ceremonies and works, and people flocked to hear the eloquent public lectures given by leading thinkers. It became an essential ingredient of that *paideia* that literate men held up as the ideal of their idle lives. On tombs, the image of a man of letters reading might equally well represent a philosopher, an amateur of belles-lettres, or a rhetor. The distinctions were irrelevant. For the ancients, a man's study was a sanctuary of private life. It was furnished with the works of writers and thinkers and decorated with their busts or painted portraits.

The degree to which the lettered class, including those of its members not enticed by the sects, was imbued with philosophical notions can be gauged by its capacity to reflect upon itself. Philosophy's success is demonstrated by the frequency of philosophical suicide. A senator who learned that the emperor was about to charge him with some crime and sentence him to death might choose to end his own life. Or a sick or elderly man might choose to die a decent death, one less painful than if he waited for nature to take its course. Suicide was accepted, even admired. The courage of the man who decides to end his suffering and accept eternal rest was extolled by the philosophers, for the suicide proved the truth of the philosophical notion that what matters is the quality and not the quantity of the time that one lives. Private life took refuge in self-mastery, in both senses of the term: having the strength to control the course of one's life, and granting oneself the sovereign privilege to do so rather than leaving the decision to nature or to a god. Suicide and eternal peace symbolized the ideal of private tranquillity, to be achieved by renouncing illusory riches.

The ancients sought not to retreat from social and ethical norms but to "care for the self," achieving security at the cost of pruning back the ego. In other societies private life later came to mean secession from public life, or sailing life's seas as a solitary mariner—or a pirate—tossed by the winds of individual desire, fancy, and fantasy.

Care of the Self

It is narcissistic and self-indulgent to give free rein to desire, fancy, and fantasy. Smiles are rare in Greco-Roman art. Tranquillity was bought at the price of tension and renunciation—hallmarks of the ancient world as much as of the world of the samurai or of Queen Victoria. The beliefs of the ancients may seem somewhat superficial. Their moralists, thinkers, and poets seem naive in their overestimation of the possibilities of self-censorship and facile in their underestimation of the potency of the censored material; they take a narrow view of man. The simplest example is probably the

most convincing. "Every person has his secret; in reverie, unbeknown to others, he finds peace, freedom, sorrow. There is a solitude between friends, between lovers, between all human beings." So simple a judgment would have been unthinkable in antiquity. To be sure, the second century witnessed the emergence of a new, subjective style that introduced a note of hypochondria and affectation. Aelius Aristides is obsessed with his health; Fronto exchanges letters of the tenderest (and most unequivocal) sort with his pupil Marcus Aurelius; and Herodius Atticus makes a ritual of·sorrow of his quite sincere grief. With the help of culture every spark of spontaneity was converted into doctrine and artifice. Prisoners of their aristocratic civism and haughtiness, the cultivated had no escape other than philosophy, which imprisoned them even more closely in prudence and self-mutilation. They completely lacked the ability to "rework, in consciousness, the broadest possible range of experience"; this adventurer's ideal would have seemed unnatural. Our modern passion is to "have an experience" in order to taste its flavor and judge its effects; such an idea apparently never occurred to the Romans. As

Masterpiece of an identified workshop, ca. A.D. 200. At the extreme left, the handsome shepherd Endymion has fallen asleep. The amorous Luna, haloed by her veil, descends majestically from her chariot to gaze at him. At right, winged Zephyr is frozen at the sight of such a handsome man. Upper left, Morphius pours poppies on Endymion. At right, the rustic scene situates Luna's loves in the innocence of pastoral. (Genoa, Doria Palace.)

Heidegger says, the Greeks went to the games at Olympia because they were interesting and an institution. None of them said, "This is an experience that I absolutely must have." Indeed, to want to explore the unknown was considered a vicious temptation, something to be feared, and was called "curiosity." This was the vice to which those who indulged in magic were prone, and it always ended badly.

Accordingly, no ancient, not even the poets, is capable of talking about himself. Nothing is more misleading than the use of "I" in Greco-Roman poetry. When an ancient poet says "I'm jealous, I love, I hate," he sounds more like a modern pop singer than a modern poet. The modern singer and the ancient poet do not recount their loves and sorrows; rather they set Jealousy and Love on a stage. When an ancient poet says, "Wealth means nothing to me," he is stating what one ought to think about wealth. He speaks in the name of all and makes no claim that his readers should be interested in his own personal state of mind. To talk about oneself, to throw personal testimony into the balance, to profess that personal conviction must be taken into account provided only that it is sincere is a Christian, indeed an eminently Protestant idea that the ancients never dared to profess.

Paganism was something more than this and continues to inspire dreams. With censorship came elegance. The art, the books, even the writing of the ancients were beautiful. Compare a Greek or Latin inscription of the first century, done in a style worthy of our greatest typographers, with an inscription of the Late Empire or Middle Ages. The decline began in the second century. The world became increasingly ugly to look at, while inwardly man ceased to avert his eyes from his own unstylized suffering, impotence, and abysmal depths. He ceased to be an elegant fool, a purveyor of empty advice. Christianity placed its bets on the less constricted, less sophisticated anthropology that it invented in the psalms. This would prove more comprehensive and popular, but also more authoritarian. For fifteen centuries pastoral authoritarianism, ecclesiastic government of souls, would arouse greater appetites and more revolts and, all things considered, shed more blood than class struggle or even patriotism had ever done.

The Imagery of Death

Sarcophagus, 2nd century or first half of 3rd century. Castor and Pollux, wearing conical hats, kidnap two beautiful women, whose attendants flee. Two warriors attempt to do battle with the armed companions of the two heroes. (Rome, Vatican Museums.)

The Roman Empire was the property of an urban nobility, if not by right of blood then at least by the fact of wealth and by virtue of an aristocratic cast of mind cloaked in civic trappings. As besotted by vanity as any of Saint-Simon's contemporaries, Roman notables hesitated for quite a long time between the old ideal of *homo civicus* and the new ideal of *homo interior*.

As proof of this, let me point, paradoxically, to imagery from which Frantz Cumont's many disciples have drawn precisely the opposite conclusion: the mythological images decorating the sumptuous sarcophagi of the wealthy. May they be the last images that the reader takes with him from the ancient city! From the second century A.D. wealthy Romans

chose to be buried in sarcophagi decorated with bas-reliefs. There was nothing morbid about these decorations, which represented a wide variety of myths. Their style, even less morbid than their subject matter, has the conventional academicism of the "ancients," the graceful, serene humanism of the Greek arch. When a sculptor gives pathetic animation to one of his figures, the emotion that comes through is that which a good storyteller imparts to his tales. These funerary decorations speak of subjects other than death and the deceased. A good example, on display in the Louvre, is the nude Diana surprised in her bath by the indiscreet hunter Actaeon, whom the chaste goddess thereupon has her dogs devour.

What are such graceful, if gratuitous, images doing on a tombstone? Nothing is easier or more tempting than to interpret symbolism. Cumont ascribed eschatological significance to this mythology. Statues in the Louvre of Jupiter abducting the handsome Ganymede to heaven, where he will serve as the god's pet, and of Castor and Pollux abducting the daughters of King Leucippus are described as allegories depicting the immortal soul being wafted off to heaven. The trouble is that such ingenious interpretations can be invented for only some of the myths represented on tombs, and not necessarily those that occur most frequently. Not to mention the fact that they clash with the style.

If the mythological decorations on the sarcophagi are not symbolic, must we conclude that they are simply decorative? No. Iconography in the manner of Panofsky has limits; the meaning of imagery is not just conceptual or doctrinal. The mythology on the sarcophagi did not only fill space; it plunged viewers into an unprosaic, nonrealistic atmosphere. It matters little which myth is represented; the point is that the Romans fled death through myth. The beautiful imagery of mythology (so unlike the pathos in the portrait art of the same period) was a way of aestheticizing death, of avoiding melancholy. In this respect the imagery is pregnant with meaning. It was the last flowering of the Apollonian spirit of ancient Greece. How does the viewer react to a sarcophagus with mythological decoration? The fear of death is eclipsed by a sense of the marvelous, the fabulous, and the voluptuous, by thoughts of carnal humanity. Costly, richly decorated tombs and moral ease in the face of the afterlife were privileges that went together. Refined Apollonian sentiments coupled with self-imposed censorship; self-satisfied wealth confused with virtue; conscious but secretly puritanical quietism and aestheticism: in these things a whole world stands revealed.

Notes

Bibliography

Acknowledgments

Index

Notes

1. The importance of gymnastics and music in Greek-inspired education during the imperial period (see Marcus Aurelius, I, 6) was confirmed by Louis Robert, in the proceedings of the international congress on epigraphy held in Athens in 1982 (I, 45). The basic reference on Hellenistic and Roman education is Ilsetraut Hadot, *Arts libéraux et Philosophie dans la pensée antique* (Paris: Etudes augustiniennes, 1984).

2. Bacchic imagery is more than decorative and less than religious (in the full sense). The key to this problem is an idea attributable to Jean-Claude Passeron, which seems to me of great theoretical importance. The language of images, Passeron says, is not "assertoric." An image can neither affirm nor deny what it depicts, nor can it add modifiers such as "a little," "perhaps," "tomorrow," and so on. Bacchic imagery is an attractive proposition that requires no response and leaves the question of its reality in suspense. The point is not, as is often said, that all symbolism is fluid and admits of a thousand different interpretations. It is rather that symbolism does not require us to respond yes or no. Spectators need not know what they think about Bacchus. The image, being less than an assertion, takes no position and does not require its viewer to take a position. But to say that an image is not assertoric in no way implies that it is merely decorative.

Bibliography

Alföldy, G. *Die Rolle des Einzelnen in der Gesellschaft des römischen Kaiserreiches: Erwartungen und Wertmassstäbe.* Sitzungsberichte der Heidelberger Akademie, 1980, VIII.

Ameling, W. *Herodes Atticus.* 2 vols. Hildesheim, 1982.

André, J. *L'Alimentation et la Cuisine à Rome.* Paris: Les Belles Lettres, 1981.

André, J.-M. *Les Loisirs en Grèce et à Rome.* Paris: Presses Universitaires de France, 1984.

Andreau, J. *Les Affaires de Monsieur Jucundus.* Rome: Ecole française de Rome, 1974.

Aufstieg und Niedergang der römischen Welt. Geschichte und Kultur Roms im Spiegel der neuren Forschung, ed. H. Temprini and W. Haase. Several volumes have been published in Berlin and New York by W. De Gruyter.

Balland, A. *Fouilles de Xanthos, VII, Inscriptions d'époque impériale du Létôon.* Paris: Boccard, 1981.

Blanck, H. *Einführung in das Privatleben der Griechen und Römer.* Darmstadt: Wissenschaftliche Buchgesellschaft, 1976.

Bleicken, J. *Stattliche Ordnung und Freiheit in der römischen Republik.* Frankfurter Althistorische Studien 6. Kallmünz: Lassleben, 1972.

Blümner, H. *Die römischen Privataltertümer.* Handbuch der klassischen Altertumswisswnschaft, IV, 2, 2. Munich, 1911.

Boulvert, G., and M. Morabito. "Le droit de l'esclavage sous le Haut-Empire." *Aufstieg und Niedergang,* II, vol. XIV, p. 98.

Brödner, E. *Die römischen Thermen und das antike Badewesen.* Darmstadt: Wissenschaftliche Buchgesellschaft, 1983.

Brunt, P. A. "Aspects of the Social Thought of Dio Chrysostom and the Stoics." *Proceedings of the Cambridge Philological Society,* 1973, p. 9.

———— "Charges of Provincial Maladministration under the Early Principate." *Historia,* 10 (1961): 189.

———— *Social Conflicts in the Roman Republic.* London: Chatto and Windus, 1971.

———— "Stoicism and the Principate." *Papers of the British School at Rome,* 43 (1975): 7.

Buti, I. *Studi sulla capacità patrimoniale dei "servi."* Pubblicazioni della Facoltà di giurisprudenza dell'università di Camerino. Naples: Jovene, 1976.

Cagnat, R., and V. Chapot. *Manuel d'archéologie romaine.* 2 vols. Paris, 1916.

Canas, B. A. "La femme devant la justice provinciale de l'Egypte romaine." *Revue historique de droit* (1984): 358.

Christes, J. *Bildung und Gesellschaft: die Einschätzung der Bildung und ihrer Vermittler in der grichisch-römischen Antike.* Darmstadt: Wissenschaftliche Buchgesellschaft, 1975.

Cockle, H. "Pottery Manufacture in Roman Egypt." *Journal of Roman Studies,* 71 (1981): 87.

Corbier, M. "Les familles clarissimes d'Afrique proconsulaire." *Epigrafia e Ordine senatorio,* 5 (1982).

———— "Ideologie et pratique de l'héritage (ler siècle avant Jésus Christ – IIe siècle après Jésus Christ)." *Index,* 1984. Proceedings of the GIREA colloquium, 1983.

Cotton, H. "Documentary Letters of Recommendation in Latin from the Roman Empire," *Beiträge zur klassischen Philologie.* Hain: Königstein, 1981.

Crook, J. *Law and Life of Rome.* Ithaca, N.Y.: Cornell University Press, 1967.

Daremberg, Saglio and Pottier. *Dictionnaire des Antiquités grecque et romaine.* Paris, 1877–1918.

D'Arms, J. H. *Commerce and Social Standing in Ancient Rome.* Cambridge, Mass.: Harvard University Press, 1981.

David, J.-M. "Les orateurs des municipes à Rome: intégration, réticences, et snobismes," *Les Bourgeoises municipales italiennes.* Paris and Naples: Centre Jean Bérard, 1983.

De Marchi, A. *Il Culto privato di Roma antica.* 2 vols. Milan, 1896–1903.

De Robertis, F. *Lavoro e Lavoratori nel mondo romano.* Bari: Laterza, 1963.

Dill, S. *Roman Society from Nero to Marcus Aurelius.*

New York, 1904. Reprint. New York: Meridian, 1957.

Dunbabin, K. *The Mosaics of Roman North Africa. Studies in Iconography and Patronage.* Oxford: Oxford University Press, 1978.

Etienne, R. *La Vie quotidienne à Pompeii.* Paris: Hachette, 1966.

Eyben, E. "Family Planning in Graeco-Roman Antiquity." *Ancient Society,* 11–12 (1980–1981): 5.

Fabre, G. *Libertus, recherches sur les rapports patron-affranchi à la fin de la République romaine.* Rome: Ecole française de Rome, 1981.

Finley, M. I. *The Ancient Economy.* Berkeley: University of California Press, 1973.

——— ed. *Slavery in Classical Antiquity.* Cambridge, England: Cambridge University Press, 1960.

Flory, Marleen B. "Family and Familia: A Study of Social Relations in Slavery." Ph.D. dissertation, Yale University, 1975.

Foucault, M. *Histoire de la sexualité,* vol. 2, *L'Usage des plaisirs;* vol. 3, *Le Souci de soi.* Paris: Gallimard, 1984.

Friedländer, L. *Darstellungen aus der Sittengeschichte Roms in der Zeit von August bis zum Ausgang der Antonine.* 9th ed. Edited by G. Wissowa. 4 vols. Leipzig, 1920.

Frier, B. W. *Landlords and Tenants in Imperial Rome.* Princeton: Princeton University Press, 1980.

Gabba, E. "Ricchezza e classe dirigente roman." *Rivista storica italiana,* 93 (1981): 541.

Galbraith, J. K. *The Nature of Mass Poverty.* Cambridge, Mass.: Harvard University Press, 1979.

Gagé, J. *Les Classes sociales dans L'Empire romain.* 2d ed. Paris: Payot, 1971.

Garnsey, P. "Independent Freedmen and the Economy of Roman Italy under the Principate." *Klio,* 63 (1981): 359.

——— ed. "Non-slave Labour in the Graeco-Roman World." *Cambridge Philological Society,* supplement VI, 1980.

Goldschmidt, V. *La Doctrine d'Epicure et le Droit.* Paris: Vrin, 1977.

——— *Le Système stoicien et l'Idée de temps.* Paris: Vrin, 1953.

Gombrich, E. *The Image and the Eye.* Oxford: Phaidon, 1982.

Gourevitch, D. *Le Triangle hippocratique dans le monde gréco-romain: le malade, sa maladie et son médecin.* Rome: Ecole française de Rome, 1984.

Hadot, I. *Seneca und die grichisch-römische Tradition der Seelenleitung.* Berlin: W. De Gruyter, 1969.

——— "Tradition stoïcienne et idées politiques au temps des Grecques." *Revue des études latines,* 48 (1970): 133.

Hadot, P. *Exercices spirituels et Philosophie antique.* Paris: Etudes augustiniennes, 1981.

Hands, A. R. *Charities and Social Aid in Greece and Rome.* London: Thames and Hudson, 1968.

Harris, H. A. *Sport in Greece and Rome.* London: Thames and Hudson, 1972.

Helen, T. *Organization of Roman Brick Production in the First and Second Centuries A.D.* Helsinki, 1975.

Hengstl, J. *Private Arbeitsverhältnisse freier Personen in den hellenistischen Papyri bis Diokletian.* Bonn: Habelt, 1972.

Jerphagnon, L. *Vivre et Philosopher sous les Césars.* Toulouse: Privat, 1980.

Kampen, N. *Image and Status. Roman Working Women in Ostia.* Berlin: Mann, 1981.

Kaser, M. *Das römische Privatrecht,* vol. 1, *Das altrömische, das vorklassische und klassische Recht.* Handbuch der Altertumswissenschaft, III, 3, 1. 2nd ed. Munich: Beck, 1971.

——— *Das römische Zivilprocessrecht.* Handbuch der Altertumswissenschaft, III, 4. Munich: Beck, 1966.

Kelly, J. M. *Roman Litigation,* Oxford: Oxford University Press, 1966.

Kleiner, D. *Roman Group Portraiture: The Funerary Reliefs of the Late Republic and Early Empire.* London and New York: Garland, 1977.

Koch, G., and H. Sichtermann. "Römische Sarkophage," *Handbuch der Archäologie.* Munich, 1982.

Krenkel, W. *Der Abortus in der Antike.* Wissenschaftliche Zeitschrift der Universität Rostock, 20, 1971, p. 443.

La Rocca, E., M. de Vos, and F. Coarelli. *Guida archeologica di Pompei.* Milan: Mondadori, 1976.

Laubscher, H. P. *Fischer und Landleute. Studien zur hellenistischen Genreplastik.* Mainz: von Zabern, 1982.

Leveau, P. *Caesarea de Maurétanie, une ville romaine et ses campagnes.* Rome: Ecole française de Rome, 1984.

Lewis, N. *Life in Egypt under Roman Rule.* Oxford: Oxford University Press, 1983.

Lilja, S. "Homosexuality in Republican and Augustan Rome." *Societas scientiarium Fennica, Commentationes humanarum litterarum,* 74, 192.

Linnott, A. W. *Violence in Republican Rome.* Oxford: Oxford University Press, 1968.

MacMullen, R. "The Epigraphic Habit in the Roman Empire." *American Journal of Philology,* 103 (1982): 233.

——— *Paganism in the Roman Empire.* New Haven: Yale University Press, 1981.

——— *Roman Social Relations, 50 B.C. to A.D. 284.* New Haven: Yale University Press, 1974.

Mallwitz, A. *Olympia und seine Bauten.* Munich: Prestel, 1972.

Marquardt, J. *Das Privatleben der Römer.* Handbuch der römischen Altertümer, VII. 2d ed. 2 vols. Leipzig, 1886.

Marrou, H.-I. *Histoire de l'éducation dans l'Antiquité.* Paris: Seuil, 1965, expanded 6th ed. For a non-functional methodological approach to the history of education, see M. Nilsson, *Die hellenistische Schule.* Munich, 1955, which reaches different conclusions.

―――― "Mousikos Aner," *Etude sur les scènes de la vie intellectuelle figurant sur les monuments funéraires romains.* Rome: Erma, 1965.

Martin, R. "La vie sexuelle des esclaves d'après les 'Dialogues rustiques' de Varron," in J. Collart, ed., *Varron, grammaire antique et stylistique latine.* Paris: Les Belles Lettres, 1978, p. 113.

―――― "Pline le Jeune et les problèmes économiques de son temps." *Revue des études anciennes,* 69 (1967): 62.

Mocsy, A. "Die Unkenntnis des Lebensalter im römischen Reich." *Acta antiqua Academiae scientiarum Hungaricae,* 14 (1966): 387.

Moreau, P. "Structures de parenté et d'alliance d'après le *Pro Cluentio*," *Les Bourgeoises municipales italiennes.* Paris and Naples: Centre Jean Bérard, 1983.

Nardi, E. *Procurato abortoneal mondo greco-romano.* Milan: Giuffrè, 1971.

Neraudau, J.-P. *Etre enfant à Rome.* Paris: Les Belles Lettres, 1984.

Nilsson, M. *Geschichte der griechischen Religion,* vol. 2, *Die hellenistische und römische Zeit.* Handbuch der Altertumswissenschaft, V, 2. 2nd ed. Munich, Beck, 1961.

Nock, A. D. *Essays on Religion and the Ancient World.* 2 vols. Oxford: Clarendon, 1972.

Nörr, D. "Zur sozialen und rechtlichen Bewertung der freien Arbeit in Rom." *Zeitschrift der Savigny-Stiftung, Roman. Abt.,* 82 (1965): 67.

Paoli, U. E. *Vita romana. La vie quotidienne dans la Rome antique,* trans. J. Rebertat. Paris: Desclée de Brouwer, 1955.

Pauly-Wissowa. *Realencylopädie der klassischen Altertumswissenschaft.* Stuttgart, 1893–1981.

Picard, G.-C. *La Civilisation de l'Afrique romaine.* Paris, Plon, 1959.

Pleket, H. W. "Collegium juvenum Nemesiorum: A Note on Ancient Youth Organization." *Mnemosyne,* 22 (1969): 281.

―――― "Games, Prizes, Athletes, and Ideology: Some Aspects of the History of Sport in the Greco-Roman World," *Arena,* 1 (1976) 49.

―――― "Urban Elites and Business in the Greek Part of the Roman Empire," in Garnsey et al. *Trade in the Ancient Economy.* London, 1983, p. 131

―――― "Zur Soziologie des antiken Sports," *Mededelingen van het Nederlands Instituut te Rome,* 36, (1974): 57.

Pohlenz, M. *Die Stoa, Geschichte einer geistigen Bewegung.* 5th ed. Göttingen: Vandenhoeck und Ruprecht, 1978.

Pomeroy, Sarah B. *Goddesses, Whores, Wives, and Slaves: Women in Classical Antiquity.* New York: Schocken, 1975.

Prachner, M. *Die Sklaven und die Freigelassenen im arretinischen Sigillatagewerbe.* Wiesbaden: Steiner, 1980.

Quet, M.-H. "Remarques sur la place de la fête dans le discours des moralistes grecs." *La Fête, pratique et discours. Annales littéraires de l'université de Besançon. Centre de recherches d'histoire ancienne,* 42 (1981): 41.

Rabbow, P. *Seelenführung Methodik der Exerzitien in der Antike.* Munich: Kösel, 1954.

Raepset-Charlier, M.-T. "Ordre sénatorial et divorce sous le Haut-Empire." *Acta classica universitatis scientiarum Debrecenensis,* 17–18 (1981–1982): 161.

Ramin, J., and P. Veyne, "Les hommes libres qui passent pour esclaves et l'esclavage volontaire." *Historia,* 30 (1981): 472.

Rawson, B. "Family Life among the Lower Classes at Rome," *Classical Philology,* 61 (1966): 71.

―――― "Roman Concubinage and Other De Facto Marriages." *Transactions of the American Philosophical Association,* 104 (1974): 279.

Reekmans, Tony. "Juvenal's Views on Social Change." *Ancient Society,* 2 (1971): 117–161.

Robert, J., and L. Robert. *Bulletin épigraphique,* in *Revue des études grecques* since 1938 (collected in indexed volumes since 1971). Contains a wealth of facts and ideas, the majority of which pertain to Greek areas of the Roman Empire or under Roman domination.

Robert, L. *Opera minora selecta.* 4 vols. Amsterdam: Hakkert, 1974.

Saller, R. P. *Personal Patronage under the Early Empire.* Cambridge, England: The Cambridge University Press, 1982.

San Nicolo, M. *Aegyptisches Vereinswesen zur Zeit der Ptolemäer und Römer.* Munich: Beck, 1972.

Schmitt-Pantel, P. "Le festin dans la fête de la cité hellénistique,"*La fête, pratique et discours. Annales littéraires de l'université de Besançon. Centre de recherches d'histoire ancienne,* 1981, vol. 62, p. 85.

Schuller, W., ed. *Korruption im Altertum.* Munich: Oldenburg, 1982.

Syme, R. *Roman Papers.* Oxford: Oxford University Press, 1979.

———— "Greeks Invading the Roman Government." *Brademas Lectures.* Brookline, Mass.: Hellenic College Press, 1982.

Thomas, Y. *Paura dei padri e Violenza dei figli: immagini retoriche e norme di diritto.* In Pellizer and Zoerzetti, *La Paura dei padri nella società antica e medievale.* Bari: Laterza, 1983.

———— "Remarques sur le pécule et les *honores* des fils de famille." *Mélanges d'archéologie et d'histoire de l'Ecole française de Rome. Antiquité,* 93 (1981): 529.

Toynbee, J. M. C. *Death and Burial in the Roman World.* London: Thames and Hudson, 1971.

Turcan, R. A. *Mithra et le Mithriacisme.* Paris: Presses Universitaires de France, 1981.

Vallat, J.-P. "Architecture rurale en Campanie septentrionale," *Architecture et Société.* Rome: Ecole française de Rome, 1983, p. 247.

Versnel, H. S., ed. *Faith, Hope and Worship. Aspects of Religious Mentality in the Ancient World.* Leyden: Brill, 1981.

Veyne, P. *L'Elégie érotique romaine.* Paris: Seuil, 1983.

———— "Le folklore à Rome et les droits de la conscience publique sur la conduite individuelle." *Latomus,* 42 (1983): 3.

———— "Suicide, Fisc, esclavage, capital et droit romain." *Latomus,* 40 (1981): 217.

———— "Les saluts aux dieux et le voyage de cette vie." *Revue archéologique,* 1985.

———— "Mythe et réalité de l'autarcie à Rome." *Revue des études anciennes,* 81 (1979): 261.

Ville, G. *La Gladiature en Occident, des origines à la mort de Domitien.* Ecole française de Rome, 1981.

Wissowa, G. *Religion und Kultur der Römer.* Handbuch der Altertumswissenschaft, IV, 5. 2nd ed. Munich: Beck, 1971.

Acknowledgments

The sites and objects illustrated in this book (on the pages noted) are found in various locations, as follows: Aquitaine Museum, Bordeaux, 81; Archaeological Museum, Aquileia, 73, 109, 126, 133, 157; Archaeological Museum, Milan, 97; Archaeological Museum, Naples, 6, 32, 36, 38, 60, 71, 72, 87, 89, 203, 208, 213, 216, 221; Archaeological Museum, Ostia, 10, 18, 122, 167, 190, 211; Archaeological Museum, Venice, 204; Arezzo Museum, 161; Bardo Museum, Tunis, 88, 193; Berlin Museum, 125; Bibliothèque Nationale, Cabinet des Médailles, Paris, 46, 209; British Museum, London, 74, 127, 198; Calvet Museum, Avignon, 180; Church of San Vittore, Ravenna, 127; Doria Palace, Genoa, 231; Dresden Museum, 121; Ducal Palace, Mantua, 165; Estonian Museum, 124; Landesmuseum, Trier, 138, 143, 144; Lapidary Museum, Arles, 76; Lateran Museum, Rome, 24 (now at Vatican), 118; Louvre, Paris, 8, 14, 16, 19, 22, 42, 44, 46, 77, 114, 170, 187, 197; Marburg Museum, 13; Metropolitan Museum, New York, 224; Museum of Ancona, 86, 130; Museum of Antiquities, Leyden, 220; Museum of the Aquila, 104; Museum of the Baths, Rome, 15, 39, 54, 58, 78, 80, 84, 120, 195, 206, 222; Museum of Beirut, 187; Museum of Benevento, 50; Museum of the Conservators, Rome, 26, 43, 47, 94, 96, 106, 135, 143, 225; Museum of Gallo-Roman Civilization, Lyons, 11; Museum of National Antiquities, Saint-Germain-en-Laye, 140; Museum of Parma, 182; Museum of Plovdiv, 188; Museum of Portogruaro, 102; Museum of Saint Paul's Outside-the-Walls, Rome, 66; Museum of Syracuse, 99; National Archaeological Museum, Athens, 28; Ny Carlsberg Glypotek, Copenhagen, 200; Palace of the Sforza, Milan, 147; Palazzo Colonna, Rome, 30; Palazzo Salviati, 145; Petit Palais, Dutuit Collection, Paris, 4, 48, 49, 59, 62, 90, 93, 142, 143, 175, 212, 213, 214; Prado, Madrid, 196; Torlonia Collection, Rome, 116, 148, 201; Uffizi, Florence, 83; Vatican Museums, Rome, 16, 34, 53, 56, 135, 160, 162, 168, 184, 199, 227, 232; Villa Albani, Rome, 41, 111.

Photographs were supplied by the following agencies and individuals: Bulloz, 4, 48, 49, 58, 59, 62, 70, 90, 93, 140, 142, 175, 212, 213, 214; G. Dagli Orti, 13, 15, 18, 30, 36, 38, 39, 41, 50, 54b, 56, 58, 66, 72, 78, 81, 87, 99, 104, 111, 116, 120, 121, 122, 125, 126, 127b, 143c, 147, 150, 152, 154, 183, 187b, 190, 192, 200, 201, 203, 208, 210, 213a; Edimédia, 74; Giraudon, 8, 16a, 18, 19, 22, 42, 46b, 209; Alinari-Giraudon, 14, 26, 32, 53, 54a,c, 60, 82, 83, 102, 106, 108, 124, 127, 145, 148; Anderson-Giraudon, 6, 70, 94, 118, 154, 160, 184, 196, 206; M. Langrognet, 216; Roger-Viollet, 76, 98, 100, 164b, 166, 188, 211; Alinari-Viollet, 28, 89, 168, 197; Anderson-Viollet, 35, 195, 199; Scala, Florence, 128; R. Tournus, 77; private collections, 47, 86, 97, 109, 161, 169, 185, 193.

Index

44 28

DATE DUE DAYS

AUG 1 7 2004		
SEP 0 7 2004		
SEP 1 5 2004		
OCT 2 9 2004		
	WITHDRAWN	
GAYLORD		PRINTED IN U.S.A.